Teen Finance Series

CASH, CREDIT AND CREDIT REPAIR INFORMATION FOURTH EDITION

CASH, CREDIT AND CREDIT REPAIR INFORMATION FOURTH EDITION

Tips for a Successful Financial Life

Including Facts about Earning Money, Budgeting, Banking, Shopping, Financial Technology, Using Credit, and Avoiding Financial Pitfalls

OMNIGRAPHICS
An imprint of Infobase

Bibliographic Note

Because this page cannot legibly accommodate all the copyright notices, the Bibliographic Note portion of the Preface constitutes an extension of the copyright notice.

* * *

OMNIGRAPHICS
An imprint of Infobase

132 W. 31st St.
New York, NY 10001
www.infobase.com
James Chambers, *Editorial Director*

* * *

Copyright © 2022 Infobase

ISBN 978-0-7808-1852-1
E-ISBN 978-0-7808-1853-8

Library of Congress Cataloging-in-Publication Data

Names: Chambers, James (Editor), editor.

Title: Cash, credit and credit repair information for teens: tips for a successful financial life: including facts about earning money, budgeting, banking, shopping, financial technology, using credit, and avoiding financial pitfalls /edited by James Chambers. Other titles: Cash and credit information for teens.

Description: Fourth edition. | New York, NY: Omnigraphics, An imprint of Infobase, [2022] | Series: Teen finance series | Earlier edition published as: Cash and credit information for teens: tips for a successful financial life: including facts about earning, spending, and borrowing money, with topics such as budgeting, consumer rights, banks, paychecks, taxes, loans, credit cards, and more. | Includes bibliographical references and index. | Audience: Ages 13 | Audience: Grades 7-9 | Summary: "Provides tips for a successful financial life including facts about earning money, paying taxes, budgeting, banking, shopping, using credit and debit cards, and avoiding scams, identity theft, and other financial pitfalls"-- Provided by publisher.

Identifiers: LCCN 2021018688 (print) | LCCN 2021018689 (ebook) | ISBN 9780780818521 (library binding ; alk. paper) | ISBN 9780780818538 (ebook)

Subjects: LCSH: Teenagers--Finance, Personal--Juvenile literature. | Finance, Personal--Juvenile literature.

Classification: LCC HG179.C346 2021 (print) | LCC HG179 (ebook) | DDC 332.02400835--dc23

LC record available at https://lccn.loc.gov/2021018688
LC ebook record available at https://lccn.loc.gov/2021018689

TABLE OF CONTENTS

Part 4 | Smart Spending

Part 5 | Understanding Latest Trends in Financial Technology

Part 6 | Avoiding Financial Pitfalls

Part 7 | If You Need More Help or Information

PREFACE

About This Book

Today's teens are spending their own money, and they are spending a lot of it. But, the challenges that come with managing and spending that money have never been more daunting. Faced with greater personal responsibility for managing their own money, and changing technology that has created both opportunity and risk, today's teens face economic challenges unlike any previous generation. Unfortunately, many teens are lacking the basic financial literacy needed to meet those challenges. As a result, the majority of today's teens remain unaware of basic financial principles, such as earning, budgeting, saving, establishing credit and managing debt. In addition, many teens are unaware of the risks that come with the technology that while making their lives easier, also makes their personal and financial information more vulnerable than ever before.

Cash, Credit and Credit Repair Information for Teens, Fourth Edition provides an updated look at how teens can earn and manage money. It provides practical information about receiving income, and budgeting. It also discusses choosing appropriate banking services, managing a checking account, using credit and debit cards, and making informed shopping decisions. It provides information about the latest trends in financial technology such as electronic banking, mobile wallets, online shopping, cryptocurrency, etc. A section on avoiding financial pitfalls provides facts about predatory lending practices, identity theft, and common financial scams. The book concludes with a directory of resources for additional information.

How to Use This Book

This book is divided into parts and chapters. Parts focus on broad areas of interest; chapters are devoted to single topics within a part.

Part 1: Earning Money begins by outlining the five key principles of making money. It continues with information about career planning and common ways teens can acquire money including jobs, apprenticeship, internships, and through entrepreneurship. Information about taxes on income and other earnings is also included.

Part 2: Managing Your Money discusses the essentials of money management and budgeting. It describes banking basics, and offers tips on how to choose a right bank account. It also offers suggestions on how to save and grow your money. A chapter on how you can use your money to help others is also provided.

Part 3: Managing Credit and Debt talks about the basics of borrowing money and what you need to know about credit. It explains how credit works and the importance of building a good credit history. Information on choosing and managing a credit card is also provided. It explains how to deal with debt and offers information about credit counseling.

Part 4: Smart Spending provides tips about shopping and spending money wisely. Individual chapters discuss some of the purchase challenges many teens face and explain how social media influences the shopping decisions of the teens.

Part 5: Understanding Latest Trends in Financial Technology talks about the latest technologies that aim at enhancing financial services and processes. The benefits and risks of electronic banking, mobile wallets, and online shopping are discussed. A special chapter on cryptocurrency is provided to help teens understand the basics of new age digital currency.

Part 6: Avoiding Financial Pitfalls explains some of the most common problems that threaten financial well-being, including predatory lending practices and identity theft. It also cautions readers about the risks associated with various frauds, such as lottery scams, charity scams, investment scams, pyramid and Ponzi schemes, and telemarketing scams.

Part 7: If You Need More Information includes a directory of resources for additional information about personal finance.

Bibliographic Note

This volume contains documents and excerpts from publications issued by the following U.S. government agencies: Apprenticeship.gov; Board of Governors of the Federal Reserve System; Consumer Financial Protection Bureau (CFPB); Federal Communications Commission (FCC); Federal Deposit Insurance Corporation (FDIC); Federal Student Aid; Federal Trade Commission (FTC); Internal Revenue Service (IRS); MyCreditUnion.gov; MyMoney.gov; Securities and Exchange Commission (SEC); Small Business Administration (SBA); U.S. Bureau of Labor Statistics (BLS); U.S. Department of Justice (DOJ); USA.gov; and Youth.gov.

It also contains original material produced by Infobase.

The photograph on the front cover is © Vasin Lee/Shutterstock.

PART 1 | EARNING MONEY

PART 1 | EARNING MONEY

CHAPTER 1
THE FIVE PRINCIPLES OF MAKING MONEY

About This Chapter: This chapter includes text excerpted from "My Money Five," MyMoney.gov, Financial Literacy and Education Commission (FLEC), June 1, 2013.

My Money Five

Making the most of your money starts with five building blocks for managing and growing your money – The MyMoney Five. Keep these five principles in mind as you make day-to-day decisions and plan your financial goals.

Earn

The Earn principle is about more than the amount you are paid through work. This principle is about knowing the fine print and details about your paycheck, including deductions and withholdings. To put it another way: In order to make the most of what you earn, it helps to understand your pay and benefits.

Actions You Can Take

- Learn about the details of your paycheck, including any deductions.
- Review the taxes that are withheld, including Social Security and Medicare taxes.
- Explore and sign up for workplace benefits.
- Invest in your future – with education and training.

Hints and Tips

- Remember, your employer has to subtract certain taxes and other items from your wages every pay period. Your take-home pay (net income) is what you receive after any taxes and deductions are subtracted.
- Usually, your deductions and withholdings include federal, state and city income taxes, Social Security and Medicare taxes, your contributions for retirement savings, and payments for health insurance provided as part of your job.

- Be sure you take advantage of all the credits and deductions that help lower your taxes.
- It is a good idea to sign up if your employer offers a retirement savings program. If so, you can arrange to have retirement savings automatically moved from your paycheck to a retirement account. Many employers will match part of every dollar you save this way, and you will benefit from it when you retire.

Save and Invest

Saving is a key principle. People who make a habit of saving regularly, even saving small amounts, are well on their way to success. It is important to open a bank or credit union account so it will be simple and easy for you to save regularly. Then, use your savings to plan for life events and to be ready for unplanned or emergency needs.

Actions You Can Take

- Start saving, form a savings habit, and pay yourself first!
- Open and keep an account at a bank or credit union that meets your needs.
- Track your savings and investments, and monitor what you own.
- Plan for short-term and long-term goals.
- Build up emergency savings for unexpected events.
- Consult with a qualified professional on investments and other key financial matters.
- Save for retirement, children's education and other major items.

Hints and Tips

- An easy way to save is to pay yourself first. That means each pay period, before you are tempted to spend money, commit to putting some in a savings account. See if you can arrange with your bank to automatically transfer a certain amount from your paycheck or your checking account to savings every month.
- People who keep track of their savings often end up saving more, because they have it on their minds. New phone apps are available to help people pass up purchases they do not really need – you might want to try one!
- If you are making investments, it is good to consult with a qualified professional about your plans. Before you purchase investments, be sure to build an emergency savings fund to cover your needs for at least three months. Keep the savings in an insured bank or credit union account that you can access if you need it.
- Many professionals call themselves "financial planners." Before you hire one, ask for a description of the services offered. A good place to check the credentials of an investment advisor is your state's consumer protection office, the state's Attorney General's office, or the issuing agency for any professional licenses or certifications.

Protect

The Protect principle means taking precautions about your financial situation. It stresses the importance of accumulating savings in case of an emergency, and buying insurance. Be vigilant about identity theft, and keep aware of your credit record and the credit score.

Actions You Can Take

- Keep your financial records in order.
- Watch out for fraud and scams, and protect your identity.
- Choose insurance to meet your needs, including healthcare insurance.

Hints and Tips

- A good system for keeping personal money records will include copies of important documents such as your will, property ownership documents, information about savings and insurance, and other document. It should include overview of what happens to property after a major life event occurs.
- Assume that any offer that "sounds too good to be true" – especially one from a stranger or an unfamiliar company – is probably a fraud.
- Look at your bank statements and bills as soon as they arrive and report any discrepancy or anything suspicious, such as an unauthorized withdrawal or charge.
- Be wary of request to "update" or "confirm" personal information, especially your Social Security number, bank account numbers, credit card numbers, personal identification numbers, your date of birth or your mother's maiden name in response to an unsolicited call, letter, or e-mail.

Spend

The fundamental concept of Spend is: Make a budget or a plan for using your money wisely. It is helpful to set short- and long-term financial goals and manage your money to meet them.

Actions You Can Take

- Live within your means.
- Be a smart shopper, and compare prices and quality.
- Track your spending habits and develop a budget or spending plan.
- Plan for short-term and long-term financial goals.

Hints and Tips

- A good way to take control of your spending is to set the maximum amounts you plan to spend each week or each month. Once you have set the maximum, stick with your plan.
- It is helpful to track your spending over a few weeks or months to get a handle on how you are using your dollars and cents. Look into using online systems or phone apps for keeping track of your spending – you will be amazed at what you will learn about your habits!
- Be careful not to let a sale or discount coupon persuade you to purchase something you do not really need and that is not in your spending plan.
- When planning a big purchase, take time to comparison shop and check prices at a few different stores, by phone or online.

Borrow

Sometimes it is necessary to Borrow for major purchases such as an education, a car, a house, or maybe even to meet unexpected expenses. Your ability to get a loan generally depends on your credit history, and that depends largely on your track record at repaying what you have borrowed in the past and paying your bills on time. So, be careful to keep your credit history strong.

Actions You Can Take

- Track your borrowing habits.
- Pay your bills on time.
- When you need to borrow, be sure to plan, understand and shop around for a loan with a low annual percentage rate (APR).
- Learn about credit and how to use it effectively.
- Pay attention to your credit history, as reflected by your credit score and on your credit report.

Hints and Tips

- Borrowing money is a way to purchase something now and pay for it over time. But, you usually pay "interest" when you borrow money. The longer you take to pay back the money you borrowed, the more you will pay in interest.
- It pays to shop around to get the best deal on a loan. Compare loan terms from several lenders, and it is okay to negotiate the terms.
- When repaying a loan, it may be better to pay more than the minimum amount due each month, so you will have to pay less in interest over the life of the loan.
- One of your most important aids when shopping for a loan is the APR – the annual percentage rate. This is the total cost, including interest charges and fees, described as a yearly rate.

- Paying your bills on time will help increase your credit score. Even if you fell into trouble with borrowing in the past, you can get on solid footing and rebuild your credit history by making regular payments as agreed.
- You are entitled to a free copy of your credit report every 12 months from each of the three nationwide credit bureaus. Go to www.AnnualCreditReport.com or call toll-free 877-322-8228 to order the free reports. Beware of imposter sites.

CHAPTER 2
CAREER EXPLORATION AND SKILL DEVELOPMENT

About This Chapter: This chapter includes text excerpted from "Career Exploration and Skill Development," Youth.gov, October 16, 2016.

Finding a job can be a challenge for youth. They must determine what careers are available, what their interests are, and what skills they have or need to develop. Numerous resources are available to help youth get a sense of their interest and skills as well as gain employment experience and learn about employment opportunities.

Mentoring

Mentoring – matching youth or "mentees" with responsible, caring "mentors," usually adults – has been found to be an important support for youth as they transition to adulthood and the workforce. Mentoring provides opportunities for youth to develop emotional bonds with mentors who have more life experience and can provide support, guidance, and opportunities to help them succeed in life and meet their goals.

Train for a Career

Career preparation should start in high school, but it should not end with graduation: Most occupations require some type of training or education after high school. On-the-job training, apprenticeships, certificates, nondegree awards, and various levels of college degrees are typically required for entry-level jobs.

Which type of training you need depends on the career you want to pursue. Your high school may offer opportunities for getting career training or college credits before you graduate. And after graduation, your training options expand even more. The closer you get to entering the workforce, the more you will want to narrow your choices.

(Source: "Career Planning for High Schoolers," U.S. Bureau of Labor Statistics (BLS), U.S. Department of Labor (DOL).)

Mentoring relationships can be formal or informal, with substantial variation, but the essential components include creating caring, empathetic, consistent, and long-lasting relationships, often with some combination of role modeling, teaching, and advising. One form of mentoring, called "instrumental" or "topic-focused mentoring," focuses on a particular problem and aims at helping mentees reach specific goals, such as improving academic performance or preparing for employment opportunities.

Career-focused mentoring, a type of instrumental or topic-focused mentoring, can take a variety of forms and may focus on different pieces of career development and employment. Some examples include assisting with the following:

- Writing resumes and cover letters
- Conducting mock interviews and providing support for answering interview questions
- Exploring possible careers and assisting with job, internship, or program searches
- Developing on-the-job skills (soft skills or technical skills)
- Modeling behavior, attitudes, or skills in the workplace (job-shadowing)
- Career planning and goal setting

Apprenticeships and internships can provide on-the-job opportunities to integrate mentoring into employment experiences for youth. You can find out more about both apprenticeships and internships for youth below. Learn more about mentoring and the benefits for youth and their mentors.

Assessment, Testing, and Counseling

Self-assessments help teach youth about themselves so that they can find a career that is a good fit for their interests and skills. They allow youth to explore:

- What they do and do not like
- How they react to certain situations
- Their skills
- Values

A professional, such as a counselor at a high school, trade or vocational school, college, or career training center, can help in selecting an appropriate assessment, interpreting the results, and providing career counseling.

The U.S. Department of Labor (DOL), Employment and Training Administration (ETA) sponsors two valuable resources to assist youth identify career pathways. CareerOneStop (www.careeronestop.org) is a website that provides a range of career-exploration help:

- Up-to-date information on job, salary and benefit information and related education and training opportunities

- Job search tools, resumes, and interview resources, and people and places to help jobseekers virtually, such as *What's My Next Move*, a guide to exploring careers for youth

The American Job Centers (AJCs), also known as "One Stop Centers," provide job referrals, counseling, and other supportive services to help with both job search and location of training and education resources. AJCs have locations across the United States.

The National Collaborative on Workforce and Disability (NCWD) provides a range of assessments that can help with the transition from school to employment. In addition to their focus on career planning, these resources recognize unique challenges faced by students with disabilities.

An additional online resource, Students and Career Advisors, allows students, career advisors, and parents to learn more about potential career opportunities. This resource provides opportunities for students to explore their interests, learn about potential careers, learn how to get job experience, and find additional educational opportunities to support career development.

Individualized Learning Plans
The goal of an Individualized Learning Plan (ILP), can also be known as "Individual Service Strategy" (ISS), is to connect what youth are doing in the classroom with their career and college goals and aspirations. ILPs help youth discover their skills and interests, match their interests with degrees and careers, set goals, and follow through in a thoughtful and meaningful way. The Office of Disability Employment Policy has a number of resources and information about ILP.

Job Search Assistance
Finding available jobs can be difficult. It is important for youth to recognize that finding a job often takes time and it is important to develop a plan, schedule, and goals when conducting a search. Many sources list available jobs, from newspapers to listservs to online directories. CareerOneStop (www.careeronestop.org) has online job listings that provide information on various employment options. Tools such as GetMyFuture (www.careeronestop.org/GetMyFuture), which allows youth to search for career opportunities based on past employment experiences, can help young people identify future careers that may be available based on their previous work experience. College career centers and CareerOneStop can help youth prepare their resumes, write cover letters, and practice interviewing. College career centers can also provide valuable resources for students as they search for jobs and internships.

Soft and Technical Skill Development and Training
Soft skills are generally defined as personal qualities, not technical, that translate to good job performance. They have been named by employers to be most important

for successful job performance. Soft skills can be learned through a variety of means, including classroom instruction, youth programs, volunteering, and service learning.

More than 50 percent of manufacturers who completed the 2005 skills gap survey reported that technical skills will play an important role in meeting the needs of employers in the upcoming years. Vocational training courses or work-study programs can teach marketable technical or occupational skills. CareerOneStop can make referrals to local postsecondary institutions and youth-serving agencies when training and other services are needed. Not only are the people there know about these resources, but they also can approve vouchers to defray training costs. The Center for Employment Training (CET) is a nonprofit organization that has partnerships with the DOL. The CET has pioneered the practice of open-ended, competency-based training that uses the workplace as the context for simulations. The individualized training allows youth to train at their own pace and explore career options firsthand. The majority of training is provided through hands-on experience. The Office of Vocational and Adult Education within the U.S. Department of Education (ED) also helps states, schools, and community colleges support technical and vocational education.

Apprenticeships

Youth apprenticeship programs grew out of the school-to-work movement and offer youth classroom instruction combined with structured on-the-job training with a mentor. The training is split between academic courses and vocational training, while the on-the-job portion provides opportunities for practice in and understanding of work-based contexts for classroom instruction. Youth apprenticeships may lead to admission to adult registered apprenticeship programs after graduation. The DOL sponsors registered apprenticeship programs that meet its standards. The minimum requirement for participation in a registered apprenticeship program may vary by the skills demanded for the program, but to be eligible, youth must be at least 16. Because of restrictions, some hazardous jobs are limited to individuals over 18. Participation in apprenticeships allows youth to receive the following:

- **A paycheck.** From day one, youth earn a paycheck guaranteed to increase over time as they acquire new skills.
- **Hands-on career training.** Apprentices receive practical on-the-job learning in a wide selection of programs, such as healthcare, construction, information technology, and geospatial careers.
- **An education.** Apprentices receive hands-on learning and related instruction to supplement the hands-on-learning and have the potential to earn college credit, even an associate's or bachelor's degree, in many cases paid for by the employer.
- **A career.** Once the apprenticeship is completed, youth are on their way to successful long-term careers with competitive salaries and little or no educational debt.

- **National industry certification.** When an apprentice completes a Registered Apprenticeship program, she or he will be certified and can take that certification anywhere in the United States.
- **The opportunity to work with recognizable partners.** Many of the nation's most recognizable companies, such as CVS Health and UPS, have Registered Apprenticeship programs.

For an example of a youth apprenticeship program, visit the Wisconsin Department of Workforce Development (DWD): Youth Apprenticeship Program Information.

The Office of Disability Employment Policy (ODEP) provides a toolkit and other resources to increase the capacity of programs to provide integrated inclusive apprenticeship training to youth and young adults with a full range of disabilities, including those with the most significant disabilities. ODEP also provides guidance on how to use the increased flexibilities in the DOL apprenticeship regulations.

Internships

Internships, both paid and unpaid, provide youth with short-term, practical experiences to learn about careers, develop networks, and experience the workplace. The Wage and Hour Division at the DOL has identified six criteria to help determine whether interns must be paid the minimum wage and overtime under the Fair Labor Standards Act. Internships are available in a diverse array of career fields and can be formal or informal. Internships give youth the opportunity to explore what they like and do not like about certain careers. They allow youth who might not know what career they want to pursue with a chance to see whether a certain environment, job, or management style fits their needs. Both on-the-job experience and the application process allow youth to develop skills so that they are able to enter the job market with relevant career experience.

CHAPTER 3
WORKING DURING COLLEGE

Working while in college may seem challenging, but it has its own perks. It can not only help students take care of their personal expenses but also provide opportunity to gain work experience. Some students have on-campus, work-study jobs that are part of a financial aid package. Others work at part-time, off-campus jobs to earn extra spending money. Many companies offer tuition assistance to help cover the cost of higher education for employees who want to increase their skills.

The biggest drawback to working during college is that jobs take time that you might otherwise spend studying, participating in extracurricular or social activities, or even sleeping. After all, working at a job for 10–20 hours per week is the equivalent of taking one to two additional classes. If the time commitment prevents you from taking a full load of classes, staying healthy, enjoying your college experience, or graduating on time, then working during college may not be worth it. However, employment during college also offers benefits that may outweigh the costs. Some of the advantages you may gain by working include the following:

- **Better academic performance.** Studies have shown that college students who work between 1 and 12 hours per week have higher graduation rates than students who do not work. The working students tend to perform as well or even better academically than their nonworking peers. Many students find that the business challenges and workplace issues they face in their jobs apply directly to their college classes and enhance the learning experience. Some students also use ideas from their college classes to solve problems in the workplace.
- **Time management skills.** Keeping up with the demands of college and a job forces you to manage your time effectively. You learn to stay organized, stick to a schedule, prioritize tasks, and develop good work and study habits. Building these critical time-management skills in college helps prepare you for a fast-paced, demanding career after graduation.

- **Less student-loan debt.** Most students who work during college do so in order to help pay for their education. Although many still need student loans to cover the costs of tuition and room and board, employment income can reduce the amount they need to borrow. By paying for books and basic living expenses out of their earnings, working students may be able to graduate with less student-loan debt than nonworking students.
- **More independence.** Some students must work to help cover education-related expenses. Others choose to work because they want to have cash available to spend on clothes, travel, eating out, entertainment, and other treats. If your parents are already paying for your education, you may feel guilty asking them for more funds. Earning your own spending money can give you greater independence. In addition, you can avoid the financial trap of applying for student credit cards to cover your extra expenses.
- **Money management skills.** Students who work during college gain valuable knowledge of personal finance. Earning an income allows you to take responsibility for establishing a budget, keeping track of expenses, paying bills, and managing your money. These skills will prove valuable once you graduate from college and launch your career.
- **Career experience.** Part-time jobs – even ones that may seem menial or meaningless – offer valuable work experience that can help you gain skills, build self-confidence, and meet potential references or networking contacts. Students who find part-time jobs or internships within their field of study also have an opportunity to clarify their career goals and add to the list of qualifications on their resumes. During job interviews, you can provide real-world examples of your ability to solve problems, work independently, and take responsibility. For many employers, work experience during college sets you apart from other recent graduates and improves your chances of landing a full-time job after graduation.

Starting with Smart Choices

Heading off to college is a time for new experiences, exploring academic interests, meeting new people and embracing newfound financial independence. However, financial independence comes with its share of risks and rewards. Are you prepared to make wise and informed financial decisions? Do you know how to recognize predatory credit offers? Can you properly manage a checking account? Do you have a savings plan? Do you understand your financial aid and how it will be repaid?

Smart financial choices you make today could help you achieve your future financial goals, like traveling or buying a car or home. However, money mistakes when you are just starting out can leave you in debt and negatively impact your credit score for a long period of time.

(Source: "Going to College," MyCreditUnion.gov.)

References

1. Dumbauld, Beth. "Six Things You Should Know about Working While Going to College," Straighter Line, October 20, 2016.
2. Higuera, Valencia. "Five Benefits of Working a Job While in College," Money Crashers, 2017.
3. Levy, David. "The Benefits of Working While in College," Edvisors, 2017.
4. "Pros and Cons of Work-Study in College," The Prospect, 2014.

CHAPTER 4

SUMMER EMPLOYMENT: A SNAPSHOT OF TEEN WORKERS

About This Chapter: "Summer Employment: A Snapshot of Teen Workers," © 2022 Infobase.

Summer jobs offer teens the opportunity to explore the work environment. Although teens may work all year in different part-time jobs, the summer months provide an opportunity for teens to work on a full-time basis while schools are out of session. Hence, summer is the right time for teens to earn more money, get introduced to the 40-hour work week, and gain valuable experience, responsibility, and skills through summer employment.

Finding a Summer Job

Teens can identify job leads for summer employment through various sources:

- Internet
- Classified ads section in the local newspaper
- Job boards
- School counselors
- Recommendations from friends and family members

If you are interested in working at a specific place, then do not hesitate to contact the manager and inquire about possible job openings. Although there will likely be plenty of job openings for teens during the summer months, the competition will also be very high, so try to be the early bird. It is better to begin your job search well before the onset of summer.

Common Summer Jobs for Teens

There will be many openings in minimum-wage service industries for teenagers during the summer months. Before you jump into the process of job hunting, make a list of your likes and dislikes and try to find a job that suits you the best. Choosing the right summer job often sets you on the right career path in adulthood. Some common summer employment opportunities available for teens are as follows:

- **Camp counseling.** A camp counselor guides and mentors kids during outdoor camp programs and events. This job will suit older teens who are natural leaders and those who wish to spend more time outdoors.
- **Tutoring.** Some students use the summer months to catch up on school work and prepare for tests. Academically inclined teens can use this opportunity to teach such kids.
- **Golf caddying.** The game of golf picks up in the summer and there will be plenty of openings for golf caddying. This job involves a lot of walking and carrying heavy bags of golf clubs.
- **Swimming pools/amusement parks.** Swimming pools and amusement parks are in action during the summer months. They provide job opportunities for teens in many areas, including ticket sales, park tours, swimming pool cleaning, food stalls, and so on. Teens who are strong swimmers can also work as lifeguards. Since lifeguarding is a challenging position with a lot of responsibility, it requires Red Cross certification.
- **Childcare.** Working parents often look for safe, secure, and reliable childcare for their young children during the months when school is not in session. Teens who enjoy spending time with children can consider babysitting or working at daycare centers.
- **Gardening.** Some people may not have the time or may be physically incapable of taking care of their lawns. Teens can assist them with planting, fertilizing, lawn mowing, and repairing irrigation systems. Gardening is in high demand during the summer months and may extend into the fall.
- **Retail sales.** Teens can find a great deal of opportunity as retail salespeople in fast-food restaurants, malls, grocery stores, and so on.
- **House sitting.** Many people travel during the summer vacation months and will be looking for responsible house sitters to look after their homes in their absence. The responsibilities of a house sitter include keeping the house clean, collecting mail and newspapers, watering plants, and taking care of the safety of the house.

Do Not Give Up

Some teens tend to give up too easily when they do not receive a reply from a potential employer after applying for a job. Persistent and polite followups can be an effective tool in such situations. However, due to heavy competition, not all teens end up getting a job. If you do not find a suitable job, you have other options to consider.

- **Volunteering.** Volunteering means providing service without getting paid. Teens can volunteer at schools, hospitals, and welfare organizations. Like paid jobs, you can find volunteering opportunities online.

Financial Empowerment

Financial empowerment is building the knowledge and ability of individuals to manage money and use financial services products that work for them.

Financially-empowered individuals are both informed and skilled. They know where to get help with their financial challenges and can access and choose financial products and services that meet their needs. This sense of empowerment can build confidence that they can effectively use their financial knowledge, skills, and resources to reach their goals.

(Source: "A Financial Empowerment Toolkit for Community Volunteers," Consumer Financial Protection Bureau (CFPB).)

- **Internships** are short-term, hands-on training opportunities offered by companies and businesses to bright students. Some internships may pay their interns a nominal salary, but most of them do not. However, if you perform well during the internship, then there is a good chance that you may be offered a full-time job.

Although most of the volunteering jobs and internships do not pay you a salary, they serve as a great way to build your knowledge and experience and look good on a resume. They can be helpful to land a high-paying job in the future.

References

1. "Teen Summer Jobs," *Houston Chronicle*, August 7, 2018.
2. "Finding a Summer Job or Internship," The Nemours Foundation/KidsHealth®, June 2017.
3. "15 Great Summer Jobs for Teens," Investopedia, May 12, 2017.
4. "Mistakes Teens Make in Looking for Summer or Part-Time Jobs," LiveCareer, January 4, 2013.

CHAPTER 5
APPRENTICESHIP AND INTERNSHIP

About This Chapter: Text under the heading "Apprenticeship" is excerpted from "Apprenticeship: Earn While You Earn," U.S. Bureau of Labor Statistics (BLS), U.S. Department of Labor (DOL), 2013; Text under the heading "Internship" is excerpted from "Internships: Previewing a Profession," U.S. Bureau of Labor Statistics (BLS), U.S. Department of Labor (DOL), 2006; Text under the heading "What Is the Difference between an Apprenticeship and an Internship?" is excerpted from "What Is the Difference between an Apprenticeship and an Internship?" Apprenticeship.gov, U.S. Department of Labor (DOL), April 5, 2019.

Apprenticeship
What Is Apprenticeship?*

Apprenticeship is an industry-driven, high-quality career pathway where employers can develop and prepare their future workforce, and individuals can obtain paid work experience, classroom instruction, mentorship, and a portable credential.

The length of an apprenticeship program can vary depending on the employer, complexity of the occupation, industry, and the type of program.

Text excerpted from "Help – Apprenticeship.gov," Apprenticeship.gov, U.S. Department of Labor (DOL), August 30, 2018.

Getting an Apprenticeship

Getting an apprenticeship is similar to getting a job: you need to find a program, apply for an opening, and qualify for selection.

Finding Apprenticeships

Apprenticeships involve commitment, so you will need to find and choose a program that is right for you.

Search for programs. You can look for apprenticeship openings in a variety of ways. State apprenticeship agencies are often a good resource and usually keep lists of apprenticeships. Another way to identify apprenticeship programs is to visit an American Job Center.

You might also search for apprenticeships advertised in a newspaper or online. Or you can contact a local union or other apprenticeship sponsor directly to ask about opportunities. DOL's Office of Apprenticeship website provides contact information for all of the sponsors in the registered apprenticeship database, searchable by state and county.

In addition, community colleges and other schools sometimes post openings for available apprenticeships, which may be offered as part of an educational program. Some workers approach their employer about creating an apprenticeship position in a job they already have.

Special programs. Some programs are designed for specific groups. For example, school-to-apprenticeship programs allow high schoolers in some states to get started in an apprenticeship while they are students. Apprenticeships for active-duty service members provide training in some military occupations. And some correctional institutions offer programs for inmates.

Preapprenticeship programs are another option. These programs help people qualify and prepare for apprenticeships. Participants might learn about career options and what an apprenticeship involves, for example, while they develop occupational skills.

Choosing a program. Apprenticeships vary in their schedules, pay, costs, technical instruction, and other details. Costs, for example, might include application fees, union dues, school tuition, books, and tools or other equipment, such as safety boots or uniforms.

Before you choose a program, it is important to learn about the occupation you are interested in. Talk to people in the occupation or tour a jobsite to get a better sense of the work culture and tasks.

Application and Selection

To get an apprenticeship, you must first apply for one. Apprentices are typically chosen through a competitive process, which often involves interviews, rankings, and other factors.

Applying. Apprenticeship requirements vary by sponsor and program. For many programs, you must be at least 18 years old and have a high-school diploma or equivalent.

You might also need to have completed certain classes in school or to pass an aptitude test in subjects such as math, physics, and reading comprehension. Related work experience is sometimes necessary. And some programs require drug tests or a physical exam to verify that you are able to do key tasks in the occupation.

When you apply for an apprenticeship program, you may need to pay a fee of about $20 to $45 and submit other material. This supplemental material might include written recommendations, school transcripts, and proof of identification, such as a birth certificate or driver's license.

Interviews. Applicants who meet the initial requirements usually have one or more interviews with their prospective sponsor. Interviewers want to know more about your qualifications, that you will be reliable, and whether you are really interested in doing the work.

Prepare for an apprenticeship interview as you would for a job interview: dress nicely, think about how you will answer common interview questions, and be ready to discuss your work-related skills and interests.

In addition, sponsors usually want to know that you understand the work involved in the occupation you will train for.

Rankings. Qualified apprenticeship applicants are often ranked on factors such as aptitude test results, interview performance, education, and work experience. As sponsors need apprentices, the most competitive applicants – those with the highest rankings – are chosen first. Applicants with lower rankings might need to wait until there is another opening.

The wait may last several weeks to several years.

Networking. For apprenticeship applicants, like for jobseekers, networking can be beneficial. It allows you to meet people in the occupations you might be apprenticing for and helps you to learn more about a program. Applicants might also gain a better sense of what to expect in an apprenticeship. In addition, your networking contacts may recommend you to sponsors.

Advantages of an Apprenticeship

Apprenticeship programs have many advantages, including a paycheck, hands-on training, technical instruction – which is often free – and a solid start to a career.

A paycheck. Apprentices start earning money right away, which is a big draw for many who choose this type of career preparation. In addition to wages, some apprentices are eligible for health insurance or other employee benefits. Apprentices usually make at least minimum wage. As apprentices' skills progress, their wages typically increase.

Hands-on training. While on the job, apprentices learn practical skills from experienced workers. By the end of their apprenticeship, people usually have had experience with all of the major aspects of their occupation.

Technical instruction. Apprentices receive related technical instruction that they use on the job. Apprentices' technical instruction is usually provided by people who work in the industry, and their sponsor frequently pays. Completed classes may count toward certification or licensure requirements, which help boost apprentices' credentials and are sometimes necessary to work in an occupation. Some apprentices earn college credits or an associate's or bachelor's degree during their program.

And apprentices often appreciate how much they gain from the instruction.

Build a career foundation. At the end of their programs, apprentices earn a certificate of completion, issued by DOL or a state apprenticeship agency. This certificate

> ## What Are the Differences between Industry-Recognized Apprenticeship Programs and Registered Apprenticeship Programs?
>
> Industry-Recognized Apprenticeship Programs (IRAPs) are high-quality apprenticeship programs recognized by industry and/or workforce leaders known as "SREs." IRAPs were designed to give the additional flexibility necessary to expand the apprenticeship model and to address the diverse workforce needs of different industries and occupations. A Registered Apprenticeship Program (RAP) is a proven model of apprenticeship that has been validated by the Department of Labor or State Apprenticeship Agency. RAPs are known for their structure, rigor, and quality and are designed for organizations interested in receiving the DOL or state seal of approval and funding opportunities made available by DOL.
>
> *(Source: "How Can We Help You?" Apprenticeship.gov, U.S. Department of Labor (DOL).)*

is recognized by employers around the country. Because apprentices' credentials are widely accepted, people who have finished an apprenticeship program frequently have increased occupational mobility.

During the course of an apprenticeship program, apprentices are encouraged to make contacts in their industry. This networking may help them get a job when they reach journey-level status. Some apprentices finish the program and then start a career with the same employer who sponsored them.

Internship

An ounce of experience can be worth a ton of research – especially when it comes to exploring careers. Internships are one of the best ways to get that experience and to test a career choice. And later, when it is time to get a job, internships attract employers. Internships provide short-term, practical experience for students, recent graduates, and people changing careers. Most internships are designed for college students, but many are open to high schoolers; others welcome career changers seeking exposure to a new field.

Internship positions are available in a number of disciplines. They can be arranged through your school or the organization for which you will work. And they often provide either pay or academic credit – sometimes, both.

Regardless of how it is coordinated, completing an internship increases your chances of getting a job that you will enjoy. Not only do you discover your job likes and dislikes, but you enter the job market with experience that is related to your career goals.

This overview is geared toward college students. It discusses the who, where, which, and how of pursuing an internship.

Who Should Pursue an Internship?

Almost anyone – both students and nonstudents who are yet to settle into a career – can benefit from doing an internship, no matter what their motivations are. A liberal arts major, for example, may have a less obvious career path than, say, a nursing student. But, even well-directed students can benefit from the practical experience that an internship provides: After all, a hospital emergency room, a pediatrician's office, and a nursing home each provide different work environments for nurses.

College students often take part in a summer internship after their junior year. Other students might work as interns during the school year, receiving academic credit toward their degree. Some students participate in more than one internship over the course of their academic careers.

Part of an internship's value comes from the opportunity for experiential learning. Whether students have some, little, or no idea about the kind of work that they want to do, they can get firsthand knowledge about a particular type of work or work environment.

Where Are Internships Located?

Internships may be located anywhere in the world. It is probably easier for students to arrange something closer to their homes or schools than to set up something halfway around the world. But with a little effort, an internship can be created just about any place.

There are several ways to locate available internship opportunities. Public libraries, career centers, and offices of school counselors usually have resources that contain hundreds, even thousands, of national listings. These internships include positions with fashion designers, publishing companies, biotechnology research firms, software developers, and federal and state government agencies, to name a few examples.

Job fairs can also be a source of information about internship opportunities, as can the Internet.

In addition, colleges and universities usually maintain local listings of employers who hire interns. Career counselors and academic advisors may be aware of possibilities, and professors may know what types of internships students in a particular field of study have had in the past. Programs that offer academic credit typically have an internship coordinator who oversees placement and monitors interns' progress.

Some companies have formal internship programs. Others accept informal arrangements. Directly contacting companies, or visiting the career section of their websites, is usually the best way to learn whether they offer internships. Students might also be able to propose and set up their own internships.

Which Internships Are Best?

The best internships allow students to learn by doing, helping them to focus their career goals. Not surprisingly, most students choose an internship that is related to their major or to their career objectives.

But, many students are not sure what they want to major in, let alone what they want to do for a career. And the differences between one internship and another can be hard to discern, particularly for students who are new to the working world. Making several important decisions can help students choose the best internship for them.

Perhaps most important, and most difficult, for some students is to decide which fields or occupations they are interested in. Career counselors, academic advisors, and vocational guidance publications, including the Occupational Outlook Handbook (available online at www.bls.gov/oco), can aid in the process.

A related decision that students must make is which industry to work in. Occupations, and their related internships, differ from one industry to the next: An internship for a would-be management analyst would be much different in a bank, for example, than in a nonprofit organization. The Career Guide to Industries, online at www.bls.gov/oco/cg, provides in-depth information about many industries.

Internship duties often vary, but any position can be worthwhile. Whether interns do odd jobs around the office or do challenging work that is related to their fields of study, they get a feel for workplace culture and make contacts that may be valuable for career networking.

How Do You Apply for an Internship?

Start early when applying for internships. Deadlines for turning in application materials vary, but many summer internships require that applications be submitted by February or March. Career counselors often say that Thanksgiving break is a good time to start gathering materials and researching opportunities for a summer internship. Other experts suggest starting the process a few semesters before the desired internship period.

Applying for an internship might seem overwhelming, especially for those who have never written a resume or cover letter. But, preparing these documents when applying for an internship means not having to start from scratch when applying for a job.

In addition to requiring a resume and cover letter, internship sponsors might request other items, such as a completed application, transcripts, coursework samples, and references. Applying for several internships increases the chance for success. Because high-profile employers are likely to get many applications, students who use personal or school contacts are most likely to stand out.

Reviewing application materials for accuracy and completeness before submitting them is a must. The most careful students have someone else read over their application as well. Materials should be sent on time, with a followup telephone call confirming that the application was received.

Some internship sponsors might require candidates to appear for an interview. To prepare for such a meeting, students should read up on employment interviewing, participate in mock interviews, and attend interviewing workshops offered at their school. And students who follow up with a thank-you note after the interview make a good impression. Career counselors, books, and other resources can be helpful in the application and interviewing process.

What Is the Difference between an Apprenticeship and an Internship?

The U.S. Department of Labor (DOL) does not have an official definition of internship or externship. However, generally speaking, differences between internships and apprenticeships include:

- **Length of time.** Internships are usually short term (1–3 months) and apprenticeships are longer term (1–3 years).
- **Structure.**
  - Apprenticeships include a structured training plan, with a focus on mastering specific skills an employer needs to fill an occupation within their organization.
  - Internships are not structured and often focus on entry-level general work experience.
- **Mentorship.** Apprentices receive individualized training with an experienced mentor who walks them through their entire process. Internships do not always include mentorship.
- **Pay.** Apprenticeships are paid experiences that often lead to full-time employment. Internships are often unpaid and may not lead to a full-time job.
- **Credential.** Apprenticeships lead to an industry-recognized credential. Internships typically do not lead to a credential.
- **College credit.** Internship and apprenticeship experiences may both lead to college credit, although some apprenticeship programs will lead to a debt-free college degree.

CHAPTER 6
SCHOLARSHIPS FOR STUDENTS

About This Chapter: This chapter includes text excerpted from "Find and Apply for as Many Scholarships as You Can – It's Free Money for College or Career School!" Federal Student Aid, U.S. Department of Education (ED), December 22, 2019.

Scholarships are gifts. They do not need to be repaid. There are thousands of them, offered by schools, employers, individuals, private companies, nonprofits, communities, religious groups, and professional and social organizations.

What Kinds of Scholarships Are Available?

Some scholarships for college are merit-based. You earn them by meeting or exceeding certain standards set by the scholarship-giver. Merit scholarships might be awarded based on academic achievement or on a combination of academics and a special talent, trait, or interest. Other scholarships are based on financial need.

Many scholarships are geared toward particular groups of people; for instance, there are scholarships for women or graduate students. And some are available because of where you or your parent work, or because you come from a certain background.

A scholarship might cover the entire cost of your tuition, or it might be a one-time award of a few hundred dollars. Either way, it is worth applying for, because it will help reduce the cost of your education.

How Do You Find Scholarships?

You can learn about scholarships in several ways, including contacting the financial aid office at the school you plan to attend and checking information in a public library or online. But, be careful. Make sure scholarship information and offers you receive are legitimate; and remember that you do not have to pay to find scholarships or other financial aid.

Try these free sources of information about scholarships:
- The financial aid office at a college or career school
- A high school or TRIO counselor

- The U.S. Department of Labor's FREE scholarship search tool (www.careeronestop.org/toolkit/training/find-scholarships.aspx)
- Federal agencies
- Your state grant agency (www2.ed.gov/about/contacts/state/index.html)
- Your library's reference section
- Foundations, religious or community organizations, local businesses, or civic groups
- Organizations (including professional associations) related to your field of interest
- Ethnicity-based organizations
- Your employer or your parents' employers

When Do You Apply for Scholarships?

That depends on each scholarship's deadline. Some deadlines are as early as a year before college starts, so if you are in high school now, you should be researching and applying for scholarships during the summer between your junior and senior years. But if you have missed that window, do not give up! Look at scholarship information to see which ones you can still apply for now.

How Do You Apply for Scholarships

Each scholarship has its own requirements. The scholarship's website should give you an idea of who qualifies for the scholarship and how to apply. Make sure you read the application carefully, fill it out completely, and meet the application deadline.

How Do You Get Your Scholarship Money?

That depends on the scholarship. The money might go directly to your college, where it will be applied to any tuition, fees, or other amounts you owe, and then any leftover funds given to you. Or it might be sent directly to you in a check. The scholarship provider should tell you what to expect when it informs you that you have been awarded the scholarship. If not, make sure to ask.

How Does a Scholarship Affect Your Other Student Aid?

A scholarship will affect your other student aid because all your student aid added together cannot be more than your cost of attendance at your college or career school. So, you will need to let your school know if you have been awarded a scholarship so that the financial aid office can subtract that amount from your cost of attendance (and from certain other aid, such as loans, that you might have been offered). Then, any amount left can be covered by other financial aid for which you are eligible. Questions? Ask your financial aid office.

CHAPTER 7
WANT TO BE YOUR OWN BOSS?

About This Chapter: Text beginning with the heading "Is Self-Employment for You?" is excerpted from "Self-Employment: What to Know to Be Your Own Boss," U.S. Bureau of Labor Statistics (BLS), U.S. Department of Labor (DOL), June 2014; Text under the heading "Characteristics of Entrepreneurship" is excerpted from "Characteristics of Entrepreneurship," Small Business Administration (SBA), August 21, 2014.

Is Self-Employment for You?

People choose to become self-employed for many reasons, including greater independence and flexibility. But, they also consider the downsides, such as the long hours and lack of benefits.

As part of your decision-making process, you should weigh the pros and cons of starting a business, along with your own reasons for seeking self-employment. For example, hoping to make a lot of money quickly can lead you into trouble. But, if you feel passionately about developing an idea, self-employment may be right for you.

Rewards

For many self-employed workers, autonomy is the biggest reward. They are able to make their own decisions, such as what kind of work they do, whom they do it for, where and when they do it – and even how much to pay themselves.

Self-employed workers usually take on many different tasks, learning to do each as the need arises. For example, a self-employed barber needs to find a suitable location for opening a shop, attract clients, and price services, in addition to cutting hair.

Many workers find that self-employment allows them not only to expand their professional skills, but also to enrich themselves personally. "I learned a lot more about business and life than I ever expected," says Megan Lebon, a physician who owns a practice in Atlanta, Georgia.

Self-employment can bring other rewards, too. Some workers enjoy creating a new business and watching it grow. They feel good about working for something they believe in.

Challenges

Self-employment is hard work, especially during the first few years. Workers may have difficulty finding clients, earning a steady income, securing business loans, and navigating laws. These challenges add up to financial risk and uncertainty.

And, with income frequently unpredictable, workers may try to handle all or most parts of the business themselves. "You end up working a lot more than you think, oftentimes way more than when you were working for someone else," says Vicki James, owner of a marketing business in Rochester, New York. This schedule can make balancing work and personal life difficult.

Another challenge with self-employment is lack of benefits. Public and private employers typically contribute to retirement, health, and other benefits, offering affordable options to their employees. But, self-employed workers must find these benefits and pay for them entirely out of pocket. And there is no paid leave for vacation or illness: A day off work is a day without pay. These types of burdens may overstretch limited financial resources.

Get Started

Even after you choose an occupation for starting a business, becoming self-employed is not as easy as deciding to work for yourself. You need certain skills and a lot of preparation before you can focus on setting up and growing a business.

But, if getting started seems daunting, remember that you do not have to do everything at once and that help is available. Focus on taking one step at a time.

Skills and Knowledge

One of the most important requirements for self-employment, business experts say, is having the technical skills and knowledge you need to do the work you want to do. For example, a graphic design freelancer needs to know color theory and how to use design software. It is a bad idea to start a business in something you do not understand well.

Other technical skills, such as bookkeeping and marketing, are helpful for operating a business. You can learn these skills in a class, at school, with the help of a mentor, or on your own. Higher education, although not a prerequisite for success, is often useful.

Some occupations have specific entry requirements, regardless of whether workers are self-employed. Physicians, for example, must have a bachelor's degree and complete a medical degree program, residency, and licensure requirements. And real estate agents need to become licensed in their state.

Experts suggest that, in addition to having technical skills, you focus on improving "soft" skills, such as time management and people skills. And, regardless of what you do, having a passion for the work is key.

Time Management

Self-employed workers often have multiple responsibilities and keep long hours. Being able to manage time efficiently – for example, through multitasking and scheduling – is crucial. These skills help you determine how much time you need to complete tasks and whether you can take on additional work.

People Skills

Good people skills, such as communication and customer service, help you attract and retain both employees and clients – especially in the beginning. "Early on, you are the chief salesperson," says Dennis Wright, a small-business mentor in Santa Ana, California. "You have to sell people on your abilities and the value of your product or service."

Passion

Experts say that a passion for what you do can give you the belief, motivation, and commitment you need to overcome the challenges that self-employment may present. "You must like and be committed to what you are doing," Wright says, "or you are likely to give up when you hit bumps in the road."

Preparation

No matter how skilled and knowledgeable you are about the product or service you want to sell, you still need to prepare to ensure success in self-employment. Experts recommend that before you invest any money, you take some time to figure out what motivates you to become self-employed, do your research, and ask for help as you plan your business.

Understand Why

Experts say that self-employed workers often feel discouraged, especially when just getting started. Understanding your motivations for becoming self-employed can help sustain you in times of struggle. "The reasons why are the catalyst that will push you forward," says James. "They will help you overcome the moments of doubt."

The reasons for becoming self-employed differ for everyone. Consider what your reasons are, and make note of them. Then, refer to them when you face challenges, to remind yourself of why you pursued self-employment.

Research

Researching your potential business is a way of evaluating whether your idea is marketable. Through research, you can also learn more about your potential customers, competitors, and collaborators. Experts suggest examining the prospective market for your product or service so that you can answer essential questions, such as the following:

- Who and where is the customer?
- How can your potential customers benefit from the product or service you are offering?

- Who are your competitors?
- What will set you apart from your competition?

Professional journals, focus groups, surveys, business clubs, seminars, and current business owners are among the sources that can provide answers to these questions. You may even find reports written by people who have done similar research.

But, not every business idea is a winner. Experts suggest moving on when your research shows that an idea would not work. Your next idea might be the right one.

And be careful not to let research stop you from actually getting started. "I thought I first needed to know everything about running a business," James says. "Find the courage to make mistakes, and learn from them as you go."

Ask for Help

Many of the principles of business are the same, so people who have already had success with self-employment are often good sources of information to those who are considering it. They may share tips and mistakes, experts say, or make valuable suggestions you had not considered. "Learn from people smarter and more experienced than you," says Luyk.

Another possible advantage in asking for help is finding a mentor: someone who offers guidance, encouragement, advice, and emotional support throughout the life of your business. You may meet a potential mentor informally or through a business organization.

Setting Up Shop

After you have determined that your business idea is viable, it is finally time to set up shop, right? Not quite; you still have work to do. For starters, you need to write a business plan, ensure that you meet all legal and tax requirements, and prepare to limit your legal and financial liability. These steps also apply if you decide to freelance, even if you get started quickly out of your own home.

The process of setting up a business can be confusing and difficult. You will need to complete a lot of paperwork to ensure that you are complying with different laws and regulations, for example. Experts recommend consulting an accountant and a lawyer for help, and they say that this investment in your future business is money well spent. "Be upfront about what you want and what you can afford," says Luyk. "These professionals will save you money in the end."

Another difficulty is a lack of money early on. Experts suggest that, before you get started, you should save up enough money to last a couple of years so that you avoid financial pitfalls.

Write a Business Plan

A business plan describes what service you will provide or product you will make, along with how and when you will do it. "If you do not set goals, you would not achieve them," says business mentor Jack Bernard. "You will just chase your tail." Use your research to set goals for the business within specific timeframes. Your business plan should explain in detail every part of your business, including the following:

- Your business values and vision for the future
- Your business's strengths, weaknesses, opportunities, and threats
- Financial projections
- The experience and achievements of key staff

Business plans are important when you seek funding, which may include loans and grants. Most reputable creditors require applicants to have a business plan, a solid credit score, and a criminal background check before agreeing to lend or invest money in a business startup.

There are plenty of free resources available to help you write your plan. For example, you can find step-by-step guides and templates online or at your local library. And some business organizations offer individualized business counseling.

Meet Legal Requirements

To legally operate a business, you need a business license, as well as permits from the city and county, or both, in which the business is located. Local governments have many different requirements, but common ones include health and zoning permits.

You also need to meet Internal Revenue Service requirements. These include registering for an employer identification number, reporting wages and taxes withheld, and verifying employees' eligibility to work in the United States.

Other federal requirements may apply, depending on your business product or service. For example, a business that sells produce throughout the country needs a permit from the U.S. Department of Agriculture (USDA) to ensure that the food is safe.

Limit Liability

The way you structure your business affects your legal and financial responsibilities. For example, a sole proprietor is someone who owns a business and is accountable for all of its assets, obligations, and so on. And sole proprietors take a great risk by assuming all responsibility for their business; lenders can take control of personal assets of a sole proprietor who fails to repay a business loan.

Some business structures are designed to limit personal liability. The most common are a limited liability company (LLC) and an S corporation. Both of these arrangements protect personal assets by risking only what is invested in the business. Generally speaking, an LLC is easier to set up and manage, but an S corporation allows for the sale of business stock to investors.

Growing the Business

After you have completed the necessary steps for self-employment, you will need to focus on growing the business. Networking, staying competitive, making adjustments, and working through challenges will increase your chances of success.

Network

Experts say that networking is one of the best ways for self-employed people to spend their time. Among other benefits it provides, networking offers opportunities for self-employed workers to reach potential clients, meet business mentors, and test ideas to gauge interest. "You have to make yourself visible to your market," Lebon says. "People can only do business with you if they can find you first."

People usually network at business events, clubs, and meetings. Volunteering with a professional organization or serving on a community board also can be useful. And networking does not have to be formal. "Sometimes I just have coffee with people and share ideas, without worrying about business," says Ryan Schwartz, a freelance communications specialist in Portland, Oregon.

Some self-employed workers also use traditional marketing tools, such as creating a website or advertising in a local paper, to attract clients. But, experts caution against relying too heavily on marketing, which often is expensive and yields mixed results. "There is no better form of advertising than word of mouth," Wright says. "Give your customers a positive experience, and they will come back with a friend."

Stay Competitive

Competition is a part of being in business. To stay competitive with other businesses that are like yours, you have to stand out in areas such as price, quality, and service. "If you cannot define what makes you better," says Bernard, "your customers certainly would not know, and they will take their business elsewhere."

Updating your research will help keep you informed about competition in your market. After starting her cleaning business, for example, Luyk asked potential clients what they liked and disliked about their existing cleaning service. She used their feedback to improve her business.

When trying to set yourself apart from other small businesses, do not compete on price, say experts. Large businesses often offer lower prices because they have some advantages, such as the ability to buy in bulk at reduced cost, that small businesses do not. Lowering prices also reduces profit, which makes it harder to stay in business. "There's always someone willing to undercut your prices," says James. "Be better in other ways."

Make Adjustments

As your business evolves, it may outgrow your original vision. Keep up with developments by making adjustments, as necessary. For example, you may have planned to run your business from home for several years, but brisk sales might allow you to rent office space sooner than expected.

Experts often recommend adding workers to your payroll as one of the first tweaks you make after your business is established. "Hire people to help you as soon as you can afford them," says Luyk. "Then you can spend your time working on your business – not in the business."

It is important to hire employees who have experience and skills that you do not have. For example, opening an eatery to showcase your culinary skills can be risky if you have never run a restaurant. Employing a manager will offset your lack of management experience and let you focus on your strengths, such as cooking or designing the menu.

Persevere

Working for yourself is not easy. The business might take longer than you expect to turn a profit, for example, or you might have trouble making rent or paying your employees.

As most self-employed workers will tell you, it takes lots of preparation, determination, and time to achieve success in a new business. "This is a marathon," Lebon says. "Temper your expectations, take things one step a time, and do not give up."

Remember, experts say, you do not have a chance for success unless you take the first step. "People are so afraid to fail that they become paralyzed," says Luyk. "But you can learn a lot from failure. And if you do not try, you will always wonder what could have been."

Characteristics of Entrepreneurship

Becoming a successful entrepreneur requires sound planning, creativity and hard work, and it also involves taking risks, because all businesses require some form of investment, usually time or money.

To begin evaluating whether launching your own business is right for you, consider some of the following common characteristics that are typical of successful small business owners:

Innovation and Creativity

The first step to starting a business is to come up with an idea or concept. It takes innovation to develop a product or service that brings value to customers that they cannot get elsewhere. Additionally, entrepreneurs often have to find creative ways to tackle everyday business problems like suppliers shipping inventory late and ineffective marketing plans.

Persistence and Resiliency

Businesses, like all things, take time to grow. Very few people will produce mass amounts of profit within just weeks or even months of being in business. There will be things that you fail at, even if your business is successful. Inevitably, some projects fail for a variety of reasons – poor planning, competitors offering better options, market timing or other factors. To be a successful entrepreneur you need to learn and grow from your mistakes to move forward. You must be able to live with uncertainty and overcome obstacles that you did not anticipate.

Flexibility

Even the most well thought out business plans will change along the way. Changes in the market, technology, and customer tastes are going to happen and they are out of your control. Your ability to be flexible and respond to these changes will be the key to your business's survival.

Passion

As you have probably realized, entrepreneurship is not easy. If you are not passionate about what you are doing, it will be much harder to persist through all of the challenges that come your way. Your customers will also notice, it is harder to sell something you are not passionate about yourself. Mollie Breault-Binaghi, who was named Vermont's Young Entrepreneur of the Year in 2011 by the SBA, said it best: "You have to be passionate about it. Otherwise it is not worth doing. Owning your own business is not easy and it is not going to make you rich quick. You are going to be in it for the long haul so it is got to be something you love."

Other characteristics that are helpful to an entrepreneur are persuasiveness, self-confidence, and being visionary. While it is not essential you have all of these qualities, it is a good idea to think about them and determine if entrepreneurship is really right for you.

CHAPTER 8
TAX INFORMATION FOR STUDENTS

About This Chapter: Text in this chapter begins with excerpts from "Your First Job," Internal Revenue Service (IRS), December 7, 2020; Text beginning with the heading "Do You Have to File a Return?" is excerpted from "Tax Guide 2020 – for Individuals," Internal Revenue Service (IRS), February 11, 2021; Text under the heading "Wages and Salaries" is excerpted from "Topic No. 401 Wages and Salaries," Internal Revenue Service (IRS), March 5, 2021; Text under the heading "Tips for Teenage Taxpayers with Summer Jobs" is excerpted from "IRS Offers Tips for Teenage Taxpayers with Summer Jobs," Internal Service Revenue (IRS), May 25, 2021; Text under the heading "Scholarships, Fellowship Grants, and Other Grants" is excerpted from "Topic No. 421 Scholarships, Fellowship Grants, and Other Grants," Internal Service Revenue (IRS), March 16, 2021.

At the end of your first week on the job, you get your paycheck only to find out that a chunk of money is gone. Your employer has taken out – or withheld – the taxes you owe. Employers withhold money for federal income taxes, Social Security taxes, and state and local income taxes in some states and localities.

Taxes are payments of money to the government that provide public goods and services for the community. Some examples of public goods are national defense, street lights, and roads and highways. Public services include welfare programs, sanitation, law enforcement, and education.

When you start a new job, your employer will ask you to provide information on Form W-4 PDF, Employee's Withholding Certificate. This will help your employer determine how much money to withhold from your wages.

By January 31 of each year, your employer (even if you do not work there anymore) will give you an IRS Form W-2, Wage and Tax Statement, showing how much you earned in wages, tips and other compensation from the previous year. It will also show the state and federal taxes, Social Security, Medicare wages, and tips withheld. You will need this form when you file your tax return.

Do You Have to File a Return?
You must file a federal income tax return if you are a citizen or resident of the United States or a resident of Puerto Rico and you meet the filing requirements for any of the following categories that apply to you.

- Individuals in general. (There are special rules for surviving spouses, executors, administrators, legal representatives, U.S. citizens and residents living outside the United States, residents of Puerto Rico, and individuals with income from U.S. possessions.)
- Dependents
- Certain children under age 19 or full-time students
- Self-employed persons
- Aliens

The filing requirements apply even if you do not owe tax.

Who Should File?

Even if you do not have to file, you should file a federal income tax return to get money back if any of the following conditions apply.

- You had federal income tax withheld or made estimated tax payments
- You qualify for the earned income credit
- You qualify for the additional child tax credit
- You qualify for the premium tax credit
- You qualify for the health coverage tax credit
- You qualify for the American opportunity credit
- You qualify for the credit for federal tax on fuels

What Happens after You File

After you send your return to the IRS, you may have some questions. This section discusses concerns you may have about recordkeeping, your refund, and what to do if you move.

What Records Should You Keep?

You must keep records so that you can prepare a complete and accurate income tax return. The law does not require any special form of records. However, you should keep all receipts, canceled checks or other proof of payment, and any other records to support any deductions or credits you claim.

If you file a claim for refund, you must be able to prove by your records that you have overpaid your tax.

Why Keep Records

Good records help you:

- **Identify sources of income.** Your records can identify the sources of your income to help you separate business from nonbusiness income and taxable from nontaxable income.
- **Keep track of expenses.** You can use your records to identify expenses for which you can claim a deduction. This helps you determine if you can itemize deductions on your tax return.

- **Keep track of the basis of property.** You need to keep records that show the basis of your property. This includes the original cost or other basis of the property and any improvements you made.
- **Prepare tax returns.** You need records to prepare your tax return.
- **Support items reported on tax returns.** The IRS may question an item on your return. Your records will help you explain any item and arrive at the correct tax. If you cannot produce the correct documents, you may have to pay additional tax and be subject to penalties.

Electronic Filing

If your adjusted gross income (AGI) is less than a certain amount, you are eligible for Free File, a free tax software service offered by IRS partners, to prepare and e-file your return for free. If your income is over the amount, you are still eligible for Free File Fillable Forms, an electronic version of IRS paper forms. IRS e-file uses automation to replace most of the manual steps needed to process paper returns. As a result, the processing of e-file returns is faster and more accurate than the processing of paper returns. However, as with a paper return, you are responsible for making sure your return contains accurate information and is filed on time.

If your return is filed with the IRS e-file, you will receive an acknowledgement that your return was received and accepted. If you owe tax, you can e-file and pay electronically. The IRS has processed more than one billion e-filed returns safely and securely. Using an e-file does not affect your chances of an IRS examination of your return.

Using Your Personal Computer

You can file your tax return in a fast, easy, and convenient way using your personal computer. A computer with Internet access and tax preparation software are all you need. Best of all, you can e-file from the comfort of your home 24 hours a day, 7 days a week.

IRS-approved tax preparation software is available for online use on the Internet, for download from the Internet, and in retail stores.

Through Employers and Financial Institutions

Some businesses offer free e-file to their employees, members, or customers. Others offer it for a fee. Ask your employer or financial institution if they offer IRS e-file as an employee, member, or customer benefit.

Free Help with Your Return

The Volunteer Income Tax Assistance (VITA) program offers free tax help to people who generally make $57,000 or less, persons with disabilities, and limited-English speaking taxpayers who need help preparing their own tax returns. The Tax Counseling for the Elderly (TCE) program offers free tax help for all taxpayers, particularly those who are 60 years of age and older. TCE volunteers specialize in answering questions about pensions and retirement-related issues unique to seniors.

You can go to IRS.gov to see your options for preparing and filing your return.

Using a Tax Professional

Many tax professionals electronically file tax returns for their clients. You may personally enter your PIN or complete Form 8879, IRS e-file Signature Authorization, to authorize the tax professional to enter your PIN on your return.

Note: Tax professionals may charge a fee for IRS e-file. Fees can vary depending on the professional and the specific services rendered.

Wages and Salaries

All wages, salaries and tips you received for performing services as an employee of an employer must be included in your gross income. Amounts withheld for taxes, including but not limited to income tax, Social Security and Medicare taxes, are considered "received" and must be included in gross income in the year they are withheld. Generally, your employer's contribution to a qualified pension plan for you is not included in gross income at the time it is contributed. Additionally, while amounts withheld under certain salary reduction agreements with your employer are generally excluded from gross income, such amounts may have to be included in wages subject to Social Security and Medicare taxes in the year they are withheld.

Your employer should provide you a Form W-2, Wage and Tax Statement showing your total income and withholding. You must include all income and withholding from all Forms W-2 you receive on your tax return, and if filing jointly, you must also include all income and withholding from your spouse's Forms W-2. Attach a copy of each Form W-2 to the front of your tax return as indicated in the instructions. Please note that self-employment income is generally reported on Form 1099-NEC, Nonemployee Compensation.

If you receive a Form W-2 after you have filed your return, file an amended tax return.

Tips for Teenage Taxpayers with Summer Jobs

Students and teenagers often get summer jobs. This is a great way to earn extra spending money or to save for later. The Internal Revenue Service (IRS) offers a few tax tips for taxpayers with a summer job:

- **Withholding and estimated tax.** Students and teenage employees normally have taxes withheld from their paychecks by the employer. Some workers are considered self-employed and may be responsible for paying taxes directly to the IRS. One way to do that is by making estimated tax payments during the year.
- **New employees.** When a person gets a new job, they need to fill out a Form W-4, Employee's Withholding Allowance Certificate. Employers use this form to calculate how much federal income tax to withhold from the employee's pay. The IRS Withholding Calculator tool on IRS.gov can help a taxpayer fill out the form.
- **Self-employment.** A taxpayer may engage in types of work that may be considered self-employment. Money earned from self-employment is taxable. Self-employment work can be jobs like baby-sitting or lawn care. Keep good records on money received and expenses paid related to the work. IRS rules may allow some, if not all, costs associated with self-employment to be deducted. A tax deduction generally reduces the taxes you pay.
- **Tip income.** Employees should report tip income. Keep a daily log to accurately report tips. Report tips of $20 or more received in cash in any single month to the employer.
- **Payroll taxes.** Taxpayers may earn too little from their summer job to owe income tax. Employers usually must withhold Social Security and Medicare taxes from their pay. If a taxpayer is self-employed, then Social Security and Medicare taxes may still be due and are generally paid by the taxpayer, in a timely manner.
- **Newspaper carriers.** Special rules apply to a newspaper carrier or distributor. If a person meets certain conditions, then they are self-employed. If the taxpayer does not meet those conditions, and are under age 18, they may be exempt from Social Security and Medicare taxes.
- **Reserve Officers' Training Corps (ROTC) pay.** If a taxpayer is in a ROTC program, active duty pay, such as pay for summer advanced camp, is taxable. Other allowances the taxpayer may receive may not be taxable.
- **Use IRS free file.** Taxpayers can prepare and e-file their federal income tax return for free using IRS Free File. Free File is available only on IRS.gov. Some taxpayers may not earn enough money to file a federal tax return, by law, but may want to if taxes were withheld. For example, a taxpayer may want to file a tax return because they would be eligible for a tax refund or a refundable credit.

Scholarships, Fellowship Grants, and Other Grants

A scholarship is generally an amount paid or allowed to a student at an educational institution for the purpose of study. A fellowship grant is generally an amount paid or allowed to an individual for the purpose of study or research. Other types of grants include need-based grants (such as Pell Grants) and Fulbright Grants.

Tax-Free

If you receive a scholarship, a fellowship grant, or other grant, all or part of the amounts you receive may be tax-free. Scholarships, fellowship grants, and other grants are tax-free if you meet the following conditions:

- You are a candidate for a degree at an educational institution that maintains a regular faculty and curriculum and normally has a regularly-enrolled body of students in attendance at the place where it carries on its educational activities; and
- The amounts you receive are used to pay for tuition and fees required for enrollment or attendance at the educational institution, or for fees, books, supplies, and equipment required for courses at the educational institution.

Taxable

You must include in gross income:

- Amounts used for incidental expenses, such as room and board, travel, and optional equipment.
- Amounts received as payments for teaching, research, or other services required as a condition for receiving the scholarship or fellowship grant. However, you do not need to include in gross income any amounts you receive for services that are required by the National Health Service Corps (NHSC) Scholarship Program, the Armed Forces Health Professions Scholarship and Financial Assistance Program, or a comprehensive student work-learning-service program (as defined in section 448(e) of the Higher Education Act of 1965) operated by a work college.

How to Report

Generally, you report any portion of a scholarship, a fellowship grant, or other grants that you must include in gross income as follows:

- If filing Form 1040 or Form 1040-SR, include the taxable portion in the total amount reported on the "Wages, salaries, tips" line of your tax return. If the taxable amount was not reported on Form W-2, enter "SCH" along with the taxable amount in the space to the left of the "Wages, salaries, tips" line.
- If filing Form 1040-NR, report the taxable amount on the "Scholarship and fellowship grants" line.

Estimated Tax Payments

If any part of your scholarship or fellowship grant is taxable, you may have to make estimated tax payments on the additional income.

PART 2 | MANAGING YOUR MONEY

CHAPTER 9
ESSENTIAL MONEY MANAGEMENT

About This Chapter: Text under the heading "Checklist for Opening a Bank or Credit Union Account" is excerpted from "Checklist for Opening a Bank or Credit Union Account," Consumer Financial Protection Bureau (CFPB), August 1, 2015; Text under the heading "Ways to Receive Your Money" is excerpted from "Ways to Receive Your Money," Consumer Financial Protection Bureau (CFPB), August 1, 2015; Text under the heading "Ways to Pay Your Bills" is excerpted from "Ways to Pay Your Bills," Consumer Financial Protection Bureau (CFPB), August 1, 2015.

Checklist for Opening a Bank or Credit Union Account

You may decide that a checking or savings account is the right product for you. If you do, opening an account at a bank or credit union is quite simple.

Opening an Account at a Bank or Credit Union

First, you may want to get a recommendation from a trusted friend or family member for a bank or credit union. Find out about:
- The fees they charge
- The services they offer, like online bill payment
- The interest they pay for savings accounts

You will usually need between $25 and $100 to open a savings or checking account. You will deposit this money into your account.

You will also need two forms of identification to open an account. Some banks or credit unions will take one form of identification and a bill with your name and address on it. You will usually be required to present:

A U.S. or state government-issued identification with your photo on it, such as a driver's license, U.S. Passport, or military identification.

If you do not have a U.S. government-issued form of identification, some banks and credit unions accept foreign passports and Consular IDs, such as the Matricula Consular card.

Additionally, you will need one of the following:

- Your Social Security card
- A bill with name and address on it
- Your birth certificate

A Matricula Consular is an official Mexican government identification document. Other countries, such as Guatemala and Argentina, offer similar IDs. Consulates in the United States offer them. If you come from another country and do not have a U.S. or state government issued ID, visit your country's consulate for more information about how to get an ID card, and check with the banks and credit unions about whether they accept it.

ITIN and Interest-Bearing Accounts

Interest on your savings or checking accounts is considered income. If you earn interest, you must pay taxes on it. That is why you must have a Social Security number or an Individual Taxpayer Identification Number (ITIN) to open an account that pays interest.

Checklists for Opening a Checking Account

Use the checklists on the following page to ensure you have what you need to open an account at a bank or credit union.

Items Needed to Open a Checking Account

- A U.S. or foreign government-issued form of identification with your picture on it. Note that each bank or credit union has its own policy on which foreign IDs it accepts.
- A second form of identification: Your Social Security card, a bill with your name and address on it, or your birth certificate.
- A Social Security number or ITIN; if not, you may only be able to open a no-interest account.
- Money to open the account

Questions to Ask Your Representative

- Minimum balance required to avoid monthly service fees
- Monthly service fees
- Direct deposit and whether it eliminates the monthly fee
- Per-check or transaction fees

- Fees associated with use of automated teller machines (ATMs)
- Internet banking access and any costs
- Online bill pay access and any costs
- How to avoid overdraft fees
- Low balance alert notifications

Ways to Receive Your Money

You can receive your wages in different ways, for example, you can be paid in cash, paper paychecks, direct deposit, or with a payroll card.

Each of these ways to receive money has some potential benefits and risks, especially when it comes to fees, security, and convenience. Knowing how these products work, how much it costs to use them, and when you will be charged extra fees can help you make the most of your money.

Cash

Cash is money that you have in hand.

Benefits

- Accepted almost everywhere

Risks

- Difficult or impossible to recover if lost or stolen
- Can be tempting to spend cash on hand
- Can be hard to track spending for personal budgeting purposes

Paper Paychecks

Paycheck is a check for your salary or wages made out to you.

Benefits

- You can deposit into a checking or a savings account. A bank or credit union where you have an account will also cash your paycheck for free.
- Safer than carrying cash. If lost or stolen, your employer may cancel and reissue the check if you report it quickly enough.

Risks

- If you do not have a bank account, you may have to pay to cash your paychecks.
- If you deposit a paycheck in a bank or credit union account, you may not be able to access all the funds immediately.

Direct Deposit: Checking or Savings Account

Your salary or wages are sent straight to your bank or credit union account electronically without the use of a paper check. May not be offered by all employers.

Benefits

- Reduces your risk of loss or theft, compared to carrying cash or getting a check
- The account has consumer protections for funds taken by electronic error or theft.
- Funds are usually available to you immediately.
- Funds can be accessed via a debit card, ATM card, or personal checks.
- Many employers allow you to split your deposit between a checking and savings account. This can help you build savings.
- There are no fees to deposit your check. Many banks and credit unions also offer checking and savings accounts with no monthly fees when you set up direct deposit.

Risks

- Keeping your money in a bank account requires you to go to an ATM or storefront location to withdraw cash when cash is needed.

Payroll Cards

Prepaid debit cards arranged by an employer. Your salary or wages are automatically sent to your payroll card electronically, without the use of a paper check.

Benefits

- Reduces your risk of loss or theft, compared to carrying cash or checks
- The payroll card has consumer protections for funds taken by electronic error or theft.

Risks

- Many cards charge fees for inactivity, purchases, ATM use, monthly fees, etc.
- Potential overdraft fees if employee uses card without enough funds.
- You have to go to an ATM or storefront to withdraw cash when cash is needed.
- There may also be fees if you do not use ATMs from the bank or credit union that issued the card. You may not be able to deposit other funds in the account.

Prepaid Cards

Your salary or wages are electronically sent to your prepaid card without the use of a paper check.

Benefits

- May be safer and more secure than carrying cash or checks

Risks

- The card does not have the same consumer protections as a checking account or payroll card for funds taken by electronic error or theft.

- You might be limited in the types of transactions you can use the card for. For example, you might not be able to use your prepaid card to pay bills.
- Many cards charge fees for inactivity, purchases, ATM use, monthly fees, etc.
- You have to go to an ATM or storefront to withdraw cash when cash is needed.

Ways to Pay Your Bills

When you move to a new place, it does not take long for bills to start coming.

You may pay some bills such as rent, utilities, and other payments each month. You may also have one-time bills, like a security deposit when you rent an apartment.

In many cases, you will have one or more options you can choose from to make these payments. The list below helps you understand different bill payment options and their potential advantages and disadvantages. Knowing how they work could help you avoid some fees, including fees from late or missed payments.

Check

Checks are forms that you fill out to pay for something from a checking account.

You write the amount and the name of the person or company that you wish to pay on the check. The amount comes out of your bank checking account when the person or company who receives the check deposits it or cashes it. You can also get a similar account from a credit union.

Benefits
- Convenient once you apply for and the account is set up at a bank or credit union
- Can be mailed
- Easy to prove payment if there is a dispute.
- Funds are held in the checking account until you write out the check and the check is deposited. Unlike cash, if a check is lost or stolen or someone forges your signature, you have protection for the money in your account. But, it can be hard to stop a check if the person who receives it deposits it quickly.

Risks
- If you pay bills by check without enough money in your account, the bank or company you send the check to may charge you fees.
- You have to remember to pay a bill using a check each time it is due (not automated).
- Postage costs of mailing the payment

Automatic or Direct Debit

You provide the merchant or service provider (e.g., your cell phone provider or utility company) with your checking account information and they take the funds from your account each time the bill is due (e.g., every month).

> **Warning:** When money is automatically taken from your account, you could accidentally spend more than you have. If you do not have enough money in your account to cover an automatic payment or other charges you have made, you may have to pay costly fees. To stop automatic withdrawals, contact both the merchant and your bank.

Benefits

- Convenient, free, and saves time
- You may pay a lower interest rate for loans if you make your payments via automatic debit.
- Makes it easy to pay for bills that are frequent and consistent
- Reduces chance of being late – once you set it up, it is automatic
- You have the right to end automatic payments.
- Easier to prove payment should a dispute arise
- If the amount of the bill changes each month you may get a notice before the transfer is made to pay the bill.

Risks

- If you pay bills by automatic debit without enough money in your account, the bank or company you are paying to may charge you fees.

Online Bill Payment

You give your bank the merchant or service provider's information, and your bank makes the payment according to the amount and schedule you set up.

Benefits

- Convenient and saves time
- Makes it easy to pay for bills that are frequent and consistent
- You can choose between making one-time payments each billing cycle or setting up recurring (automatic) payments using your bank or credit union's online web services.
- Reduces chance of being late – once you set it up, it is automatic
- Easier to prove payment should a dispute arise.
- Easier to stop an unintended or erroneous payment.

Risks

- Takes time to set up and learn
- If you pay bills by online bill payment without enough money in your account, the bank or service provider may charge you fees.
- If you have set up recurring payments and the amount changes, you may pay the wrong amount. If you pay less than the full amount of the bill, you may have to pay fees.

Money Order

A money order can be used instead of a check. You can buy a money order to pay a business or other party.

Benefits

- Easy to understand
- Can be mailed
- No personal banking information appears on the money order

Risks

- May be inconvenient because you have to buy a money order
- Cost to buy money order and to mail the payment
- May be hard to prove payment unless you have the money order receipt and a receipt for payment
- Funds are difficult or impossible to recover if lost or stolen
- You have to remember to pay the bill each time it is due (not automated).

Credit Card

A credit card allows you to borrow money up to an approved credit limit. You will pay interest if you carry a balance, and you can be charged other fees based on the terms of the contract. You can expect to make a minimum monthly payment and you may want to pay more than the minimum to pay it off sooner.

Benefits

- Can use a credit card to pay bills over the phone or online
- Easy to prove payment should a dispute arise
- Protects you from having to pay for some or all the charges if your card or information is stolen or lost and you report the theft
- Can be set up to automatically pay recurring bills
- Can help build your credit history if you make payments on time and do not get close to your credit limit

Risks

- Costs more than paying for the purchase with cash or a check if you cannot pay the credit card balance in full every month. If you carry a balance, you have to pay interest on the balance.
- Creates another bill you have to pay
- Creates debt – you are borrowing money to pay for bills and other items

Cash

Cash is money that you have in hand.

Benefits

- Often no fees associated with paying cash directly to the company if paying the full amount owed. Buying or using a special product such as a money order or prepaid cards may cost money.
- When you use cash, you are not incurring debt.
- No risk of overdrawing your account

Risks

- Not all bill payments can be made in cash.
- Can be inconvenient and costly to travel to the company to pay the bill in person
- May be hard to prove payment unless you have a receipt
- Cash is difficult or impossible to recover if lost, stolen or destroyed.
- You have to remember to pay the bill each time it is due (not automated).

CHAPTER 10

HOW PARENTS CAN HELP TEENS MANAGE MONEY

> About This Chapter: This chapter includes text excerpted from "Teenagers and Young Adults," Consumer Financial Protection Bureau (CFPB), September 7, 2018.

Teens and young adults generally start to earn money and make decisions on their own. Adult supervision, guidance, and feedback can help them navigate successfully.

Talking with your child about money can go smoother if you keep the conversation age appropriate. The conversation starters and activities here can help you find the words.

Teenagers and Earning
Conversations about Earning
"Your paychecks might be smaller than you expect because taxes are taken out first."
- Discuss the difference between gross pay (before taxes are taken out) and net pay (the amount you take home).
- Explain that the W-4 form, which you fill out when starting a job, determines the amount of taxes taken out of a paycheck.
- Explain that tax brackets vary depending on how much you earn.
- Discuss what taxes pay for, including schools, road maintenance, and medical help for the elderly.
- Walk through your teen's paycheck together, item by item, to figure out what is being deducted and where the money goes.

> Skills such as setting a goal, looking up missing facts, and following through help children (and adults) achieve financial well-being in adulthood. These skills are a foundation for deliberate financial decision-making, such as financial planning, research, and intentional decisions.

Teenagers and Saving
Conversations about Saving
"A good rule of thumb is to save 10 percent of what you earn, and have at least three months' worth of living expenses saved up in case of an emergency."

- Once your teen has a steady job, help him set up a savings program so that at least 10 percent of earnings goes directly into his savings account.
- Help your teen track what she/he actually spends in a month. Talk about how to estimate three months' worth of expenses, and how much to save from each paycheck to build up his savings.
- Talk about how to keep money in a safe place, such as a federally-insured bank or credit union.
- Explain that, if possible, it is better to have more savings – like six to nine months' worth of living expenses, instead of only three.
- Discuss how much your child can save. What will she/he gain? What will she/he have to give up? Is it worth it?
- Explain to your child that once she/he starts a job, she/he may be offered an account at work called a "401(k)." Some employers provide matching contributions as an incentive to save, so it is smart to save at least enough for the maximum matching contribution.

Teenagers and Planning
Conversations about Planning
"You can save up for short-term goals, and you may want to invest money to achieve long-term goals."

- Your child should think of a short-term goal as something she/he wants within the next year or two. Savings accounts are safe and help your child feel sure the money will be there when she/he needs it.
- Long term usually refers to something that is more than five years away, such as buying a first home or eventually retiring. Investments can give your child's money more power to grow and compound over the long term, but there is risk of losing money.
- Ask your child to think about goals. Attending college? Purchasing a car in the next couple years? Moving to a new city? Buying a home sometime later in life? Define two financial goals for the long-term future, and help your child plan a few steps to help achieve them.
- Explain that IRAs and 401(k)s are ways to save up money for the far future, and the earlier your child can start saving, the more powerful these accounts can be.

Teenagers and Shopping
Conversations about Shopping

"When you invest for the long term, it is worthwhile to comparison shop."

- Recognize that your child might not use investing knowledge for years, but talking about how to compare investments can help build comfort and confidence.
- Talk about the benefits, risks, and costs of investing. For example, for a stock mutual fund, the benefit is the potential for long-term growth, the risk is the potential for losing money, and the costs include fees paid to the mutual fund company regardless of gain or loss.
- Share with your child the idea of not putting all your eggs in one basket and the advantages of a mix of stocks, bonds, and cash.
- Share your own stories about long-term investing and what you have learned.

"College graduates tend to earn more than people who did not go to college."

- Discuss how much you can contribute to your child's college tuition and expenses each year.
- Compare college costs, graduation rates, loan default rates, average monthly loan payments, and employment prospects by using the Department of Education's College Scorecard (collegescorecard. ed.gov).
- See what schools cost by finding the "net price calculator" on their websites; know that most families do not pay the tuition sticker price.
- Use the CFPB's Paying for College tool (www.consumerfinance.gov/paying-for-college) to compare financial aid offers.
- To estimate your child's financial aid, use the FAFSA4caster tool (fafsa. ed.gov/spa/fafsa4c/?locale=en_US#/landing).
- Visit Federal Student Aid (studentaid.gov) to research additional loans, scholarships, and grants, and use the calculators to estimate your child's monthly loan payments.

Teenagers and Borrowing
Conversations about Borrowing

"Pay off your credit card balance each month."

- When a parent cosigns for a child's credit card, any late payments the child makes also affect the parent's credit history.
- Explain that paying bills late can hurt your child's credit history and affect her or his chances of getting a job and an apartment.
- After reaching age 18, your teen can get free credit reports once a year.

- Shop for a credit card with your teen, comparing interest rates and annual fees. If your child's college or university offers a credit card, take care to review the terms offered.
- Explain that there may be an emergency expense that your child cannot pay immediately and needs to charge, and that is why it is important not to charge everyday items.
- Explore credit card repayment calculators with your child, to see how long it could take to repay a $1,000 credit card debt by making the minimum monthly payments.

Teenagers and Protecting
Conversations about Protecting
"Your health and your property need protection, and most people buy insurance to avoid high costs when something goes wrong."
- Remind your teen to comparison shop for insurance like she/he would for any other product.
- Your teen may be able to stay on your health insurance, if you have it – with some exceptions, she/he is entitled to, by law, until she/he turns 26.
- Discuss disability insurance, which can help provide income if your child cannot work because of an injury or disability.
- If your child rents an apartment, help him comparison shop for renter's insurance and talk about whether or not it is worthwhile.
- If your child owns, leases, or rents a car, help him comparison shop for auto insurance.

CHAPTER 11
PREPARING A BUDGET

About This Chapter: Text in this chapter begins with excerpts from "Not Sure How to Handle Your Finances and Student Aid (Grants, Scholarships, Loans, Work-Study) While You Are in School?" Federal Student Aid, U.S. Department of Education (ED), August 5, 2015; Text beginning with the heading "Never Tried to Live on a Budget Before?" is excerpted from "Never Tried to Live on a Budget Before?" Federal Student Aid, U.S. Department of Education (ED), April 10, 2014.

While you are in college or career school, you will need to learn how to manage your finances, plan for changes, and prepare for the unexpected. Budgeting will help you build decision-making skills and reach your financial and academic goals.

Why Should You Create a Budget?

A budget is a guide that keeps you on the path to reach your financial goals. Budgeting keeps your finances under control, shows when you need to make adjustments to your spending, and helps you decide where your money goes instead of wondering where it all went.

Budgeting helps you answer these important questions:
- Where does all my money go?
- Is there a way to spend less?
- How will I handle unexpected expenses such as replacing a broken cell phone or repairing my car?
- How can putting money into savings help me with some of my bigger financial goals?

Budgeting Helps You Achieve Academic and Financial Goals

Writing down your goals is the first step in creating a plan to make them realities. A budget will also help you prepare for unexpected expenses and obstacles. Budgeting involves challenging decision-making, but setting goals will make the tough choices a little easier.

As you create a budget, you will want to set short-, medium-, and long-term goals and track your progress toward achieving them.

Short-Term Goals

Budgeting helps you achieve academic and financial goals.

Medium-Term Goals

Medium-term goals involve thinking a bit farther into the future, perhaps the next one to three years. These goals could include buying a new laptop computer, saving $1,000 for an emergency fund, completing your program of study, or saving $5,000 for a down payment on a car.

Long-Term Goals

What do you want to do beyond three years and into the future? Long-term goals could include paying off your student loans after graduation, saving toward a down payment on a house, or saving for retirement.

Budgeting Makes It Easier to Plan, to Save, and to Control Your Expenses

When you set up your budget, you will be able to see whether your expenses exceed your income and, if so, then you can identify expenses that can be reduced. Once you are paying attention to your income and spending, you can make informed decisions that will help you meet your financial goals.

Plus, if you have problems keeping your spending under control, a budget will help you manage your spending. Following a budget can help you free up money for the things that really matter to you.

Budgeting Can Help You Avoid Debt and Improve Your Credit

When you stick to a budget, you avoid spending more than you earn and you can avoid or reduce your credit card debt. If you have received student loans to help with the cost of college or career school, then a budget will help you make the most of the money you have borrowed and can help you determine how long it will take to repay your debt and how much it will cost. If you do borrow, being able to pay what you owe on time each month will have a positive impact on your creditworthiness and your financial future.

How Do You Create a Budget?

Creating a budget is pretty straightforward and starts with this simple equation:

What you earn (your income) minus what you spend (your expenses).

The steps involved in creating a budget include:

- Determining your timeframe and setting goals,
- Finding a budgeting tool that works for you,
- Identifying your income and expenses,
- Subtracting your expenses from your income to see if you have money left over or if you have a shortfall, and
- Making any needed adjustments.

Budgeting is not just a one-time event. You will need to track your spending over time and update your budget as needed.

How Do You Balance a Job and School?

For some students, working while in college is a necessity; for others, it is a way to build a résumé or earn extra money for luxuries. Whatever the reason, it is important to know the pros and cons of working while you are attending school.

If you have a job, determine how many hours a week you will be able to work and still be able to stay on track with school demands. For example, if you want to earn more money and potentially reduce your need for student loans (or reduce the amount that you borrow), then you could consider working more hours. Managing a schedule with limited free time is an excellent way to prepare for your future. But remember, you may also need to take fewer classes to accommodate your work schedule. Keep in mind that part-time enrollment will delay your graduation, postpone your ability to earn a higher income, and possibly impact your eligibility for some federal aid. Tuition and fees may also be higher for part-time enrollment.

You may opt to work fewer hours and maximize the benefit of your student loans by taking a heavier class load instead of the minimum requirements. By taking extra classes, you may be able to graduate earlier. Alternatively, you may find that taking classes during the summer leaves you better able to balance work and school during the academic year and still stay on track to graduate on time. Keep in mind that the longer it takes to complete your program of study, the more you will pay in total.

What Should You Know about Budgeting after You Leave School?

Your expenses will change after you leave school. For example, if you recently graduated, you usually would not be required to begin paying off your student loans for six months, but when that payment is added to your monthly expenses, it will have a big impact on your budget. When you leave school, you will want to update your budget to include student loan payments, as well as your new income and living costs. Leaving school can be an exciting (and stressful) time, but you do not want to stop tracking and managing your finances.

As you move through changes in your life, you will need to constantly reevaluate your income and expenses. Your goals will change as well. You may want to buy a car, get married, have children, continue your education, or start a business, and all these activities affect your budget in some way. Think of your budget as a living document. You have the power to revise it at any time to keep track of your finances and reach your goals.

Never Tried to Live on a Budget Before?

Get tips to help you start budgeting, manage your budget, and stay on track.

As you create and maintain your budget, you will want to keep some important tips and suggestions in mind.

Get Started

Here are some important points to keep in mind as you build your budget and identify what goes into your income and expenses.

- **Overestimate your expenses.** It is better to overestimate your expenses and then underspend and end up with a surplus.
- **Underestimate your income.** It is better to end up with an unexpected cash surplus rather than a budget shortfall.
- **Involve your family in the budget planning process.** Determine how much income will be available from family sources such as parents or your spouse. Discuss how financial decisions will be made.
- **Prepare for the unexpected by setting saving goals to build your emergency fund.** Budgeting will help you cover unusual expenses and plan for changes that may happen while you are in school.
  - Planning to move off campus? Short-term budgeting goals for the year can include saving for the rent deposit and furniture for your new apartment.
  - Starting an internship next semester? Adjust your budget to save for buying new clothes to wear to work and paying increased transportation costs.
  - Finishing school in the next year? Budget to include job search expenses such as résumé preparation, travel to interviews and job fairs, and professional exam fees. Also, you may need to think about how you will manage your money between leaving school and finding a job – this is a time when an emergency fund can really help out.

Differentiate between Needs and Wants

One benefit of budgeting is that it helps you determine if you have the resources to spend on items that you want versus those you need.

- Start by making a list of things you would like to save up for.
- Identify whether each item on the list is something you absolutely need or is really a want.
- If you decide you want something, ask yourself if you will still be happy you bought the item in a month.
- Next, prioritize each item on the list.
- Once you have set your priorities, you can then determine whether you should incorporate each item into your budget.

Table 11.1. Needs and Wants

First Step My Needs and Wants	Second Step Need or Want?	Third Step Priority Importance? 1=must have 2=really want 3=would be nice
Save for a vacation	Want	3
Buy a new computer	Want	2
Go to college	Need	1
Buy a better car	Want	2
Save for an emergency fund	Need	1
Save money for a down payment on a house	Need	3
Pay off credit cards	Need	1

Pay Yourself First!
Include "Savings" as a recurring expense item in your monthly budget. Small amounts that you put away each month do add up.

Manage Your Budget

Keeping track of all of your spending may seem like a lot of work. But if you are organized, keep good records, and use some of the following tips, you will find it is easier than you may think. And, do not be too hard on yourself if you slip up.

- **Record your actual expenses.** Have you noticed how fast your cash disappears? To get a handle on where you cash is going, carry a small notebook or use a phone app to record even the smallest expenditures such as coffee, movie tickets, snacks, and parking. Some expenses that are often ignored include music downloads, charges for extra cell phone usage, and entertainment expenses. Search for an online tool to assist you – many are free!

- **Organize your records.** Decide what system you are going to use to track and organize your financial information. There are mobile apps and computer-based programs that work well, but you can also track your spending using a pencil and paper. Be sure to be consistent and organized, and designate a space to store all your financial information. Good record-keeping saves money and time!

- **Create a routine.** Manage your money on a regular basis, and record your expenses and income regularly. If you find that you cannot record your expenses every day, then record them weekly. If you wait longer than two weeks to record information, you may forget some transactions and be overwhelmed by the amount of information you need to enter.

- **Include a category in your budget called "unusual."** There will be some expenses every month that would not fall neatly into one category or that you could not have planned for. An "unusual" category will help you budget for these occasional expenses.

- **Review your spending for little items that add up to big monthly expenditures.** The daily cup of coffee and soda at a vending machine will add up. Consider packing your lunch rather than eating out every day. Spending $10 a day eating out during the week translates to $50 a week and $200 a month. A $5 packed lunch translates into a savings of $1,200 a year. Save even more by looking for ways to manage and reduce your transportation and entertainment expenses.

- **Make your financial aid credit balance refund last.** If your school applies your financial aid to your tuition and fees and there is money left over, the school will refund that money to you so you can use it for other education-related expenses (textbooks, transportation, food, etc.). Remember that your financial aid is supposed to help you cover your cost of attendance for the whole semester or term, so be sure to make that refund stretch over time rather than spending it all as soon as you get it.

- **Comparison shop.** Comparison shopping is simply using common sense to compare products in an attempt to get the best prices and best value. This means doing a little research before running out to buy something, especially when it comes to more expensive items. Make the most of tools like phone apps for comparing prices and value.

- **Use credit cards wisely.** Think very carefully before you decide to get your first credit card. Is a credit card really necessary, or would another payment option work just as well? If you receive a credit card offer in the mail, do not feel obligated to accept it. Limit the number of cards you get.

- **Do not spend more on your credit card than you can afford to pay in full on a monthly basis.** Responsible use of credit cards can be a shopping convenience and help you establish a solid credit rating and avoid financial problems. Consider signing up for electronic payment reminders, balance notices, and billing statement notifications from your credit card provider.

CHAPTER 12
BUILDING AN EMERGENCY FUND

> About This Chapter: This chapter includes text excerpted from "An Essential Guide to Building an Emergency Fund," Consumer Financial Protection Bureau (CFPB), January 9, 2020.

We have all experienced unexpected financial emergencies – a fender bender, an unexpected medical bill, a broken appliance, a loss of income, or even a damaged cell phone. Large or small, these unplanned expenses often feel like they hit at the worst times.

Setting up a dedicated savings or emergency fund is one essential way to protect yourself, and it is one of the first steps you can take to start saving. By putting money aside – even a small amount – for these unplanned expenses, you are able to recover quicker and get back on track towards reaching your larger savings goals.

What Is an Emergency Fund?

An emergency fund is a cash reserve that is specifically set aside for unplanned expenses or financial emergencies. Some common examples include car repairs, home repairs, medical bills, or a loss of income.

In general, emergency savings can be used for large or small unplanned bills or payments that are not part of your routine monthly expenses and spending.

Expect the Unexpected

Your emergency fund should be used for expenses that fall outside the categories of annual and periodic bills. Unexpected expenses are the result of life events such as job loss, illness, or car repairs. Redefine your notion of "unexpected" bills to encompass these unforeseen events rather than more common but infrequent expenses. The good news is that if you do not use your emergency fund, you will have savings – which should always be a priority when managing your finances. And, if you have to use your emergency fund, you may avoid unnecessary borrowing.

(Source: "Never Tried to Live on a Budget Before?" Federal Student Aid, U.S. Department of Education (ED).)

Why Do You Need It?

Without savings, a financial shock – even minor – could set you back, and if it turns into debt, it can potentially have a lasting impact.

Research suggests that individuals who struggle to recover from a financial shock have less savings to help protect against a future emergency. They may rely on credit cards or loans, which can lead to debt that is generally harder to pay off. They may also pull from other savings, such as retirement funds, to cover these costs.

How Much Do You Need in It?

The amount you need to have in an emergency savings fund depends on your situation. Think about the most common kind of unexpected expenses you have had in the past and how much they cost. This may help you set a goal for how much you want to have set aside.

If you are living paycheck to paycheck or do not get paid the same amount each week or month, putting any money aside can feel difficult. But, even a small amount can provide some financial security.

Keep reading to find the savings strategy, or strategies, that work best for you.

How Do You Build It?

There are different strategies to get your savings started. These strategies cover a range of situations, including if you have a limited ability to save or if your pay tends to fluctuate. It may be that you could use all of these strategies, but if you have a limited ability to save, managing your cash flow or putting away a portion of your tax refund are the easiest ways to get started.

Create a Savings Habit

Building a savings of any size is easier when you are able to consistently put money away. It is one of the fastest ways to see it grow. If you are not in a regular practice of saving, there are a few key principles to creating and sticking to a savings habit:

- **Set a goal.** Having a specific goal for your savings can help you stay motivated. Establishing your emergency fund may be that achievable goal that helps you stay on track, especially when you are initially getting started.
- **Create a system for making consistent contributions.** There are a number of different ways to save, and as you will read below, setting up automatic recurring transfers is often one of the easiest. It may also be that you put a specific amount of cash aside each day, week, or payday period. Aim to make it a specific amount, and if you can occasionally afford to do more, you will watch your savings grow even faster.
- **Regularly monitor your progress.** Find a way to regularly check your savings. Whether it is an automatic notification of your account balance or

writing down a running total of your contributions, finding a way to watch your progress can offer gratification and encouragement to keep going.

- **Celebrate your successes.** If you are sticking with your savings habit, do not miss the opportunity to recognize what you have accomplished. Find a few ways that you can treat yourself, and if you have reached your goal, set your next one.

Who is this helpful for: Anyone, but particularly those with consistent income. If you know you have a regular paycheck or money consistently coming in, you can create a habit to put some of that money towards an emergency savings fund.

Manage Your Cash Flow

Your cash flow is essentially the timing of when your money is coming in (your income) and going out (your expenses and spending). If the timing is off, you can find yourself running short at the end of the week or month, but if you are actively tracking it, you will start to see opportunities to adjust your spending and savings.

For example, you may be able to work with your creditors (such as your landlord, utility companies, or credit card companies) to adjust the due dates for your bills, or you can use the weeks when you have more money available to move a little extra into savings.

Who is this helpful for: Anyone. This is one important first step in managing your money, regardless of whether you are living paycheck to paycheck or having a tendency to spend more than your budget allows.

Take Advantage of One-Time Opportunities to Save

There may also be certain times during the year when you get an influx of money. For many Americans, a tax refund can be one of the largest checks they receive all year. There may be other times of the year, such as a holiday or birthday, that you receive a cash gift.

While it is tempting to spend it, saving all or a portion of that money could help you quickly set up your emergency fund.

Who is this helpful for: Anyone but particularly those with irregular income. If you receive a large check from a tax refund or for some other reason, it is always good to consider putting all or a portion of it away into savings.

Make Your Saving Automatic

Saving automatically is one of the easiest ways to make your savings consistent so you start to see it build over time. One common way to do this is to set up recurring transfers through your bank or credit union so money is moved automatically from your checking account to your savings account. You get to decide how much and how often, but once you have it set up, you will be making consistent contributions to your savings.

It is a good idea to be mindful of your balances, however, so you do not incur overdraft fees if there is not enough money in your checking account at the time of the automatic transaction. To help you stay mindful, consider setting up automatic notifications or calendar reminders to check your balance.

Who is this helpful for: Anyone, but particularly those with consistent income. Again, you can determine how much and how often to have money transferred between accounts, but you want to make sure you have money coming in. If your situation changes or your income changes, you can always adjust it.

Save through Work

Another way to save automatically is through your employer. In addition to employer-based contributions for retirement, you may have an option to split your paycheck between your checking and savings accounts. If you receive your paycheck through direct deposit, check with your employer to see if it is possible to divide it between two accounts. If you are tempted to spend your paycheck when you get it, this is an easy way to put money aside without having to think twice.

Who is this helpful for: Those with consistent income. Again, if you are getting a check from your employer on a regular basis, pay yourself first by putting a portion of it automatically into savings.

Where Should You Keep It?

Where you put your emergency fund depends on your situation. You want to make sure this fund is safe, accessible, and in a place where you are not tempted to spend it on nonemergencies.

Here are a few options for where to put your emergency savings, and you can choose the one that makes the most sense for you:

- **Bank or credit union account.** If you have an account with a bank or credit union – generally considered one of the safest places to put your money – it might make sense to have a dedicated account where you can keep and maintain these funds.
- **Prepaid card.** A prepaid card is a card that you can load money onto. It is not connected with a bank or credit union, and you can only spend the amount that is on your card.
- **Cash.** Another option is keeping money on hand for emergencies, either in your home or with a trusted family member or friend. Keep in mind that cash can be stolen, lost, or destroyed.

When Should You Use It?

Set some guidelines for yourself on what constitutes an emergency or unplanned expense. Not every unexpected expense is a dire emergency but try to stay consistent. Even if it is not a trip to the emergency room, you may need it to pay for a medical bill that was not covered by insurance.

Having a reserve fund for financial shocks can help you avoid relying on other forms of credit or loans that can turn into debt. If you use a credit card or take out a loan to pay for these expenses, your one-time emergency expense may grow significantly larger than your original bill because of interest and fees.

However, do not be afraid to use it if you need it. If you spend down what is in your emergency savings, just work to build it up again. Practicing your savings skills over time will make this easier.

CHAPTER 13
BANKING BASICS

About This Chapter: "Banking Basics," © 2022 Infobase.

Many parents set up bank savings accounts for their children as soon as they are born, so it is possible that you have been dealing with banks for many years. But, perhaps you have never done business with a bank, or if you had an account as a child maybe you are ready to transition to a more adult account of your own. In any case, it pays to learn a bit about the banking system so you can understand your choices and make informed decisions.

What Is a Bank?

It may seem obvious, but a bank is more than the building on the corner with a drive-through cash machine. Odds are that building houses a branch of a much larger organization that consists of many branches and an overarching corporate structure. In some cases there may be no brick-and-mortar building at all. Some banks strictly operate online, with all transactions taking place via a secure website.

Whatever its structure, a bank is a financial institution that provides a wide variety of functions for businesses and individual customers. But, its main purpose is to take in funds, pool them together, and use that money for loans and other investments. The money it earns is then paid to depositors in the form of interest.

Bank Services

Most of the many functions performed by banks probably will not concern you at the moment, but it is worthwhile to understand a few of the more common services they provide, including:

- **Savings accounts.** There are simple savings accounts that pay a relatively small amount of interest on your deposits but allow you to withdraw your money at any time. Then there are other types of accounts that earn a higher rate of interest in exchange for leaving your money in the bank for longer periods, such as money market accounts and certificates of deposit (CDs).

- **Checking accounts.** When you open a checking account you deposit funds and receive a book of checks, slips of paper that are a promise to pay a specified amount of money from your account. These days, writing physical checks is becoming something of a rarity, but checking accounts also let you make deposits and withdrawals from an ATM (automated teller machine), pay bills online, and transfer money between accounts.

- **Debit cards.** When you open a savings or checking account, the bank might issue a debit card to you. This card has a magnetic strip and an embedded microchip that can be scanned by readers at ATMs, restaurants, gas stations, and stores, allowing you to conduct transactions using funds in your accounts at the bank.

- **Loans.** One of the primary ways banks make money is by taking funds it receives from depositors and lending it to people who need it. The bank makes money by charging a higher fee for these loans than it pays out in interest.

- **Credit cards.** Credit cards are, essentially, a type of loan. Unlike with a debit card, money for credit-card purchases does not automatically come out of the customer's bank account. Rather, the bank is advancing the funds to a merchant or other payee with the understanding that the customer will pay the money back to the bank.

- **Online and mobile banking.** When you open an account, you are typically given a user ID and password to get access to the bank's secure website. Then, from any computer with an Internet connection, you can check your balances, transfer funds between accounts, and pay bills. Most banks now also have mobile apps that allow you to perform these same functions from your phone or tablet.

Advantages of Banks

As an informed consumer, it is to your benefit to learn how banks can work for you. Some advantages include:

- **You earn money.** Funds you deposit into a savings account – and some checking accounts – earn interest, which the bank pays you for letting it use your money. Generally, the interest earned on these accounts is not a lot, but it is more than you would get by keeping it in a drawer.

- **Your money is safe.** The Federal Deposit Insurance Corporation (FDIC), an independent agency created by the U.S. Congress, insures most personal bank deposits up to $250,000. There are some types of bank investments that are not covered, but customers with regular savings and checking accounts know their money is guaranteed to be there.

- **Banks help you budget.** A bank statement, either mailed to you monthly or accessed online, lets you keep track of income and expenses very easily. You can also set up different accounts for different purposes. For example, you might have one savings account where you accumulate money for a car and another for short-term use, such as school expenses.
- **Convenience.** Banks give you option of buying goods and services or paying bills as easily as possible using their various payment methods, including debit cards and online or mobile banking. They also allow you to go to the bank location to make deposits or withdrawals or take advantage of the nearest ATM to perform the same functions.

Bank Fees

Unsurprisingly, banks charge fees for many of their services. These vary depending on the bank and the type of account, so it is smart to shop around. Some bank fees can include:

- **Checking account fees.** Most banks charge a monthly fee for maintaining your checking account, usually between $10 and $20. This can often be avoided by either keeping a minimum balance in that account or by maintaining a minimum balance in a saving account at the same bank.
- **Overdraft charge.** If you use more money than you have in your checking account – either by writing a check or by using your debit card – and the bank covers the difference, you may be charged an overdraft fee of $20 to $40.
- **Returned check fee.** A returned check fee is incurred when you write a check without enough money in your account and the bank does not cover the difference. The bank may charge as much as $40 in such a case.
- **ATM fees.** Usually banks do not charge customers for using their own cash machines. But, if you use an ATM operated by another bank, the other bank will charge a fee, and in some instances your own bank may add a fee, as well. The average charge is around $3.

Other bank charges can include foreign transaction fees; paper statement fees, charged by some banks if you want hard-copies mailed to you; inactivity fees, which are sometimes incurred if an account lies dormant for a long time; check-printing fees; and lost debit-card fees.

Choosing a Bank

As with shopping for clothes, a car, or anything else, when selecting a bank it is smart to shop around. Banks vary considerably in areas such as the fees they charge, the amount of interest they pay, and the services they offer, and some are bound to meet your needs better than others. Some factors to consider:

- **Fees.** One of the most important things to learn is how much it is going to cost you to do business with a bank. Ask about account maintenance charges, ATM fees, overdraft fees, and any other charges that may be associated with the accounts you plan to open.
- **Legitimacy.** You want to be sure you are dealing with a reliable, established bank. One of the most important things is to be sure the bank is a member of the FDIC. The bank's website will usually tell you this, but you can also go to FDIC.gov and search their Bank Find tool just to be sure.
- **Location.** Even people who do not actually go to the bank building very often tend to select a bank near where they live or work. If the need arises for a personal visit, you will appreciate the convenience.
- **Size.** If you travel a lot it could be helpful to do business with a large bank that has branches in several states, or even outside the country.
- **Minimum deposit amount.** Many banks have a minimum amount required to open an account, and this can vary widely.
- **Types of services offered.** Right now, you might only be interested in opening a savings account, but at some point you may want a checking account, credit card, or car loan. It is good to know your options before you begin doing business with a bank.
- **Technology.** If you plan to make regular use of electronic banking, be sure the bank offers what you need. Ask about online fund transfers, remote deposits, text and e-mail alerts for unusual account activity, and mobile apps.

Finally, when shopping for a bank, use the Internet to your advantage. You can learn a lot about a bank from its website. There you will find information about interest rates, fees, services they offer, and special promotions they may be running (such as free check-printing for new customers). And, as with pretty much everything these days, you can Google the bank's name and find useful customer reviews and ratings.

References

1. "Banking 101," USTrust.com, 2016.
2. "Banking Basics," Indiana Department of Financial Institutions, n.d.
3. "Banking Basics 101: A Quick Lesson in Banking and Saving," CesiSolutions.org, September 21, 2013.
4. Calonia, Jennifer. "Banking," Learnvest.com, June 1, 2012.
5. Campisi, Natalie. "Banking 101 Guide: Tips and Terms to Know before Opening Your First Account," GoBankingRates.com, August 19, 2016.
6. "Selecting a Bank," Teensguidetomoney.com, n.d.

CHAPTER 14

CHOOSING AND USING THE RIGHT BANK ACCOUNT

About This Chapter: This chapter includes text excerpted from "FDIC Consumer News Summer 2016 – Choosing and Using the Right Bank Account," Federal Deposit Insurance Corporation (FDIC), August 11, 2016.

Tips for Getting More out of Your Checking and Savings

When managing your money, the right tools can make all the difference. That is why it helps to start by opening a bank account that best fits your lifestyle and your financial goals. The FDIC Consumer News provides some simple pointers to help you choose wisely and streamline how you manage your checking and savings accounts.

Before You Open an Account

Consider what you need or want from a bank account. Think about your day-to-day life and how you like to handle your money. For example: Do you receive a fixed paycheck or pension on a regular basis or does the amount and frequency of your income vary? Do you prefer to pay for purchases using cash, credit cards, debit cards, paper checks or online bill-paying services? Is one of your personal financial goals to set aside money regularly for savings? Are you concerned about possible overdrafts and the fees you might incur as a result? The answers to questions like these will help you make an informed decision about opening a bank account that works for you.

Comparison shop. There are many types of bank products and services, and the fees, interest rates and special promotional offers will vary from institution to institution. Some banks will charge fees for using another bank's automated teller machines (ATMs), while others will not charge fees and they may even reimburse customers for fees (up to a certain dollar amount) charged by the ATM owner. So if you often withdraw cash from ATMs, you may want to look closely at how ATM fees are handled before signing up.

Also, some bank accounts may have minimum balance requirements or monthly maintenance fees. Many banks will reduce or even eliminate these requirements if you have your paycheck directly deposited or you have a minimum number of electronic transactions.

Read the agreement from the bank that describes the account's terms and conditions before making a final decision. Federal rules require certain information to be disclosed to consumers before opening an account. You can review a bank's account agreements online or by stopping by a branch. Looking at a legal document may appear intimidating or time-consuming, but many banks offer simplified disclosures and knowing how the account works is worth it to ensure that you understand all aspects of the account, including the potential fees and when they may be assessed. That is the best way to avoid surprises.

Managing an Account

Follow your transactions and balance your accounts. Some consumers use pen and paper, a check register, a computer spreadsheet, a website or an app to ensure that they stay on top of what is happening in their accounts. Whichever method you choose, track every transaction – be it a deposit, check, ATM transaction, debit card transaction or online bill payment – to handle your money effectively and avoid spending more than you are comfortable with. You also can monitor your transactions using online services provided by your bank. In addition, many banks offer alerts via e-mail or text to notify customers when their account balance drops below a specified level or when a check has cleared.

Understand how to avoid overdraft fees for withdrawing more than what is in your account. Opening a checking account has long been the way customers establish a relationship with a financial institution. However, a traditional checking account may not be for everyone and can quickly become harmful to your finances if you are not careful about incurring fees, including overdraft fees.

Today, many financial institutions offer a "checkless" checking account. These types of accounts generally do not come with the ability to write paper checks, but enable customers to pay bills, make purchases and otherwise withdraw money electronically by banking online or using debit cards or mobile apps.

Checkless accounts may be a great option for consumers who prefer to use their computer, smartphone or other mobile device for banking. Generally, these accounts do not come with the ability to be overdrawn, so users will not be subject to the high overdraft or insufficient funds fees that come with many traditional checking accounts.

For those who prefer typical checking accounts, a careful decision should be made regarding whether or not to "opt-in" (agree) to overdraft coverage. Most banks offer overdraft programs that allow customers to make ATM withdrawals or perform certain debit card transactions that exceed the customer's available balance. These overdraft transactions trigger fees that may reach $35 or more per overdrafted item, but banks are only allowed to assess fees for paying an ATM or one-time debit card transaction if the customer has opted in to overdraft coverage.

If you choose not to opt in, be aware that ATM and one-time debit card transactions that go over the amount of funds in your account will be declined.

Another option is to ask your bank if you can link your savings account to your checking account to automatically transfer funds to cover transactions when you do not have enough money in your checking account. A bank may charge a fee for this automatic transfer service, but the fee is typically smaller than an overdraft fee. Find out how the fees compare by reviewing the bank's account agreement or fee schedule. These documents are usually available online or can be picked up at a local bank branch.

The easiest way to avoid overdraft charges is to keep a close eye on your account balance and on how much you plan to spend. Also, make sure you have enough in the account to cover any automatic (typically monthly) payments you have set up.

Direct deposit your pay and benefit checks. Direct deposit allows your money to be safely and securely electronically deposited into your bank account. With this feature you do not have to worry about finding time to make deposits yourself. Using the service may also help you with savings, as you can set up your direct deposit to have a certain amount from each check automatically sent to your savings account.

In addition, some banks offer incentives if you sign up for direct deposit, such as increasing the account's interest rate or waiving certain minimum balance requirements and fees.

Earn more interest, but be mindful of any conditions. If you have money in your checking account that you do not expect to use right away, moving it to a savings account or a certificate of deposit (for a set period of time) can be a good personal-finance strategy for building short-term savings and earning more interest. But before switching accounts, find out if there may be restrictions or requirements.

"Be aware of limitations on how soon you can withdraw funds from a certificate of deposit without paying a penalty, and restrictions on the number of withdrawals during a month from a savings account," said Luke W. Reynolds, chief of the FDIC's Outreach and Program Development Section. "Your institution may also offer a different checking account product that pays a higher rate of interest, but you might need to meet certain requirements, such as having a set number of debit card withdrawals post to your statement during the month. Be sure you are likely to meet any requirements based on how you normally handle your finances."

Help guard your accounts from theft and fraud. Check your accounts regularly for suspicious transactions. Protect your passwords and PINs. Also avoid clicking on links or responding to e-mails requesting personal information such as Social Security and bank account numbers, no matter how legitimate they may look. That is because criminals create fictitious websites and e-mails claiming to be from government agencies or trusted companies. In general, legitimate companies will never contact you unprompted requesting sensitive information. Contact your bank to learn more about the security features it offers or tips it suggests for customers.

The bottom line: Having a bank account brings important benefits, including access to safe and affordable financial services in good times and bad. If you choose well and manage wisely, your banking relationship can evolve and grow as you do – affording you access to more options for credit, savings and investment when you are ready and when you need them.

CHAPTER 15

WHAT YOU SHOULD KNOW ABOUT CHECKING ACCOUNTS

About This Chapter: This chapter includes text excerpted from "Managing Your Checking Account," Consumer Financial Protection Bureau (CFPB), February 3, 2016.

Once you have your checking account, you need to manage it in order to keep it. Good account management helps you to avoid unnecessary fees and helps you to maintain the account. If you have trouble keeping enough money in your account to cover your payments or withdrawals, your bank or credit union might close the account and report you to a checking account reporting company. If there is a negative report, you could have trouble opening a new checking account with a financial institution for up to 7 years. Checking account reporting companies must comply with the Fair Credit Reporting Act (FCRA). This means, for example, that they must follow reasonable procedures to maximize the accuracy of the information that they provide to banks, and they cannot include most information that is more than 7 years old. They can choose a shorter time period, and the checking account reporting companies typically disregard information that is more than five years old.

Here are some tips for reducing the fees on your checking or prepaid account.

Pay Attention to Monthly Service Fees
Many financial institutions waive monthly service fees if you maintain a minimum balance or sign up for direct deposit. Some institutions waive these fees for senior citizens, students, or members of the military. Be sure to ask about these products if you think you might be eligible.

Keep Track of Your Balance and Any Outstanding Payments
Keep track of your account balance and your account activity to avoid spending more than you have in your account. Keeping track of your balance also helps you to keep the

minimum balance you need in your account to avoid monthly fees. Some of the steps you can take are:

- Monitor your account online or on your phone.
- Check your balance by phone or online before you withdraw cash at an ATM.
- Check your balance by phone or online before you write a big check or make a big payment.
- Sign up for transaction alerts and low-balance warnings via e-mail or text.
- Do not assume that the money you deposited is available immediately. Find out when the money you deposit will be available for your use. Ask if there is a "hold" on the money you deposit, and if so when the hold will be lifted.
- The payments that you make can be processed very quickly, so do not make a payment from your checking account unless the money to cover it is already in your account and past any hold period.
- Know that your payments and withdrawals are not always processed in the order in which you make them. Be sure that you have enough in your account to cover everything.
- Know when regular electronic transfers, such as a rent payment or utility bills, will be paid.

Avoid Overdraft Fees

An overdraft occurs when you spend or withdraw more money than you have in your account and the bank or credit union pays to cover the shortfall. Overdrafts can be very expensive. Fees are generally charged "per item" and often as high as $35 or more per each overdraft transaction. To resolve an overdraft, you generally have to pay back the amount of the negative balance plus all fees, and you may have to pay additional fees if you do not repay quickly.

To reduce the likelihood that you will overdraft, you can:

- Switch to a checking account that is designed not to allow overdraft. Such "no-overdraft" products can help you manage your spending, but can still charge you a fee if you overspend. For example, if you write a check or try to pay a bill when you do not have enough money in your account, even if the transaction is declined.
- Choose not to "opt-in" to debit overdraft. Your bank or credit union cannot charge you a fee for an overdraft with your debit card unless you "opt-in" to overdraft coverage for these transactions. Keep in mind that you could be charged a fee for checks and online or direct debit overdrafts even if you have chosen not to opt-in.
- Link your accounts. If you link your account, if you run out of money in your checking account, the bank will pull money from the place you have chosen. You can link your checking account to a savings account, if

> **TIP:** Do not let terminology confuse you. "No-overdraft" products are designed to help you manage your spending and reduce the likelihood that you will overdraft. Banks and credit unions also offer overdraft programs, such as "overdraft coverage" and "overdraft protection," that generally do allow overdrafts.

you have one and are able to maintain a balance in it to cover potential shortfalls. You pay a fee for this service, but the fee is usually much lower than an overdraft fee. You may also be able to link your checking account to a credit card or line of credit, if you have one. While the fee you are charged on your checking account may be much lower than an overdraft fee, you may also be charged a fee on the credit card or line of credit.

Open and Review All of the Statements from Your Bank or Credit Union

Whether you get your account statements by mail, online, or both, review account statements every month to make sure they are correct and report errors immediately. Also watch for changes in your minimum balance requirement, fees, or other account terms.

Spend Only What You Have

Never write a check or authorize an electronic payment for funds unless you know you will have enough money in your account to cover it. If you do not have the funds you will be charged a nonsufficient funds (NSFs) fee or an overdraft fee (for debit card payments and ATM withdrawals, only if you have opted in to overdraft) from the bank or credit union. Overdrawing your account or not paying fees could severely impact your ability to access financial services in the future.

Use Your Financial Institution's ATMs

When you use ATMs in your bank's or credit union's network, there is generally no charge. However, many banks and credit unions will charge you for using an out-of-network ATM, such as an ATM branded by another bank or credit union. The owner of the out-of-network ATM may also charge you a fee. Some banks and credit unions will reimburse you for fees you pay at ATMs on other networks. Many banks and credit unions offer ATM locator maps on their websites and mobile apps to help you find in-network ATMs.

CHAPTER 16
SAVINGS AND INVESTMENT

About This Chapter: This chapter includes text excerpted from "Saving and Investing for Students," Securities and Exchange Commission (SEC), October 17, 2010.

No one is born knowing how to save or to invest. Every successful investor starts with the basics – the information in this chapter.

A few people may stumble into financial security – a wealthy relative may die, or a business may take off. But, for most people, the only way to attain financial security is to save and invest over a long period of time.

As a student, you might think that saving and investing is something you do not need to consider right now. But there is a cost to waiting, and even saving a little now can add up over time and help you pay for your short- and long-term goals.

Making a Financial Plan
What Are the Things You Want to Save and Invest In?
- A car
- An education
- A comfortable social life
- Emergencies
- Periods of unemployment
- Your future goals

Make your own list and then think about which goals are the most important to you. List your most important goals first.

> ### Keys to Financial Success
> 1. Make a financial plan.
> 2. Create a budget.
> 3. Start saving and investing as soon as you have paid off your debts.

Decide how many years you have to meet each specific goal, because when you save or invest you will need to find a savings or investment option that fits your time frame for meeting each goal. Many tools exist to help you put your financial plan together.

Know Your Current Financial Situation

Sit down and take an honest look at your entire financial situation. You can never take a journey without knowing where you are starting from, and a journey to financial comfort is no different. You will need to figure out on paper your current situation – what you own and what you owe. You will be creating a "net worth statement." On one side of the page, list what you own. These are your "assets." And on the other side list what you owe other people, your "liabilities" or debts.

Subtract your liabilities from your assets. If your assets are larger than your liabilities, you have a "positive" net worth. If your liabilities are greater than your assets, you have a "negative" net worth.

You will want to update your "net worth statement" every year to keep track of how you are doing. Do not be discouraged if you have a negative net worth. If you follow a plan to get into a positive position, you are doing the right thing.

Know Your Income and Expenses

The next step is to keep track of your income and your expenses for every month. Write down what you earn, and then your monthly expenses.

Pay Yourself First

Include a category for savings and investing. What are you paying yourself every month? Many people get into the habit of saving and investing by following this advice: Always pay yourself first. Many people find it easier to pay themselves first if they allow their bank to automatically remove money from their paycheck and deposit it into a savings or investment account.

If you work, you may be eligible to participate in an employer-sponsored retirement plan such as a 401(k), 403(b), or 457(b). That automatically deducts money from your paycheck, and may reduce the taxes you are paying. Additionally, in many plans the employer matches some or all of your contribution. When your employer does that, it is offering "free money."

Any time you have automatic deductions made from your paycheck or bank account, you will increase the chances of being able to stick to your plan and to realize your goals.

Finding Money to Save or Invest

If you are spending all your income, and never have money to save or invest, you will need to look for ways to cut back on your expenses. When you watch where you spend your money, you will be surprised how small everyday expenses that you can do without add up over a year.

Small Savings Add up to Big Money

If you buy a bottle of soda every day for $2.00, that adds up to $730.00 a year. If you saved that $730.00 for just one year, and put it into a savings account or investment that earns 5 percent a year, it would grow to $931.69 after 5 years, and grow to $3,155.02 after 30 years.

That is the power of "compounding." With compound interest, you earn interest on the money you save and on the interest that money earns. Over time, even a small amount saved can add up to big money.

If you are willing to watch what you spend and look for little ways to save on a regular schedule, you can make money grow. You just did it with one bottle of soda.

If a bottle of soda can make such a huge difference, start looking at how you could make your money grow if you decided to spend less on other things and save those extra dollars.

If you buy on impulse, make a rule that you will always wait 24 hours to buy anything. You may lose your desire to buy it after a day. And try emptying your pockets and wallet of spare change at the end of each day and put that money aside. You will be surprised how quickly those nickels and dimes add up!

Pay off Credit Card or Other High-Interest Debt

Speaking of things adding up, few investment strategies pay off as well as, or with less risk than, merely paying off all high-interest debt you may have.

Many people have credit cards, some of which they have "maxed out" (meaning they have spent up to their credit limit). Credit cards can make it seem easy to buy expensive things when you do not have the cash in your pocket – or in the bank. But, credit cards are not free money.

Most credit cards charge high-interest rates – as much as 18 percent or more – if you do not pay off your balance in full each month. If you owe money on your credit cards, the wisest thing you can do is pay off the balance in full as quickly as possible. Virtually no investment will give you the high returns you will need to keep pace with an 18 percent interest charge. That is why you are better off eliminating all credit card debt before investing savings. Once you have paid off your credit cards, you can budget your money and begin to save and invest. Here are some tips for avoiding credit card debt:

Put Away the Plastic

Do not use a credit card unless your debt is at a manageable level and you know you will have the money to pay the bill when it arrives.

Know What You Owe

It is easy to forget how much you have charged on your credit card. Every time you use a credit card, write down how much you have spent and figure out how much you will have to pay that month. Keep track of your accounts online. If you know you would not be able to pay your balance in full, try to figure out how much you can pay each month and how long it will take to pay the balance in full.

Pay off the Card with the Highest Rate

If you have got unpaid balances on several credit cards, you should first pay down the card that charges the highest rate. Pay as much as you can toward that debt each month until your balance is once again zero, while still paying the minimum on your other cards. Now, once you have paid off those credit cards and begun to set aside some money to save and invest, what are your choices?

Making Money Grow

There are basically two ways to make money.

- **You work for money.** Someone pays you to work for them or you have your own business.
- **Your money works for you.** You take your money and you save or invest it.

Your Money Can Work for You in Two Ways

- **Your money earns money.** When your money goes to work, it may earn a steady paycheck. Someone pays you to use your money for a period of time. When you get your money back, you get it back plus "interest." Or, if you buy stock in a company that pays "dividends" to shareholders, the company may pay you a portion of its earnings on a regular basis. Your money can make an "income," just like you. You can make more money when you and your money work.
- **You buy something with your money that could increase in value.** You become an owner of something that you hope increases in value over time. When you need your money back, you sell it, hoping someone else will pay you more for it. For instance, you collect comic books thinking they will increase in value over time. You expect to sell them in five, ten, or even twenty years when someone will buy them from you for a lot more money than you paid. And sometimes, your money can do both at the same time – earn a steady paycheck and increase in value.

The Difference between Saving and Investing
Saving

Your "savings" are usually put into the safest places, or products, that allow you access to your money at any time. Savings products include savings accounts, checking accounts, and certificates of deposit. Some deposits in these products may be insured by the Federal Deposit Insurance Corporation (FDIC) or the National Credit Union Administration (NCUA). But, there is a tradeoff for security and ready availability. Your money is paid a low wage as it works for you.

After paying off credit cards or other high-interest debt, most smart investors put enough money in a savings product to cover an emergency, like sudden unemployment. Some make sure they have up to six months of their income in savings so that they know it will absolutely be there for them when they need it.

But, how "safe" is a savings account if you leave all of your money there for a long time, and the interest it earns does not keep up with inflation? What if you save a dollar when it can buy a loaf of bread. But, years later when you withdraw that dollar plus the interest you earned on it, it can only buy half a loaf? This is why many people put some of their money in savings but look to investing so they can earn more over long periods of time, say three years or longer.

Investing

When you "invest," you have a greater chance of losing your money than when you "save." The money you invest in securities, mutual funds, and other similar investments typically is not federally insured. You could lose your "principal" – the amount you have invested. But, you also have the opportunity to earn more money

What about Risk

All investments involve taking on risk. It is important that you go into any investment in stocks, bonds or mutual funds with a full understanding that you could lose some or all of your money in any one investment. While over the long term the stock market has historically provided around 10 percent annual returns (closer to 6 percent or 7 percent "real" returns when you subtract for the effects of inflation), the long term does sometimes take a rather long, long time to play out. Those who invested all of their money in the stock market at its peak in 1929 (before the stock market crash) would wait over 20 years to see the stock market return to the same level.

However, those that kept adding money to the market throughout that time would have done very well for themselves, as the lower cost of stocks in the 1930s made for some hefty gains for those who bought and held over the course of the next twenty years or more.

It is often said that the greater the risk, the greater the potential reward in investing, but taking on unnecessary risk is often avoidable. Investors best protect themselves against risk by spreading their money among various investments, hoping that if one investment loses money, the other investments will more than make up for those losses. This strategy, called "diversification," can be neatly summed up as, "Don't put all your eggs in one basket." Investors also protect themselves from the risk of investing all their money at the wrong time (think 1929) by following a consistent pattern of adding new money to their investments over long periods of time. Once you have saved money for investing, consider carefully all your options and think about what diversification strategy makes sense for you. While the Securities and Exchange Commission (SEC) cannot recommend any particular investment product, you should know that a vast array of investment products exists – including stocks and stock mutual funds, corporate and municipal bonds, bond mutual funds, certificates of deposit, money market funds, and U.S. Treasury securities. Diversification cannot guarantee that your investments would not suffer if the market drops. But, it can improve the chances that you would not lose money, or that if you do, it would not be as much as if you were not diversified.

What Are the Best Investments for You?

The answer depends on when you will need the money, your goals, and if you will be able to sleep at night if you purchase a risky investment where you could lose your principal. For instance, if you are saving for a long-term goal, such as a college fund for a child, you may want to consider riskier investment products, knowing that if you stick to only the "savings" products or to less risky investment products, your money will grow too slowly – or, given inflation and taxes, you may lose the purchasing power of your money. A frequent mistake people make is putting money they will not need for a very long time in investments that pay a low amount of interest. On the other hand, if you are saving for a short-term goal, five years or less, such as a car, you do not want to choose risky investments, because when it is time to sell, you may have to take a loss. Since investments often move up and down in value rapidly, you want to make sure that you can wait and sell at the best possible time.

What Are Investments All About?

When you make an investment, you are giving your money to a company or enterprise, hoping that it will be successful and pay you back with even more money.

Stocks and Bonds

Many companies offer investors the opportunity to buy either stocks or bonds. The example below shows you how stocks and bonds differ.

Let us say you believe that a company that makes computers may be a good investment. Everyone you know is buying one of their computers, and your friends report that the company's laptops rarely break down and run well for years. You either have an investment professional investigate the company and read as much as possible about it, or you do it yourself.

After your research, you are convinced it is a solid company that will sell many more computers in the years ahead. The computer company offers both stocks and bonds. With the bonds, the company agrees to pay you back your initial investment in ten years, plus pay you interest twice a year at the rate of 4 percent a year.

If you buy the stock, you take on the risk of potentially losing a portion or all of your initial investment if the company does poorly or the stock market drops in value. But, you also may see the stock increase in value beyond what you could earn from the bonds. If you buy the stock, you become an "owner" of the company.

You wrestle with the decision. If you buy the bonds, you will get your money back plus the 4 percent interest a year. And you think the company will be able to honor its

Table 16.1. The Main Differences between Stocks and Bonds

Stocks	Bonds
If the company profits or is perceived as having strong potential, its stock may go up in value and pay dividends. You may make more money than from the bonds.	The company promises to return money plus interest.
Risk: The company may do poorly, and you will lose a portion or all of your investment.	**Risk:** If the company goes bankrupt, your money may be lost. But if there is any money left, you will be paid before stockholders.

promise to you on the bonds because it has been in business for many years and does not look like it could go bankrupt. The company has a long history of making computers and you know that its stock has gone up in price by an average of 6 percent a year, plus it has typically paid stockholders a dividend of 3 percent from its profits each year.

You take your time and make a careful decision. Only time will tell if you made the right choice. You will keep a close eye on the company and keep the investment as long as the company keeps selling a quality computer that consumers want to use, and it can make an acceptable profit from its sales.

Why Some Investments Make Money and Others Do Not

You can potentially make money in an investment in a company if:
- The company performs better than its competitors.
- Other investors recognize it is a good company, so that when it comes time to sell your investment, others want to buy it.
- The company makes profits, meaning they make enough money to pay you interest for your bond, or maybe dividends on your stock.

You can lose money if:
- Consumers do not want to buy the company's products or services. The company's officers mismanage the business, they spend too much money, and their expenses are larger than their profits.
- Other investors that you would need to sell to think the company's stock is too expensive given its performance and future outlook.
- The people running the company are ensnared in fraud.
- For whatever reason, you have to sell your investment when the market is down.

Mutual Funds and Exchange-Traded Funds

Because it is sometimes hard for investors to become experts on various businesses – for example, what are the best telecommunications, pharmaceutical, or computer companies – investors often depend on professionals who are trained to investigate companies and recommend companies that are likely to succeed. Since it takes work to pick the stocks or bonds of the companies that have the best chance to do well in the future, many investors choose to invest in mutual funds and exchange-traded funds (ETFs).

What Are Mutual Funds and Exchange-Traded Funds?

A mutual fund or ETF is a pool of money run by a professional or group of professionals called the "investment adviser." In a managed fund, after investigating the prospects of many companies, the fund's investment adviser will pick the stocks or bonds of companies and put them into a fund. Investors can buy shares of the fund, and their shares rise or fall in value as the values of the stocks and bonds in the fund rise and fall. Investors may typically pay a fee when they buy or sell their shares in the fund, and those fees in part pay the salaries and expenses of the professionals who manage the fund.

Even small fees can and do add up and eat into a significant chunk of the returns a fund is likely to produce, so you need to look carefully at how much a fund costs and think about how much it will cost you over the amount of time you plan to own its shares. If two funds are similar in every way except that one charges a higher fee than the other, you will make more money by choosing the fund with the lower annual costs.

Mutual Funds and Exchange-Traded Funds without Active Management

One way that investors can obtain for themselves nearly the full returns of the market is to invest in an "index fund." This is a fund that does not attempt to pick and choose stocks of individual companies based upon the research of the fund managers. An index fund seeks to equal the returns of a major stock market index, such as the Standard & Poor's 500, the Wilshire 5000, or the Russell 3000. Through computer programmed buying and selling, an index fund tracks the holdings of a chosen index, and so shows the same returns as an index minus, of course, the annual fees involved in running the fund. The fees for index mutual funds and ETFs generally are much lower than the fees for managed funds. Historical data shows that index funds have, primarily because of their lower fees, enjoyed higher returns than the average managed fund. But, like any investment, index funds involve risk.

Watch "Turnover" to Avoid Paying Excess Taxes

To maximize your fund returns, or any investment returns, know the effect that taxes can have on what actually ends up in your pocket. Funds that trade quickly in and out of stocks will have what is known as "high turnover." While selling a stock that has moved up in price does lock in a profit for the fund, this is a profit for which taxes have to be paid. Turnover in a fund creates taxable capital gains, which are paid by the fund shareholders. All funds are now mandated by the SEC to show both their before- and after-tax returns. The differences between what a fund is reportedly earning, and what a fund is earning after taxes are paid on the dividends and capital gains, can be quite striking. If you plan to hold funds in a taxable account, be sure to check out these historical returns in the fund prospectus to see what kind of taxes you might be likely to incur.

How Can You Protect Yourself?

Many people hire an investment professional to assist in selecting investments. You can never ask a dumb question about your investments and the people who help you choose them, especially when it comes to how much you will be paying for any investment, both in upfront costs and ongoing management fees.

Here are some questions you should ask when choosing an investment professional or someone to help you:

- What training and experience do you have? How long have you been in business?
- What is your investment philosophy? Do you take a lot of risks or are you more concerned about the safety of my money?
- Describe your typical client. Can you provide me with references, the names of people who have invested with you for a long time?
- How do you get paid? By commission? Based on a percentage of assets you manage? Another method? Do you get paid more for selling your own firm's products?
- How much will it cost you in total to do business with them?

Your investment professional should understand your investment goals, whether you are saving to buy a car, or to pay for your education.

Your investment professional should also understand your tolerance for risk. That is, how much money can you afford to lose if the value of one of your investments declines? An investment professional has a duty to make sure that she or he only recommends investments that are suitable for you. That is, that the investment makes sense for you based on your other securities holdings, your financial situation, your means, and any other information that your investment professional thinks is important. The best investment professional is one who fully understands your objectives and matches investment recommendations to your goals. You will want someone you can understand, because your investment professional should teach you about investing and investment products.

How Should You Monitor Your Investments?

Investing makes it possible for your money to work for you. In a sense, your money has become your employee, and that makes you the boss. You will want to keep a close watch on how your employee, your money, is doing.

Some people like to look at the stock quotations every day to see how their investments have done. That is probably too often. You may get too caught up in the ups and downs of the "trading" value of your investment, and sell when its value goes down temporarily – even though the performance of the company is still stellar. Remember, you are in for the long haul.

Some people prefer to see how they are doing once a year. That is probably not often enough. What is best for you will most likely be somewhere in between, based on your goals and your investments.

But, it is not enough to simply check an investment's performance. You should compare that performance against an index of similar investments over the same period of time to see if you are getting the proper returns for the amount of risk that you are assuming. You should also compare the fees and commissions that you are paying to what other investment professionals charge.

While you should monitor performance regularly, you should pay close attention every time you send your money somewhere else to work.

Every time you buy or sell an investment you will receive a confirmation slip from your broker. Make sure each trade was completed according to your instructions. Make sure the buying or selling price was what your broker quoted. And make sure the commissions or fees are what your broker said they would be.

Watch out for unauthorized trades in your account. If you get a confirmation slip for a transaction that you did not approve beforehand, call your broker. It may have been a mistake. If your broker refuses to correct it, put your complaint in writing and send it to the firm's compliance officer. Serious complaints should always be made in writing.

Remember, too, that if you rely on your investment professional for advice, she or he has an obligation to recommend investments that match your investment goals and tolerance for risk. Your investment professional should not be recommending trades simply to generate commissions. That is called "churning," and it is illegal.

How Can You Avoid Problems?

Choosing someone to help you with your investments is one of the most important investment decisions you will ever make. While most investment professionals are honest and hardworking, you must watch out for those few unscrupulous individuals. They can make your life's savings disappear in an instant. Securities regulators and law enforcement officials can and do catch these criminals. But, putting them in jail does not always get your money back. Too often, the money is gone. The good news is you can avoid potential problems by protecting yourself. Make sure the investment professional and her firm are licensed and registered using the free database on Investor.gov. You can find additional information by visiting the website of the North American Securities Administrators Association (NASAA) at www.nasaa.org or by calling 202-737-0900.

You should also find out as much as you can about any investments that your investment professional recommends. First, make sure the investments are registered. Keep in mind, however, the mere fact that a company has registered and files reports with the SEC does not guarantee that the company will be a good investment.

Be wary of promises of quick profits, offers to share "inside information," and pressure to invest before you have an opportunity to investigate. These are all warning signs of fraud. Ask your investment professional for written materials and prospectuses, and read them before you invest. If you have questions, ask your investment professional.

- How will the investment make money?
- How is this investment consistent with my investment goals?
- What must happen for the investment to increase in value?
- What are the risks?
- Where can I get more information?

Finally, it is always a good idea to write down everything your investment professional tells you. Accurate notes will come in handy if ever there is a problem.

CHAPTER 17

ANOTHER GOOD USE OF YOUR MONEY: HELPING OTHERS

About This Chapter: Text under the heading "Helping the Less Fortunate" is excerpted from "FDIC Consumer News Summer 2006 – Start Smart: Money Management for Teens," Federal Deposit Insurance Corporation (FDIC), June 12, 2014; Text under the heading "Before Giving to a Charity" is excerpted from "Before Giving to a Charity," Federal Trade Commission (FTC), May 2021.

Helping the Less Fortunate

You may think the most important reason to save and manage money is to take good care of yourself. It is, but you should also consider using some of your money (and some of your time) to help others less fortunate than you in your town or around the world.

How can you get more involved sharing your time and money with others? Here are some possibilities:

- Donate part of your allowance or gift money to a charity you admire.
- Ask friends and family to donate to a charity instead of giving you birthday or holiday gifts.
- Join or start an organization at school or in your community that helps others.
- Coordinate with friends and parents on a lemonade sale, car wash, a toy or food collection, or some other event for a local charity.
- Volunteer to mow the lawn, rake leaves or handle another chore for an ill or elderly neighbor.
- Help your parents when they volunteer for a good cause or donate items to a charity.
- Participate in a walk or run that raises money for a charity.

Need more ideas or direction? Start by talking to your parents and other family members. Also, your city or county government may have websites that list local charities and volunteer opportunities.

Before Giving to a Charity

You want your donations to count, so it is important to do some research before giving to a charity. Here are some things you can do to learn more about a charity and avoid donating to a scam.

Things to Do before You Donate to a Charity

- Search online for the cause you care about – like "hurricane relief" or "homeless kids" – plus phrases like "best charity" or "highly rated charity." Once you find a specific charity you are considering giving to, search its name plus "complaint," "review," "rating," "fraud," or "scam." If you find bad reviews, it might be best to find another organization.
- **Check out the charity's website.** Does it give you details about the programs you want to support or how it uses donations? How much of your donation will go directly to support the programs you care about? If you cannot find detailed information about a charity's mission and programs, be suspicious.
- **Use one of these organizations that help you research charities:**
  - BBB Wise Giving Alliance (www.give.org)
  - Charity Navigator (www.charitynavigator.org)
  - CharityWatch (www.charitywatch.org)
- **Find out if the fundraiser and the charity are registered.** Some states require that charities register with the state regulator. Check to see if a fundraiser and the charity they are calling on behalf of are registered with your state's charity regulator.
- **Check if the donation will be tax deductible.** If this is important to you, confirm that the organization you are donating to is registered with the IRS as a tax-exempt organization. Look up the organization in the IRS's Tax Exempt Organization Search.

Phone Calls Asking You to Donate

If someone calls asking you to donate, ask important questions:

- **What is the charity's exact name, web address, and mailing address?** Some dishonest telemarketers use names that sound like large well-known charities to confuse you. You will want to confirm this information later.
- **How much of your donation will go directly to the program you want to help?** The caller is most likely a paid fundraiser, not the charity itself. So after the fundraiser gives you their answer, call the organization directly and ask them, too. Or see if the information is on the charity's website. What else does the charity spend money on? Some fundraising can be very expensive, leaving the charity with little money to spend on its programs.
- **Are you raising money for a charity or a Political Action Committee (PAC)?** Not every call seeking a donation is from a charity. Some calls might be from a PAC where donations are not deductible and the PAC will use the money in a different manner than a charity would.
- **Will your donation be tax-deductible?** To be sure, though, look up the charity in the IRS's Tax Exempt Organization Search. If donations really are tax deductible, the organization will be listed there. Remember that donations to individuals and PACs are not tax deductible.

Rules Callers Must Follow

Fundraising calls are allowed even if your number is on the National Do Not Call Registry. If you want fundraisers to stop calling, ask them to put you on the charity's do not call list.

When a charity's fundraiser calls to ask you for a donation, they have to follow some rules:

- **They can only call during specific times.** They cannot call you before 8 a.m. or after 9 p.m.
- **They have to disclose their name and purpose.** They have to tell you the name of the charity, and tell you if the reason they are calling is to seek a donation.
- **They cannot deceive you or lie about:**
  - The fundraiser's connection to the charity.
  - The mission or purpose of the charity.
  - Whether a donation is tax deductible.
  - How a donation will be used, or how much of the donation actually goes to the charity's programs.
  - The charity's affiliation with the government.
- They cannot use a robocall or prerecorded message to reach you unless you are a member of the charity or a prior donor – and even then they must offer you a way to opt out of future calls.

- **Their caller ID has to be truthful.** The caller ID on your phone has to show the name of the charity or fundraiser, along with a number that you can call to ask to be placed on the charity's do not call list.

If a fundraiser breaks any of these rules, that might be a sign of their dishonesty. It may be best to find another way to donate to the cause you care about.

How You Pay When You Donate

If You Are Ready to Donate

- **Do not pay with wire transfers or gift cards.** If someone asks you to donate by wiring money through companies like Western Union and MoneyGram, or buying gift cards and sending them the codes, do not do it. Scammers ask you to pay that way because these payment methods are hard to track.
- It is safest to donate by credit card or check – after you have done some research on the charity.
- If you are donating online, make sure the webpage where you enter your payment information has "https" in the web address. That means your information is encrypted and transmitted securely. But, encryption alone does not mean the site is legit. Scammers know how to encrypt, too.
- **Be suspicious if they insist that you donate with cryptocurrency.** If someone tells you that the only way you can donate is with cryptocurrency and that the charity does not accept checks or credit cards, it is likely a scam.

After You Have Donated

- Review your bank account and credit card statements. Make sure you are only charged the amount you agreed to donate ? and that you're not signed up to make a recurring donation if you did not mean to.
- Keep a record of all donations. You may need them later if your donations are tax deductible.

Avoid Donating to a Fake Charity

- **Do not let anyone rush you into making a donation.** Scammers rush you so there's no time to research their claims or think it through.
- **Do not trust your caller ID.** Technology makes it easy for scammers to fake caller ID information. Calls can look like they come from your local area code, or from a specific organization, even if they do not. In reality, the caller could be anywhere in the world.
- **If the fundraiser says you already pledged, stop and check.** They may lie and say – in a phone call or a mailer – that you already pledged to make the

donation, or that you donated to them last year. They think that means you will be more willing to donate.

- **Listen carefully to the name of the charity, write it down, and then research it.** Some scammers use names that sound a lot like other charities to trick you. Do some research before you give.
- **Watch out for sentimental claims with few details.** Be suspicious if you hear a lot of vague sentimental claims, for example, that the charity helps many families that cannot afford cancer treatment and veterans wounded at war who cannot work, but do not get specifics about how your donation will be used.
- **Do not donate with a wire transfer or gift card.** Anyone asking you to donate this way is a scammer.
- **Sweepstakes winning in exchange for a donation? Nope.** If someone guarantees you will win a prize or contest if you contribute, that is a scam. You will not win anything, and your donation money will go to a scammer.

Donating on Social Media and Crowdfunding Sites

The safest way to give on social media or through crowdfunding is to donate to people you know.

- **Do not assume the request is legitimate because a friend posted it.** Pay attention to who posts the request on social media. Contact your friend privately or offline to ask them about the post they shared.
- **Check where the link to donate goes.** Does it go to a crowdfunding campaign? If that is the case, any money you give will go directly to the crowdfunding organizer. Are you sure that person will pass the money on to the cause you want to support? Confirm with whoever posted the link that they know the person behind the fundraising.

Donating Things Instead of Money

Have you ever donated clothes or home goods to a charity? Those noncash donations to a charity are called "gifts-in-kind." Sometimes the gifts-in-kind can be large ticket items, such as a car or medical equipment that is not being used.

When a charity uses and reports these donations properly, gifts-in-kind can be an important part of a charity's programs. But, a dishonest charity might mark up the value of donated goods to make their organization appear more financially successful than it really is.

When you research the charity, pay attention to how the organization spends its cash, not just the value of gifts-in-kind. If a charity is using gifts-in-kind to inflate its operations, but then spends most of its cash to pay executives or cover operating expenses, you may want to consider donating to a different organization.

Report Charity Scams

Report scams to:

- The FTC at ReportFraud.ftc.gov
- Your state charity regulator. Find who that is at nasconet.org.

When you report a charity scam, share any information you have – like the name and phone number of the organization or fundraiser, how the fundraiser contacted you, and what the fundraiser said.

PART 3 | MANAGING CREDIT AND DEBT

CHAPTER 18
WHAT YOU NEED TO KNOW ABOUT CREDIT

About This Chapter: This chapter includes text excerpted from "Credit, Loans and Debt," Federal Trade Commission (FTC), October 1, 2012.

What Is a Credit History?

Sometimes, people talk about your credit. What they mean is your credit history. Your credit history describes how you use money:
- How many credit cards do you have?
- How many loans do you have?
- Do you pay your bills on time?

If you have a credit card or a loan from a bank, you have a credit history. Companies collect information about your loans and credit cards.

Companies also collect information about how you pay your bills. They put this information in one place: your credit report.

What Is a Credit Report?

Your credit report is a summary of your credit history. It lists:
- Your name, address, and Social Security number
- Your credit cards
- Your loans
- How much money you owe
- If you pay your bills on time or late

People sometimes confuse the words debt and credit because they are both connected to borrowing money. Credit is your ability to borrow money if you want a loan or mortgage. Debt is the money you owe when you take on a loan.
(Source: "Your Money, Your Goals – A Financial Empowerment Toolkit for Community Volunteers," Consumer Financial Protection Bureau (CFPB).)

Why Do You Have a Credit Report?

Businesses want to know about you before they lend you money. Would you want to lend money to someone who pays bills on time? Or to someone who always pays late?

Businesses look at your credit report to learn about you. They decide if they want to lend you money, or give you a credit card. Sometimes, employers look at your credit report when you apply for a job. Cell phone companies and insurance companies look at your credit report, too.

Who Does Make Your Credit Report?

A company called a "credit reporting company" collects your information. There are three big credit reporting companies:

- TransUnion
- Equifax
- Experian

These companies write and keep a report about you.

Can You See Your Credit Report?

You can get a free copy of your credit report every year. That means one copy from each of the three companies that writes your reports.

The law says you can get your free credit reports if you:

- Call Annual Credit Report at 877-322-8228 or
- Go to AnnualCreditReport.com

Someone might say you can get a free report at another website. They probably are not telling the truth.

What Is a Credit Score?

A credit score is a number. It is based on your credit history. But, it does not come with your free credit report unless you pay for it.

A high credit score means you have good credit. A low credit score means you have bad credit. Different companies have different scores. Low scores are around 300. High scores are around 700-850.

Do You Need to Get Your Credit Score?

It is very important to know what is in your credit report. But, a credit score is a number that matches your credit history. If you know your history is good, your score will be good. You can get your credit report for free.

It costs money to find out your credit score. Sometimes a company might say the score is free. But, if you look closely, you might find that you signed up for a service that checks your credit for you. Those services charge you every month.

Before you pay any money, ask yourself if you need to see your credit score. It might be interesting. But, is it worth paying money for?

What If You Do Not Have Credit?

You might not have a credit history if:

- You have not had credit card
- You have not gotten a loan from a bank or credit union

Without a credit history, it can be harder to get a job, an apartment, or even a credit card. It sounds crazy: You need credit to get credit.

How Do You Get Credit?

Do you want to build your credit history? You will need to pay bills that are included in a credit report.

- Sometimes, utility companies put information into a credit report. Do you have utility bills in your name? That can help build credit.
- Many credit cards put information into credit reports.
- Sometimes, you can get a store credit card that can help build credit.
- A secured credit card also can help you build your credit.

Why Is Your Credit Report Important?

Businesses look at your credit report when you apply for:

- Loans from a bank
- Credit cards
- Jobs
- Insurance

If you apply for one of these, the business wants to know if you pay your bills. The business also wants to know if you owe money to someone else. The business uses the information in your credit report to decide whether to give you a loan, a credit card, a job, or insurance.

What Does "Good Credit" Mean?

Some people have good credit. Some people have bad credit. Some people do not have a credit history. Businesses see this in your credit report. Different things happen based on your credit history:

You Have a "Good" Credit

That means:

- You have more loan choices
- It is easier to get credit cards
- You pay lower interest rates
- You pay less for loans and credit cards

You Have a "Bad" Credit

That means:

- You have fewer loan choices
- It is harder to get credit cards
- You pay higher interest rates
- You pay more for loans and credit cards

You Have a "No" Credit

That means:

- You have no bank loan choices
- It is very hard to get credit cards
- You pay high-interest rates
- Loans and credit cards are hard to get and cost a lot

All this information is in your credit report.

Why Should You Get Your Credit Report?

An important reason to get your credit report is to find problems or mistakes and fix them:

- You might find somebody's information in your report by mistake.
- You might find information about you from a long time ago.
- You might find accounts that are not yours. That might mean someone stole your identity.

You want to know what is in your report. The information in your report will help decide whether you get a loan, a credit card, a job or insurance.

If the information is wrong, you can try to fix it. If the information is right – but not so good – you can try to improve your credit history.

Where Do You Get Your Free Credit Report?

You can get your free credit report from Annual Credit Report. That is the only free place to get your report. You can get it online: AnnualCreditReport.com, or by phone: 877-322-8228.

You get one free report from each credit reporting company every year. That means you get three reports each year.

What Should You Do When You Get Your Credit Report?

Your credit report has a lot of information. Check to see if the information is correct. Is it your name and address? Do you recognize the accounts listed?

If there is wrong information in your report, try to fix it. You can write to the credit reporting company. Ask them to change the information that is wrong. You might need to send proof that the information is wrong – for example, a copy of a bill that shows the correct information. The credit reporting company must check it out and write back to you.

How Do You Improve Your Credit?

Look at your free credit report. The report will tell you how to improve your credit history. Only you can improve your credit. No one else can fix information in your credit report that is not good, but is correct.

It takes time to improve your credit history. Here are some ways to help rebuild your credit.

- Pay your bills by the date they are due. This is the most important thing you can do.
- Lower the amount you owe, especially on your credit cards. Owing a lot of money hurts your credit history.
- Do not get new credit cards if you do not need them. A lot of new credit hurts your credit history.
- Do not close older credit cards. Having credit for a longer time helps your rating.

After six to nine months of this, check your credit report again. You can use one of your free reports from the Annual Credit Report.

How Does a Credit Score Work?

Your credit score is a number related to your credit history. If your credit score is high, your credit is good. If your credit score is low, your credit is bad.

There are different credit scores. Each credit reporting company creates a credit score. Other companies create scores, too. The range is different, but it usually goes from about 300 (low) to 850 (high).

It costs money to look at your credit score. Sometimes a company might say the score is free. But usually, there is a cost.

What Goes into a Credit Score?

Each company has its own way to calculate your credit score. They look at:

- How many loans and credit cards you have
- How much money you owe
- How long you have had credit
- How much new credit you have

They look at the information in your credit report and give it a number. That is your credit score.

It is very important to know what is in your credit report. If your report is good, your score will be good. You can decide if it is worth paying money to see what number someone gives your credit history.

How Do You Check Your Credit Report?

This is easy to do by phone:

- Call Annual Credit Report at 877-322-8228.
- Answer questions from a recorded system. You have to give your address, Social Security number, and birth date.
- Choose to only show the last four numbers of your Social Security number. It is safer than showing your full Social Security number on your report.
- Choose which credit reporting company you want a report from. (You get one free report from each company every year.)

That company mails your report to you. It should arrive 2-3 weeks after you call.

What Do You Do with a Credit Report?

Read it carefully. Make sure the information is correct:

- **Personal information.** Are the name and address correct?
- **Accounts.** Do you recognize them?
- Is the information correct?
- **Negative information.** Do you recognize the accounts in this section of the report?
- Is the information correct?
- **Inquiries.** Do you recognize the places you applied for credit?

(If you do not, maybe someone stole your identity.)

The report will tell you how to improve your credit history. Only you can improve your credit history. It will take time. But, if any of the information in your report is wrong, you can ask to have it fixed.

How Do You Fix Mistakes in Your Credit Report?

- Write a letter. Tell the credit reporting company that you have questions about information in your report.
- Explain which information is wrong and why you think so.
- Say that you want the information corrected or removed from your report.
- Send a copy of your credit report with the wrong information circled.
- Send copies of other papers that help you explain your opinion.
- Send this information to Certified Mail. Ask the post office for a return receipt. The receipt is proof that the credit reporting company got your letter.

The credit reporting company must look into your complaint and answer you in writing.

How Do You Use Credit?

When you use credit, it usually means using a credit card. It also might mean that you get a loan. A loan is another way to use credit.

Using credit means you borrow money to buy something.

- You borrow money (with your credit card or loan).
- You buy the thing you want.
- You pay back that loan later – with interest.

What Is Interest?

Interest is what you pay for using someone else's money. You repay money to whoever gave you the credit card or loan.

Credit cards and loans have different interest rates. Look for the "APR." APR means annual percentage rate. It is how much interest you pay during a whole year.

A lower interest rate means you pay less money. A higher interest rate means you pay more money.

When Can You Use Credit?

Many people use a credit card to buy everyday things. You might use a credit card to pay for:

- Gas
- Groceries
- Services – like a haircut

Loans usually are for more expensive things. You might get a loan for:

- Furniture
- Education
- A car or home

Where Can You Get a Credit Card?

Banks and credit unions offer credit cards. They usually offer credit cards to people with a good credit history.

Some stores offer credit cards. You can use a store credit card only in that store. Sometimes these cards are easier to get if you do not have a good credit history. Sometimes a store credit card is a good way to build your credit history.

What If You Cannot Get a Credit Card?

Banks and other companies offer secured credit cards. This means you deposit money with the bank. Then you spend that money by using the secured credit card.

A secured credit card works like a debit card. You use your money, not a loan from a bank. A secured credit card can help you build your credit history.

Where Can You Get a Loan?

Banks and credit unions offer loans. They usually offer loans to people with a good credit history.

Some stores offer loans to buy their product. These loans often cost more money. Why? Because interest often is higher on a store loan than on a bank loan.

What If You Cannot Get a Loan?

There are other ways to borrow money. Some people go to a payday lender. Some use the title to their car to get a loan. Some people pawn things.

These other ways to borrow are expensive. They almost always cost more than going to a bank, a credit union, or a store. Some people have problems with debt after using these ways to borrow. The charges can be very high. It is hard to pay the money back and get out of debt.

CHAPTER 19
CREDIT REPORTS AND CREDIT SCORES

About This Chapter: This chapter includes text excerpted from "Credit Reports and Credit Scores," Board of Governors of the Federal Reserve System, February 16, 2011.

Your credit history is important to a lot of people: mortgage lenders, banks, utility companies, prospective employers, and more. So it is especially important that you understand your credit report, credit score, and the companies that compile that information, credit bureaus. This brochure provides answers to some of the most common, and most important, questions about credit.

Credit Report

A credit report is a record of your credit history that includes information about:
- **Your identity.** Your name, address, full or partial Social Security number, date of birth, and possibly employment information.
- **Your existing credit.** Information about credit that you have, such as your credit card accounts, mortgages, car loans, and student loans. It may also include the terms of your credit, how much you owe your creditors, and your history of making payments.
- **Your public record.** Information about any court judgments against you, any tax liens against your property, or whether you have filed for bankruptcy.
- **Inquiries about you.** A list of companies or persons who recently requested a copy of your report.

Why Is a Credit Report Important?

Your credit report is important because lenders, insurers, employers, and others may obtain your credit report from credit bureaus to assess how you manage financial responsibilities. For example:

- Lenders may use your credit report information to decide whether you can get a loan and the terms you get for a loan (e.g., the interest rate they will charge you).
- Insurance companies may use the information to decide whether you can get insurance and to set the rates you will pay.
- Employers may use your credit report, if you give them permission to do so, to decide whether to hire you.
- Telephone and utility companies may use information in your credit report to decide whether to provide services to you.
- Landlords may use the information to determine whether to rent an apartment to you.

Who Does Collect and Report Credit Information about You?

There are three major credit bureaus – Equifax, Experian, and TransUnion – that gather and maintain the information about you that is included in your credit report. The credit bureaus then provide this information in the form of a credit report to companies or persons that request it, such as lenders from whom you are seeking credit.

Where Do Credit Bureaus Get Their Information?

Credit bureaus get information from your creditors, such as a bank, credit card issuer, or auto finance company. They also get information about you from public records, such as property or court records. Each credit bureau gets its information from different sources, so the information in one credit bureau's report may not be the same as the information in another credit bureau's report.

How Can You Get a Free Copy of Your Credit Report?

You can get one free credit report every twelve months from each of the nationwide credit bureaus – Equifax, Experian, and TransUnion – by:
- Visiting www.annualcreditreport.com
- Calling 877-322-8228

You will need to provide certain information to access your report, such as your name, address, Social Security number, and date of birth.

You can order one, two, or all three reports at the same time, or you can request these reports at various times throughout the year. The option you choose will depend on the goal of your review. A report generated by one of the three major credit bureaus may not contain all of the information pertaining to your credit history. Therefore, if you want a complete view of your credit record at a particular moment, you should examine your report from each bureau at the same time. However, if you wish to detect any errors and monitor changes in your credit profile over time, you may wish to review a single credit report every four months.

Who Else Is Allowed to See Your Credit Report?

Because credit reports contain sensitive personal information, access to them is limited. Credit bureaus can provide credit reports only to:

- Lenders from whom you are seeking credit
- Lenders that have granted you credit
- Telephone, cell phone, and utility companies that may provide services to you
- Your employer or prospective employer, but only if you agree
- Insurance companies that have issued or may issue an insurance policy for you
- Government agencies reviewing your financial status for government benefits and
- Anyone else with a legitimate business need for the information, such as a potential landlord or a bank at which you are opening a checking account

Credit bureaus also furnish reports if required by court orders or federal grand jury subpoenas. Upon your written request, they will also issue your report to a third party.

Does the Credit Bureau Decide Whether to Grant You Credit?

No, credit bureaus do not make credit decisions. They provide credit reports to lenders who decide whether to grant you credit.

How Long Does Negative Information, Such as Late Payments, Stay on Your Credit Report?

Generally, negative credit information stays on your credit report for 7 years. If you have filed for personal bankruptcy, that fact stays on your report for ten years. Information about a lawsuit or an unpaid judgment against you can be reported for seven years or until the statute of limitations runs out, whichever is longer. Information about criminal convictions may stay on your credit report indefinitely.

What Can You Do If You Are Denied Credit, Insurance, or Employment Because of Something in Your Credit Report? What Can You Do If You Receive Less Favorable Credit Terms than Other Consumers Because of Something in Your Credit Report?

If you are denied credit, insurance, or employment – or some other adverse action is taken against you, such as lowering your credit limit on credit card account – because of information in your credit report, the lender, insurance company, or employer must notify you and provide you with the name, address, and phone number of the credit bureau that provided the credit report used to make the decision. You can get a free credit report from this credit bureau if you request it within sixty days after receiving the notice. This free report is in addition to your annual free report.

In addition, lenders may use a credit report to set the terms of credit they offer you. If a lender offers you terms less favorable (e.g., a higher rate) than the terms offered to consumers with better credit histories based on the information in your credit report, the lender may give you a notice with information about the credit bureau that provided the credit report used to make the decision. Again, you can get a free credit report (in addition to your annual free report) from this credit bureau if you request it within sixty days after receiving the notice.

If you receive one of these notices, it is a good idea to get your free credit report and review the information in it right away. If you think your credit report contains inaccurate or incomplete information, follow the steps in Credit Report Errors below, to try to resolve the issue.

Credit Score

What Is a Credit Score? How Is Your Credit Score Calculated?

A credit score is a number that reflects the information in your credit report. The score summarizes your credit history and helps lenders predict how likely it is that you will repay a loan and make payments when they are due. Lenders may use credit scores in deciding whether to grant you credit, what terms you are offered, or the rate you will pay on a loan.

Information used to calculate your credit score can include:
- The number and type of accounts you have (credit cards, auto loans, mortgages, etc.),
- Whether you pay your bills on time,
- How much of your available credit you are currently using,
- Whether you have any collection actions against you,
- The amount of your outstanding debt, and
- The age of your accounts.

What Can Cause Your Credit Score to Change?

Because your credit score reflects the information in your credit report, changes to your credit report may cause your credit score to change. For instance, if you pay your bills late or incur more debt, your credit score may go down. However, if you pay down an outstanding balance on a credit card or mortgage or correct an error in your credit report, your credit score may go up.

How Can You Get Your Credit Score?

In some cases, a lender may tell you your credit score for free when you apply for credit. For example, if you apply for a mortgage, you will receive the credit score or scores that were used to determine whether the lender would extend credit to you and on what terms. You may also receive a free credit score or scores from lenders when you apply for other types of credit, such as an automobile loan or a credit card.

Are Credit Scoring Systems Reliable?

Credit scoring systems enable creditors or insurance companies to evaluate millions of applicants consistently on many different characteristics. To be statistically valid, these systems must be based on a big enough sample. They generally vary among businesses that use them.

Properly designed, credit scoring systems generally enable faster, more accurate, and more impartial decisions than individual people can make. And some creditors design their systems so that some applicants – those with scores not high enough to pass easily or low enough to fail absolutely – are referred to a credit manager who decides whether the company or lender will extend credit. Referrals can result in discussion and negotiation between the credit manager and the would-be borrower.

(Source: "Credit Scores," Federal Trade Commission (FTC).)

You may also purchase your credit score from any of the credit bureaus by calling them or visiting their websites.

- Equifax: Call 800-685-1111 or visit www.equifax.com
- Experian: Call 888-397-3742 or visit www.experian.com
- TransUnion: Call 800-493-2392 or visit www.transunion.com

Credit Report Errors

How Can You Correct Errors Found in Your Credit Report?

If you find errors in your credit report, you may dispute the information and request that the information be deleted or corrected. To do so, you should contact either the credit bureau that provided the report or the company or person that provided the incorrect information to the credit bureau.

To contact the credit bureau, call the toll-free number on your credit report or visit their website:

- Equifax (www.equifax.com/answers/correct-credit-report-errors/en_cp)
- Experian (www.experian.com/disputes/)
- TransUnion (www.transunion.com/corporate/personal/creditDisputes. page)

To contact the company or person that provided the incorrect information to the credit bureau, look on your credit report, in an account statement, or on the company's website for contact information for handling such disputes.

When disputing information on your credit report, you should:

- Provide information about yourself, such as your name, address, date of birth, and Social Security number
- Identify specific details about the information that is being disputed and explain the basis of your dispute
- Have a copy of your credit report that contains the disputed information available and

- Provide supporting documentation, such as a copy of the relevant portion of the consumer report, a police report, a fraud or identity theft affidavit, or account statements.

What Does Happen Once You Send in Information to Correct Information in Your Credit Report?

If you submit your dispute through a credit bureau or directly to the company or person that provided the incorrect information to the credit bureau, your dispute must be investigated, usually within thirty days. If you provide additional information during the thirty-day investigation, that investigation period may be extended an additional fifteen days in some circumstances. When the investigation is completed, either the credit bureau or the company or person that provided the incorrect information to the credit bureau must give you the written results of its investigation.

If the information provider finds the disputed information is inaccurate, it must notify all three nationwide credit bureaus so they can correct the information in your credit report. You can get a free copy of your report if the dispute results in a change. This free report is in addition to your annual free report. If an item is changed or deleted, a credit bureau cannot put the disputed information back in your credit report unless the company or person that provided the incorrect information to the credit bureau verifies that the information is, indeed, accurate and complete.

You can request that the credit bureau send notices of any correction to anyone who received your report in the past six months. A corrected copy of your report can be sent to anyone who received a copy during the past two years for employment purposes.

What If an Investigation Does Not Resolve Your Dispute?

If an investigation does not resolve your dispute, you can ask that a statement of the dispute be included in your future credit reports. You also can ask the credit bureau to provide your statement to anyone who received a copy of your report in the recent past, but you may have to pay a fee for this service.

CHAPTER 20
USING CREDIT WISELY

About This Chapter: "Using Credit Wisely," © 2022 Infobase.

The responsible use of credit can have a major impact on a student's future. Obviously, you need to have an established, healthy credit history if you plan to buy a car or home and make other large purchases, but the way you handle credit can also have other significant implications. For example, landlords review credit history before they will rent you an apartment, and many employers check your credit record as part of the hiring process. The smart thing to do is to begin building a positive credit history now, taking small steps to demonstrate your ability to handle money effectively. A good record of repayment will not only make it easier to get the credit you need in the future but will also result in lower interest rates when you do borrow money.

Credit Score

When someone checks your credit history, what they are looking at is your credit score. This is a number, generally from 300 to 850, tallied by large credit reporting agencies (CRAs) using information about past purchases and repayment that is obtained from various retailers and other creditors. The three largest CRAs are Equifax, Experian, and TransUnion, and prospective lenders use their scores as predictors of your likelihood to default on future credit.

There can be more than 30 factors that go into calculating a credit score, but these are generally grouped together into five major categories:

- **Credit history.** This is the most important factor and makes up 35 percent of your credit score. Unsurprisingly, lenders want to know that you regularly pay back money you owe.
- **Total indebtedness.** This makes up 30 percent of the score and is important because having a lot of debt can make it hard to pay it all back. The ratio of debt to available credit is also critical. Having a lot of available credit but

only using a small amount is good; using up all or most of your available credit hurts your score.

- **Length of credit history.** Accounting for 15 percent of the total score, this includes both how long you have had a credit record and how long individual accounts have been open. A longer history gives potential lenders a better idea of how you handle credit.
- **Type of credit.** This generally makes up 10 percent of the score, although it is more important for individuals with a short credit history. A mix of different kinds of credit shows potential lenders that you can handle various types of indebtedness responsibly.
- **New credit.** This makes up another 10 percent of the total and includes newly-opened accounts as well as "hard inquiries," which go on your record any time you apply for credit, whether you actually borrow money or not. (Soft inquiries, such as when you check your own credit record, have no impact on your score.) Lenders may see too much new credit – or applying for new credit – as an indication that you will be adding more indebtedness in the near future.

Building a Credit Record

Students building a credit history will need to start small and take carefully measured steps to demonstrate fiscal responsibility. One of the first things to do is to check your current credit history, if you have one. There are several online sites that allow you to do this, including Freecreditreport.com, Annualcreditreport.com, and Creditkarma. com, as well as the three major CRAs. Here are some suggestions for next steps:

- **Open savings and checking accounts.** It is always good to have some savings in the bank, and the regular use of a checking account and debit card shows that you can budget and handle money responsibly.
- **Pay your monthly bills.** Regular payment of phone, electric, and cable bills is another indicator of prudent financial management.
- **Pay your student loans.** Most students need loans to help pay for college, and making payments on time shows that you take your responsibilities seriously.
- **Get a student credit card.** One of the best ways to begin building credit is to select a suitable card with a low credit limit, then use it regularly and make payments in full each month. To start with, you may need a joint card with a parent or other person with established credit.

Note that not all of these go directly into a credit score. For example, the use of a debit card would not have an impact on the total. But, each of these steps provides an indication of financial responsibility and helps develop good money-management habits.

Keep in touch with your creditors. If you cannot make a payment on time, for example, ask for an extension. There is usually not a problem doing this (once, anyway), and it might help you avoid a late fee. If payments are due at a bad time of month for you, ask for a revised due date.

Types of Credit

There are a number of kinds of credit that are commonly available to students, and it is important to understand how they work. Unless you have an established credit history, it is likely that you will need a cosigner or joint account holder, but as long as your name is on the account, you will be building a positive credit history.

- **Credit cards.** These are cards, such as Visa, Mastercard, and Discover, issued by a bank or other financial institution that you can use to purchase goods or services. The card-issuer pays the merchant or service provider, then you pay back the money to the issuer. About one-third of college students have a credit card of some kind, because they are a convenient way to pay expenses and buy things on campus. But, if you do not pay off the entire balance each month, a finance charge will be added, and this will continue to build until the balance is paid off. Look for a card with no annual fee and the lowest interest rate possible.

- **Retail cards.** Also called "store cards," these are usually issued by department stores for use at their retail locations or online. They have limited use, since they can only be used with one retailer, and for that reason they are not as common as they once were. (Most retailers now partner with a major credit-card issuer for a store-branded card that can be used anywhere.) But, retail cards have the advantage of generally being easier to get than a major credit card, so they can be a good way to start building credit history.

- **Gasoline cards.** Another type of retail card, these are issued by gasoline companies for use at their own stations. Like store cards, they tend to be easier to get than major credit-card brands, and they are a good way for students with cars to keep track of fuel and maintenance expenses and build a good credit score.

- **Student loans.** Education loans most often come from government-backed sources. Some are based on need and some are open to anyone. Most of the time, repayment is deferred until you graduate or leave school, and interest may also not begin accruing until then. Other student loans come from private sources and work like any other credit instrument, such as a car loan. In either case, maintaining a regular schedule of repayment works to build a strong credit history.

Good Credit Practices

Many people get into trouble by not using credit wisely. Developing solid credit practices while avoiding some common pitfalls can help ensure that you build and maintain a good credit score and create financial health. Here are some tips:

- **Shop for credit.** Fees and interest rates vary widely, and they can really add up. Speak to several lenders and examine their websites carefully before signing anything.
- **Read the fine print.** Credit applications contain a lot of detail. Be sure you know if, for example, you are signing up for a low introductory interest rate that goes up after a period of time.
- **Do not borrow more than you can pay back.** It may seem strange, but lenders will often loan you more money than you can repay. Know your finances and live within your budget.
- **Use cash or a debit card when possible.** Credit cards are convenient, but they let you spend more than you have. Sticking to cash or debit cards limits you to the funds you have on hand.
- **Have only one credit card.** Credit-card offers are tempting, but with multiple cards you run the risk of overextending your debt, and applying for them negatively affects your credit score.
- **Avoid annual fees.** Some credit cards come with an annual fee, but so many of them do not that there is no need to pay for the privilege of having a card.
- **Avoid late fees.** If you do not make payments on time, you will be assessed a late fee. This not only costs money, it also negatively affects your credit score and may result in a higher interest rate.
- **Pay your balance every month.** By paying off the amount you charge each month, you will avoid accruing interest, which costs you money. **Note:** There is a common myth that paying the balance each month has a negative impact on your credit score. This is false. It will help build your score.
- **Do not get cash advances.** Read the fine print. Cash advances on credit cards almost always come with higher interest rates and possibly some additional fees.
- **Take advantage of points and other perks.** When shopping for a credit card, look for one that offers reward points, travel rewards, discounts, and other perks. These can save you money.
- **Check your monthly statements.** You want to be sure the lender's accounting is accurate and that there are no charges you did not initiate. If you find a discrepancy, call the lender immediately.
- **Check your credit score at least annually.** Make sure it is accurate and there are no accounts listed that you did not open. If something looks wrong, contact the lender and the CRA right away.

References

1. "10 Tips for Using Credit Wisely," BusinessWire.com, April 7, 2015.
2. "Credit Basics: Using Credit Wisely," CapitolOne.com, 2017.
3. "How to Use Credit Cards Wisely," CollegeBoard.org, 2017.
4. Irby, LaToya. "Dos and Don'ts of Using Credit Cards Wisely," TheBalance.com, June 26, 2016.
5. "Using Credit Wisely," Greenpath.com, n.d.
6. "Using Credit Wisely," HandsOnBanking.org, n.d.

CHAPTER 21
CREDIT REPAIR

About This Chapter: This chapter includes text excerpted from "Credit Repair: How to Help Yourself," Federal Trade Commission (FTC), November 2012.

Credit Repair: How to Help Yourself

You see the ads in newspapers, on TV, and online. You hear them on the radio. You get fliers in the mail, e-mail messages, and maybe even calls offering credit repair services. They all make the same claims:

"Credit problems? No problem!"

"We can remove bankruptcies, judgments, liens, and bad loans from your credit file forever!"

"We can erase your bad credit – 100% guaranteed."

"Create a new credit identity – legally."

Do yourself a favor and save some money, too. Do not believe these claims: they are very likely signs of a scam. Indeed, attorneys at the Federal Trade Commission, the nation's consumer protection agency, say they have never seen a legitimate credit repair operation making those claims. The fact is there is no quick fix for creditworthiness. You can improve your credit report legitimately, but it takes time, a conscious effort, and sticking to a personal debt repayment plan.

Your Rights

No one can legally remove accurate and timely negative information from a credit report. You can ask for an investigation – at no charge to you – of information in your file that you dispute as inaccurate or incomplete. Some people hire a company to investigate for them, but anything a credit repair company can do legally, you can do for yourself at little or no cost. By law:

- You are entitled to a free credit report if a company takes "adverse action" against you, such as denying your application for credit, insurance, or employment. You have to ask for your report within 60 days of receiving notice of the action. The notice includes the name, address, and phone number of the consumer reporting company. You are also entitled to one free report a year if you are unemployed and plan to look for a job within 60 days; if you are on welfare; or if your report is inaccurate because of fraud, including identity theft.

- Each of the nationwide credit reporting companies – Equifax, Experian, and TransUnion – is required to provide you with a free copy of your credit report once every 12 months, if you ask for it. To order, visit annualcreditreport.com, or call 877-322-8228. You may order reports from each of the three credit reporting companies at the same time, or you can stagger your requests throughout the year.

- It does not cost anything to dispute mistakes or outdated items on your credit report. Both the credit reporting company and the information provider (the person, company, or organization that provides information about you to a credit reporting company) are responsible for correcting inaccurate or incomplete information in your report. To take advantage of all your rights, contact both the credit reporting company and the information provider.

DIY

Step 1: Tell the credit reporting company, in writing, what information you think is inaccurate. Include copies (NOT originals) of any documents that support your position. In addition to including your complete name and address, your letter should identify each item in your report that you dispute; state the facts and the reasons you dispute the information, and ask that it be removed or corrected. You may want to enclose a copy of your report, and circle the items in question. Send your letter by certified mail, "return receipt requested," so you can document that the credit reporting company got it. Keep copies of your dispute letter and enclosures.

Credit reporting companies must investigate the items you question within 30 days – unless they consider your dispute frivolous. They also must forward all the relevant data you provide about the inaccuracy to the organization that provided the information. After the information provider gets notice of a dispute from the credit reporting company, it must investigate, review the relevant information, and report the results back to the credit reporting company. If the investigation reveals that the disputed information is inaccurate, the information provider has to notify the nationwide credit reporting companies so they can correct it in your file.

When the investigation is complete, the credit reporting company must give you the results in writing, too, and a free copy of your report if the dispute results in a change. If an item is changed or deleted, the credit reporting company cannot put the disputed information back in your file unless the information provider verifies that it is accurate and complete. The credit reporting company also must send you written notice that includes the name, address, and phone number of the information provider. If you ask, the credit reporting company must send notices of any correction to anyone who got your report in the past six months. You also can ask that a corrected copy of your report be sent to anyone who got a copy during the past two years for employment purposes.

If an investigation does not resolve your dispute with the credit reporting company, you can ask that a statement of the dispute be included in your file and in future reports. You also can ask the credit reporting company to give your statement to anyone who got a copy of your report in the recent past. You will probably have to pay for this service.

Step 2: Tell the creditor or other information provider, in writing, that you dispute an item. Include copies (NOT originals) of documents that support your position. Many providers specify an address for disputes. If the provider reports the item to a consumer reporting company, it must include a notice of your dispute. And if the information is found to be inaccurate, the provider may not report it again.

Reporting Accurate Negative Information

When negative information in your report is accurate, only time can make it go away. A credit reporting company can report most accurate negative information for seven years and bankruptcy information for 10 years. Information about an unpaid judgment against you can be reported for seven years or until the statute of limitations runs out, whichever is longer. The seven-year reporting period starts from the date the event took place. There is no time limit on reporting information about criminal convictions; information reported in response to your application for a job that pays more than $75,000 a year; and information reported because you have applied for more than $150,000 worth of credit or life insurance.

The Credit Repair Organizations Act

The Credit Repair Organization Act (CROA) makes it illegal for credit repair companies to lie about what they can do for you, and to charge you before they have performed their services. The CROA is enforced by the Federal Trade Commission and requires credit repair companies to explain:

- Your legal rights in a written contract that also details the services they will perform
- Your three-day right to cancel without any charge
- How long it will take to get results
- The total cost you will pay
- Any guarantees

What if a credit repair company you hired does not live up to its promises? You have some options. You can:

- Sue them in federal court for your actual losses or for what you paid them, whichever is more
- Seek punitive damages – money to punish the company for violating the law
- Join other people in a class action lawsuit against the company, and if you win, the company has to pay your attorney's fees

Report Credit Repair Fraud

State Attorneys General

Many states also have laws regulating credit repair companies. If you have a problem with a credit repair company, report it to your local consumer affairs office or to your state attorney general (AG).

Federal Trade Commission

You also can file a complaint with the Federal Trade Commission. Although the FTC cannot resolve individual credit disputes, it can take action against a company if there is a pattern of possible law violations. File your complaint online at ftc.gov/complaint or call 877-FTC-HELP (877-382-4357).

Where to Get Legitimate Help

Just because you have a poor credit history does not mean you cannot get credit. Creditors set their own standards, and not all look at your credit history the same way. Some may look only at recent years to evaluate you for credit, and they may give you credit if your bill-paying history has improved. It may be worthwhile to contact creditors informally to discuss their credit standards.

If you are not disciplined enough to create a budget and stick to it, to work out a repayment plan with your creditors, or to keep track of your mounting bills, you might consider contacting a credit counseling organization. Many are nonprofit and work with you to solve your financial problems. But, remember that "nonprofit" status does not guarantee free, affordable, or even legitimate services. In fact, some credit counseling organizations – even some that claim nonprofit status – may charge high fees or hide their fees by pressuring people to make "voluntary" contributions that only cause more debt.

Most credit counselors offer services through local offices, online, or on the phone. If possible, find an organization that offers in-person counseling. Many universities, military bases, credit unions, housing authorities, and branches of the U.S. Cooperative Extension Service operate nonprofit credit counseling programs. Your financial institution, local consumer protection agency, and friends and family also may be good sources of information and referrals.

If you are thinking about filing for bankruptcy, be aware that bankruptcy laws require that you get credit counseling from a government-approved organization within six months before you file for bankruptcy relief. You can find a state-by-state list of government-approved organizations at www.usdoj.gov/ust, the website of the U.S. Trustee Program. That is the organization within the U.S. Department of Justice that supervises bankruptcy cases and trustees. Be wary of credit counseling organizations that say they are government-approved, but do not appear on the list of approved organizations.

CHAPTER 22

CHOOSING AND MANAGING A CREDIT CARD

Credit cards are used in place of physical cash and are considered a convenient mode of payment. A credit card is a rectangular plastic or metal card that allows cardholders to borrow funds from the issuing bank or financial institution. Many businesses allow their customers to pay for their goods and services through credit cards, making a credit card payment convenient and universal. Credit cards are seemingly ideal for young adults who are starting to manage their finances. Credit cards have certain conditions, such as an applicable interest rate and additional charges paid back by the cardholder based on a billing plan. Some credit cards also offer a cash line of credit which means cardholders can access physical cash from ATMs and cash advances from credit card convenience checks. An essential aspect of credit cards is that they also come with a predetermined borrowing limit curated as per the card holder's credit rating or score.

Using a credit card is similar to taking a loan and is thus subject to interest charges charged to the card one month after the expenditure. Credit card companies must offer a minimum of 21 days which is called a "grace period," before interest is charged on the credit card. When purchasing with a credit card, the card's details are sent to the seller's bank, which then verifies your credit card with the credit card provider. Once verified, the provider can either approve or reject the transaction. If approved, money is deposited into the seller's account, and the same amount is deducted from the available credit balance in the credit card. At the end of the billing period, a statement of the transactions, and available credit is given to the card holder with details such as the minimum payment required and the due date for the same. In most cases, interest is not charged when the due is paid in full before the end of the grace period.

A credit card has an annual percentage rate (APR) that reflects the expense of carrying a balance.

Types of Credit Cards

When choosing a credit card, there are various options ranging from basic credit cards to premium cards that offer additional advantages. It is essential to choose a credit card that adapts to one's financial needs and budget. Some common types of credit cards available are:

- Standard credit cards
- Student credit cards
- Charge cards
- Rewards credit cards
- Balance transfer credit cards
- Secured credit cards
- Subprime credit cards
- Prepaid credit cards
- Business credit cards
- Limited purpose cards

Benefits of a Credit Card

Credit cards are convenient and are among the best options during a medical emergency, while traveling, for unplanned expenses, and are also great at helping increase credit scores if used responsibly. Credit cards provide a variety of advantages and benefits such as:

- Earning rewards that can help reduce direct expenditures
- Increased purchase power
- Free from foreign transaction fees
- Help in securing a hotel room or car while traveling
- Free from checking or savings account charges
- Help improve credit scores

How to Choose a Credit Card

Before deciding on a credit card provider, there are some helpful points to remember, such as:

- **Considering the credit score.** Most credit card providers require cardholders to have at least five years of good credit history. The credit score depends on many factors such as income and debt history. One must have a good credit score before applying for a credit card.
- **Understanding expenditure.** It can help to have an idea of monthly or annual expenditure. This can help decide on a credit card that offers rewards for expenditures in areas of maximum spending. For example,

if travel and groceries are the top areas of expenditure, one can choose a provider offering credit cards with rewards for purchasing airline tickets.

- **Knowledge of credit card terminology.** As young adults handling their own money, it can help to have a basic understanding of some standard terms that credit card providers use in their documents and promotions. Some terms include annual percentage rate (APR), minimum payments, perks, fees, rewards, and welcome bonus.
- **Checking for the need for a dedicated business credit card.** If there are expenses related to a self-owned business, it can help to have a separate business account and a dedicated credit card to help organize finances and in the event of a legal or tax audit.
- **Deciding on the most appropriate credit card.** After considerable research on the available types of credit cards, it can help choose one that fits the individual's financial requirements best regarding cashback and rewards. It is beneficial to select a credit card that offers a low APR or customized rewards since these are the best options for young adults and teenagers looking to choose a credit card.

When choosing between two or more competitive credit card providers, drawing up a comparison between them to come up with the best option can help. Some key points to look for when comparing credit cards are:

- APR for balance transfers, cash advances
- Annual fees
- Promotional APR terms and conditions
- Introductory bonus offer terms
- Rewards programs

How to Manage a Credit Card

Once a credit card is selected, the next step is to know how to handle the credit card responsibly. Using the credit card within limits will make it more of an asset than a financial burden in the long run.

- Use the credit card wisely for regular purchases that offer cashback and rewards. If done appropriately, one can earn or save a large sum of money. Use services that provide these returns on credit card payments and keep track of the money availed. Remember to spend within a budget and pay off the entire due at the end of the billing cycle to avoid losing earned rewards in interest payments.
- One can use the credit card to build a good credit score over time by ensuring that all dues are paid on time, and no penalties are levied. This can help in getting a quicker approval when a loan application is required in the future.

- Use the credit card to help organize spending behavior. When using the card regularly, one can also see spending patterns on the card and draw up a better budget plan that will not push towards debt but will keep the cash flow running for the month.
- Keep the credit card as an emergency line of money for sudden expenditures that may arise. As a young adult or a college student without an emergency fund, one can use a credit card for minimal purchases to keep the card active and avoid being financially stranded.
- Protect the credit card with fraud and purchase protection. These cards are ultimately safer when compared to debit cards.

Credit Card Pitfalls to Avoid

Credit cards are a valuable tool in managing money and are beneficial to everyone. This does not take away from the fact that it is prone to risks and disadvantages. There are a few pitfalls that teenagers and young people interested in purchasing a credit card must avoid at all costs to help them manage their finances. Some of these mistakes are:

- Paying only the minimum amount. Paying the due in full and not just the minimum can help avoid carrying balances to the next billing cycle.
- Skipping a payment. Late payments can lower the credit score, especially if they are delayed by more than 30 days.
- Carrying forward a balance every month. This does more damage to the credit score and can lead to large sum payments at the end of the billing cycle.
- Making use of the cash advance facility. Cash advances on credit cards are chargeable with interest.
- No knowledge of APR and other fees. One must be aware of the rates and extra costs being levied to avoid excess debt.
- Using the entire credit limit
- Purchasing a credit card too often. This leads to an inquiry on the credit score and too many in a short period can lower the credit score.
- Closing a credit card account can reduce the length of credit history and also the credit score.
- Using the wrong card for a long time. Change the card according to your needs.
- Not utilizing rewards earned on credit card purchases

References

1. Luthi, Ben. "10 Mistakes You Are Probably Making with Your Credit Card," Money Under 30, February 8, 2021.

2. White, Alexandria. "10 Common Credit Card Mistakes You May Be Making and How to Avoid Them," Select, CNBC Network, August 25, 2020.
3. Weliver, David. "How to Use a Credit Card Responsibly," Money Under 30, October 19, 2020.
4. White, Alexandria. "How to Choose the Best Credit Card in 3 Easy Steps," Select, CNBC Network, February 1, 2021.
5. Black, Michelle. "How to Choose a Credit Card," The Points Guy, March 27, 2020.
6. Weliver, David. "How to Choose a Credit Card Wisely," Money Under 30, February 25, 2020.
7. "What Are the Advantages of Credit Cards?" Discover, March 18, 2020.
8. Irby, Latoya. "10 Types of Credit Cards, and How to Use Them," The Balance, July 21, 2020.
9. Lake, Rebecca. "How Do Credit Cards Work?" Investopedia, September 28, 2020.

CHAPTER 23

OTHER PLASTIC: DEBIT CARDS, CREDIT CARDS, CHARGE CARDS, AND PREPAID CARDS

> About This Chapter: Text in this chapter begins with excerpts from "Credit, Debit, and Charge Cards," Federal Trade Commission (FTC), August 2012; Text under the heading "Prepaid Cards and Other Prepaid Accounts" is excerpted from "Prepaid Cards and Other Prepaid Accounts," Consumer Financial Protection Bureau (CFPB), April 1, 2019.

Credit, charge, or debit? Each lets you pay for products and services. Each also has unique characteristics. And if you are shopping for a credit card, it is important to compare fees, interest rates, finance charges, and benefits.

Plastic 101

Credit card. You can use a credit card to buy things and pay for them over time. But remember, buying with credit is a loan – you have to pay the money back. And some issuers charge an annual fee for their cards. Some credit card issuers also provide "courtesy" checks to their customers. You can use these checks in place of your card, but they are not a gift – they are also a loan that you must pay back. And if you do not pay your bill on time or in full when it is due, you will owe a finance charge – the dollar amount you pay to use credit. The finance charge depends in part on your outstanding balance and the annual percentage rate (APR).

Charge card. If you use a charge card, you must pay the balance in full each time you get your statement.

Debit card. This card allows you to make purchases in real-time by accessing the money in your checking or savings account electronically.

The Fine Print

When applying for credit cards, it is important to shop around. Fees, interest rates, finance charges, and benefits can vary greatly. And, in some cases, credit cards might seem like great deals until you read the fine print and disclosures. When you are trying to find the credit card that is right for you, look at the:

Annual percentage rate (APR). The APR is a measure of the cost of credit, expressed as a yearly interest rate. It must be disclosed before your account can be activated, and it must appear on your account statements. The card issuer also must disclose the "periodic rate" – the rate applied to your outstanding balance to figure the finance charge for each billing period.

Some credit card plans allow the issuer to change your APR when interest rates or other economic indicators – called "indexes" – change. Because the rate change is linked to the index's performance, these plans are called "variable rate programs." Rate changes raise or lower the finance charge on your account. If you are considering a variable rate card, the issuer also must tell you that the rate may change and how the rate is determined.

Before you become obligated on the account, you also must receive information about any limits on how much and how often your rate may change.

Grace period. The grace period is the number of days you have to pay your bill in full without triggering a finance charge. For example, the credit card company may say that you have 25 days from the statement date, provided you paid your previous balance in full by the due date. The statement date is on the bill.

The grace period usually applies only to new purchases. Most credit cards do not give a grace period for cash advances and balance transfers. Instead, interest charges start right away. If your card includes a grace period, the issuer must mail your bill at least 14 days before the due date so you will have enough time to pay.

Annual fees. Many issuers charge annual membership or participation fees. Some card issuers assess the fee in monthly installments.

Transaction fees and other charges. Some issuers charge a fee if you use the card to get a cash advance, make a late payment, or exceed your credit limit. Some charge a monthly fee if you use the card – or if you do not.

Customer service is something most people do not consider, or appreciate, until there is a problem. Look for a 24-hour toll-free telephone number.

Unauthorized charges. If your card is used without your permission, you can be held responsible for up to $50 per card. If you report the loss before the card is used, you cannot be held responsible for any unauthorized charges. To minimize your liability, report the loss as soon as possible. Some issuers have 24-hour toll-free telephone numbers to accept emergency information. It is a good idea to follow-up with a letter to the issuer – include your account number, the date you noticed your card missing, and the date you reported the loss. Keep a record – in a safe place separate from your cards – of your account numbers, expiration dates, and the telephone numbers of each card issuer so you can report a loss quickly.

Prepaid Cards and Other Prepaid Accounts

What Is a Prepaid Card?*

A prepaid card is a card you can use to pay for things. You buy a card with money loaded on it. Then you can use the card to spend up to that amount.

A prepaid card is also called a "prepaid debit card," or a "stored-value card." You can buy prepaid cards at many stores and online.

Many prepaid cards come with the Visa or MasterCard logo. These prepaid cards look just like a credit card.

Text excerpted from "Prepaid Cards," Federal Trade Commission (FTC), September 28, 2012.

Choose the Right Card for Your Situation

Prepaid cards have different features, functions, and fees. To decide which prepaid card is right for you, learn about your choices. Compare the fees to how you will use the card.

How Do You Plan to Use Your Card?

- Will you use the card regularly or only for some things?
- Will you only make purchases, or also use the card for cash withdrawals or bill payments?
- Will you have your paycheck or benefits directly deposited onto the card?

Questions to Consider When Choosing a Card

What Type of Card Is Right for You?

There are different types of prepaid cards. You can make the best choice about which card is right for you when you understand key differences.

- A **reloadable prepaid card** allows you to add more money. This type of card is sometimes called a "General Purpose Reloadable Card," or "GPR Card." Some cards start out as nonreloadable, but can be reloaded once you complete a registration process. Some prepaid cards are "nonreloadable," meaning you cannot add more money to them.
- A **payroll card** is a prepaid card you get from your employer that you receive your paycheck on.
- A **government benefit card** is a prepaid card used by a government agency to pay certain government benefits, such as unemployment insurance.
- Some **college ID cards** are also prepaid cards. Some colleges offer a card that you can only use to pay for things on campus (and maybe some nearby stores). Other schools offer a card that you can use at any retail location that accepts that network brand.
- A **gift card** may look like a prepaid card, but it is different. A gift card may have a network logo that allows you to use the card widely, or it may only be usable at certain locations. While gift cards have some protections under

federal law, they typically will not have the protections from the CFPB's 2019 prepaid rule.

What Are "Open-Loop" and "Closed-Loop" Cards?

Sometimes you might hear a card referred to as an "open-loop" or "closed-loop" card.

An open-loop prepaid card is a card with a network logo on it. Examples of networks are Visa, MasterCard, American Express, and Discover. These cards can be used at any location that accepts that card type. Most prepaid cards are open-loop cards. GPR prepaid cards, payroll cards, and some types of government benefit cards are open-loop, as are many other kinds of prepaid cards. Even some gift cards are open-loop.

A closed-loop prepaid card is a card you can only use at certain locations. For example, a closed-loop card might be good only at a specific store or group of stores, or on your public-transportation system. Most closed-loop cards do not have a network logo on them. Many gift cards are closed-loop cards.

What Fees Will the Card Charge?

Read the information about the card carefully to understand all of the fees. The CFPB's prepaid rule requires prepaid card providers to give you information about fees before you choose a card. For cards you buy at the store, important information is included on the card as well as inside the card package. (Due to phase-in rules, it may take some time for new packaging to make it to stores, so you may not see all cards with this information immediately.) Consider how you plan to use the card and shop for the one that is best for your situation.

There are different types of fees on prepaid cards. Different prepaid cards charge different types and amounts of fees. Common fees include:

- Monthly usage
- Transaction or per purchase fee
- In-network/out-of-network ATM withdrawal fee
- ATM balance inquiry fee
- Cash reload fee
- Customer service fee
- Inactivity fee
- Paper statement fee
- Decline fee
- Card-to-card transfer fee
- Bill payment fee
- Stop payment
- Card replacement fee
- Additional card fee
- Foreign transaction fee
- Card cancellation fee

> **Tip.** Think about how you plan to use the card. Then look at the fees for the ways you might use the card. The card packaging will include a chart that contains certain key fees and other information about the prepaid account, and you can use that to comparison shop between cards at the store. The packaging will also have a website where you can see a form that includes all of the fees that the card charges, as well as other key information about the card.

Not every card charges each type of fee. Some cards charge a monthly fee but not transaction fees. Other cards may skip the monthly fee but charge you transaction fees each time you use the card for certain types of transactions (such as purchases made in stores or online using the card).

What Protections Does the Card Have?

If you have registered your prepaid card, or if your card is a payroll card or a certain type of government benefit card, you have certain error resolution rights that protect you from unauthorized transactions under federal law. Network-branded prepaid card providers usually give some additional protections for loss or theft, but you should check your card provider's website or your cardholder agreement to find out the specifics.

Call your card issuer right away if your card or PIN is lost or stolen or if you see unauthorized charges.

What Are the Alternatives?

A prepaid card may or may not be the right choice for you, depending on how you plan to use the card. You may want to consider alternatives, such as a bank account.

Prepaid Cards versus Debit Cards

A prepaid card is not linked to a bank checking account or to a credit union share draft account. Instead, you are spending money you placed in the prepaid card account in advance. This is sometimes called "loading money onto the card."

Generally, you cannot spend more money than you have already loaded onto your prepaid card. Overspending can occur with a checking account for some types of uses, and with a bank account debit card if you have "opted in" to your bank's overdraft program. This means that your bank may charge you a fee for covering the cost of a purchase or ATM withdrawal that exceeds what you have in your account. Your bank will also require you to repay the overdraft.

Prepaid Cards versus Credit Cards

Prepaid cards are very different from credit cards. This can be confusing because both types of cards may have a card network logo like Visa, MasterCard, American Express, or Discover on them. When you use a credit card, you are borrowing money. Generally, when you use a prepaid card, you are spending money you loaded onto the card in advance. However, if your prepaid card provider offers credit (including overdraft) on your prepaid card, it will need to comply with the rules for other credit cards.

Do Not Forget to Register Your Card!

It is a good idea to register your prepaid card. Registration will provide you with more protections if your card is lost or stolen. Some prepaid card providers may require you to register your card and verify your identity when you buy or receive the prepaid card, or soon after. The card provider likely will limit how you can use the card until the card is registered.

Registration is also necessary for FDIC or NCUA insurance (if it is offered for your card), which protects you if the bank or credit union issuing your card goes out of business.

CHAPTER 24
LOAN OPTIONS FOR PEOPLE UNDER 18

When you are younger than 18, it can be difficult to get a loan approved, but it is not impossible. When a loan provider does a credit check on you, they will be assessing their risk and, in particular, checking to determine how likely it is that you will be able to repay the loan. However, because of your age, the lender may find it hard to judge how reliable you might be.

There are many reasons why a young person may opt for a loan. They might, for example, want to get a loan to buy their first car or to fund their studies. Other reasons include buying a house, going on a vacation, paying for a wedding, or paying off debts.

Types of Loans for Young People

There is a prime age set for borrowing based on the risk factors that age carries. To put it simply, the older you are, the less time you will have to repay your debt and the younger you are, the less income and experience you will have to indicate the likelihood that you will repay your debt. Despite these obstacles, a person younger than 18 can be eligible for certain types of loans. Some of these are listed below:

Personal Loans

If you are under 18 with little credit history, then you may be eligible for a personal loan. However, the amount that you are offered might be less, or at a higher rate of interest than advertised. This is because the lender may consider a person below the age of 18 to be a potentially risky prospect.

It is also important to note that your credit score drops each time you apply for a loan, so applying for many is unwise and a lower credit score will make it difficult to get a loan or credit product in the future.

Search tools, such as insurance.com, etc., allow you to see whether you are eligible for a loan. Since rejection of a loan adversely affects your credit score, it is always better to take advantage of online tools such as these.

Student Loans

There are three types of student loans:

- Federal loans
- Private loans
- Refinance loans (once you leave school)

Federal loans are funded by the government, while private and refinanced loans are provided by banks, credit unions, and states. Federal loans are more flexible than private loans. However, the loan that is best suited to you will be determined by several factors, including your financial need, grade point average (GPA), and credit history.

A "Free Application for Federal Student Aid" (FAFSA) application must be filled out in order to get a federal loan. A borrower usually must apply with the bank or financial institution directly for private or refinanced loans.

Cosigner Loans

Since few people under the age of 18 will be approved for a loan, they may wish to consider asking their parents, relatives, or even an older friend to be a guarantor for them. This person takes on the responsibility of repaying the loan if the borrower is unable to pay it.

Alternatives to Loans

There are other options that a person can consider before taking out a loan. Some of the options are listed below:

Check with Peers

Even though peers may not always have money they can lend, they may be able to direct you to someone who can help. Hence, checking with peers is always worth the effort.

Check with Family

If a family member or close friend is able to lend money to you, then you may wish to consider asking them. However, it is also important to remember that even if the money is being borrowed from a person of trust, it is recommended that you draw up a contract that lists details about the repayment amount, loan period, and whether or not interest will be paid on the loan.

Government Support

People who receive federal benefits may be eligible for an interest-free loan that can be used for everyday essentials such as rent; therefore, check your eligibility for such benefits.

Credit Cards

Interest-free credit cards can be used as an alternative to a loan. However, it is important to note when the interest-free period ends, or you could end up paying interest that is higher than the typical interest rate on payments made after the interest-free period ends.

Savings

If the loan is desired in order to purchase a car or move out, then start saving for the expense as early as possible. This could result in not having to take out a loan at all.

Tips for Getting a Loan at 18

Here are some suggestions to consider if you are 18 and trying to get a loan:

- Show evidence that you can save.
- Offer collateral.
- Get a letter of recommendation and/or proof of employment from your employer if employed.
- Apply for a lower amount.
- Opt for a secured loan.

Taking out a loan at a young age can give you access to quick funds and help you build a credit history, but it may come with certain negative consequences such as a high-interest rate and an increased risk of defaulting on your payment. Hence, it is always important to think of alternative ways to raise the funds before you choose to pursue a loan. Finally, if you are considering a loan, make sure you can afford to repay it.

References

1. "Loans for Young People," GoCompare, January 17, 2016.
2. "Compare Loans for 18-Year-Olds," Finder, January 5, 2020.
3. "Types of Student Loans: Which Is Best for You?" NerdWallet, June 13, 2019.

CHAPTER 25

UNDERSTANDING THE DIFFERENCE BETWEEN SECURED AND UNSECURED LOANS

About This Chapter: This chapter includes text excerpted from "Personal Loans: Secured vs. Unsecured," MyCreditUnion.gov, June 23, 2018.

Personal Loans

Loans provide you with money you might not currently have for large purchases, and let you pay back the money over a stated period of time. Many loan types are available, such as home loans, car loans, and student loans. Loans are either secured or unsecured.

Secured Loans

With secured loans, your property is used as collateral. If you cannot repay the loan, the lender may take your collateral to get its money back. Common secured loans are mortgages, home equity loans, and installment loans.

Mortgages

A mortgage loan is used to buy real estate, such as a home. Fixed-rate and adjustable-rate mortgages are the two main types of mortgages, but there is a wide variety of mortgage products available. Typical sources for mortgage loans include credit unions, commercial banks, thrift institutions, mortgage brokers, and online lenders. When shopping for a home mortgage, you should consider contacting several lenders to compare offers.

If you do not make your mortgage payments when due, foreclosure proceedings may occur. This action provides the legal means for your lender to take possession of your home. Foreclosures have a negative impact on your credit history. Beware of predatory mortgage lending, where creditors impose unfair or abusive terms on you. Deceptive mortgage lending practices can strip you of home equity and threaten foreclosure.

For more information, refer to the Looking for the Best Mortgage booklet by the U.S. Department of Housing and Urban Development. Tips on avoiding mortgage relief scams, and where to get legitimate help, are available from the Federal Trade Commission (FTC).

Home Equity Loans

A home equity loan is a form of mortgage loan where your home is used as collateral to borrow money. It is typically used to pay for major expenses (education, medical bills, or home repairs). These loans may be a one-time lump sum amount, or a more flexible revolving line of credit allowing you to withdraw funds at any time. In either case, if you cannot pay back the loan, the lender could foreclose on your home.

Installment Loans

With an installment loan, you repay the loan over time with a set number of scheduled payments. Car loans are the most common installment loans. Before you sign an agreement for a loan to buy a car, or other large purchase, make sure you fully understand all of the lender's terms and conditions.

In particular, know the dollar amount you are borrowing, payment amounts and when they are due, total finance charge (including all interest and fees you must pay to get the loan), and the rate of interest you will pay over the full term of the loan. Be aware of penalties for late payments, or for paying the loan back early. Know what the lender will do if you cannot repay the loan.

Lenders are required by federal law to provide this information before you agree to make the purchase, so you can compare different offers.

Unsecured Loans

Unsecured loans do not use property as collateral. Lenders consider these to be riskier than secured loans, so they charge a higher rate of interest for them. Two common unsecured loans are credit cards and student loans.

Credit Cards

Credit cards allow you to purchase products and services now, but you need to repay the balance before the end of your billing cycle to avoid paying interest on your purchase. The credit card issuer sets a credit limit on how much you can charge on your card. When applying for credit cards, it is important to shop around. Fees, interest rates, finance charges, and benefits can vary greatly.

For further information, visit the FTC's consumer information on Credit, Debit, and Charge Cards. Tips to help you choose the right credit card are also available from the Consumer Financial Protection Bureau (CFPB).

Seven Things to Look for in a Mortgage

- The size of the loan
- The interest rate and any associated points
- The closing costs of the loan, including the lender's fees
- The Annual Percentage Rate (APR)
- The type of interest rate and whether it can change (Is it fixed or adjustable?)
- The loan term, or how long you have to repay the loan
- Whether the loan has other risky features, such as a prepayment penalty, a balloon clause, an interest-only feature, or negative amortization

(Source: "What Is a Mortgage?" Consumer Financial Protection Bureau (CFPB).)

Student Loans

Student loans are available from a variety of sources, including the federal government, individual states, colleges and universities, and other public and private agencies and organizations. To help pay for higher education expenses, students and parents can borrow funds that must be repaid with interest. As a general rule, federal loans have more favorable terms and lower interest rates than traditional consumer loans.

CHAPTER 26
DEALING WITH DEBT

About This Chapter: This chapter includes text excerpted from "Coping with Debt" Federal Trade Commission (FTC), November 2012.

Having trouble paying your bills? Getting dunning notices from creditors? Are your accounts being turned over to debt collectors? Are you worried about losing your home or your car? You are not alone. Many people face a financial crisis at some point in their lives. Whether the crisis is caused by personal or family illness, the loss of a job, or overspending, it can seem overwhelming. But, often, it can be overcome. Your financial situation does not have to go from bad to worse.

If you or someone you know is in financial hot water, consider these options: self-help using realistic budgeting and other techniques; debt relief services, such as credit counseling or debt settlement from a reputable organization; debt consolidation; or bankruptcy. How do you know which will work best for you? It depends on your level of debt, your level of discipline, and your prospects for the future.

Self-Help
Developing a Budget
The first step toward taking control of your financial situation is to do a realistic assessment of how much money you take in and how much money you spend. Start by listing your income from all sources. Then, list your "fixed" expenses – those that are the same each month – such as mortgage payments or rent, car payments, and insurance premiums. Next, list the expenses that vary – such as groceries, entertainment, and clothing. Writing down all your expenses, even those that seem insignificant, is a helpful way to track your spending patterns, identify necessary expenses, and prioritize the rest. The goal is to make sure you can make ends meet on the basics: housing, food, healthcare, insurance, and education. You can find information about budgeting and money management techniques online, at your public library, and in bookstores. Computer software programs can be useful tools for developing and maintaining a

budget, balancing your checkbook, and creating plans to save money and pay down your debt.

Contacting Your Creditors

Contact your creditors immediately if you are having trouble making ends meet. Tell them why it is difficult for you, and try to work out a modified payment plan that reduces your payments to a more manageable level. Do not wait until your accounts have been turned over to a debt collector. At that point, your creditors have given up on you.

Dealing with Debt Collectors

Federal law dictates how and when a debt collector may contact you: not before 8 a.m., after 9 p.m., or while you are at work if the collector knows that your employer does not approve of the calls. Collectors may not harass you, lie, or use unfair practices when they try to collect a debt. And they must honor a written request from you to stop further contact.

Managing Your Auto and Home Loans

Your debts can be unsecured or secured. Secured debts usually are tied to an asset, like your car for a car loan, or your house for a mortgage. If you stop making payments, lenders can repossess your car or foreclose on your house. Unsecured debts are not tied to any particular asset, and include most credit card debt, bills for medical care, and signature loans.

Most automobile financing agreements allow a creditor to repossess your car any time you are in default. No notice is required. If your car is repossessed, you may have to pay the balance due on the loan, as well as towing and storage costs, to get it back. If you cannot do this, the creditor may sell the car. If you see default approaching, you may be better off selling the car yourself and paying off the debt: You will avoid the added costs of repossession and a negative entry on your credit report.

If you fall behind on your mortgage, contact your lender immediately to avoid foreclosure. Most lenders are willing to work with you if they believe you are acting in good faith and the situation is temporary. Some lenders may reduce or suspend your payments for a short time. When you resume regular payments, though, you may have to pay an additional amount toward the past due total. Other lenders may agree to change the terms of the mortgage by extending the repayment period to reduce the monthly debt. Ask whether additional fees would be assessed for these changes, and calculate how much they total in the long term.

If you and your lender cannot work out a plan, contact a housing counseling agency. Some agencies limit their counseling services to homeowners with FHA mortgages, but many offer free help to any homeowner who is having trouble making mortgage payments. Call the local office of the Department of Housing and Urban Development or the housing authority in your state, city, or county for help in finding a legitimate housing counseling agency near you.

Debt Relief Services

If you are struggling with significant credit card debt, and cannot work out a repayment plan with your creditors on your own, consider contacting a debt relief service such as credit counseling or debt settlement. Depending on the type of service, you might get advice on how to deal with your mounting bills or create a plan for repaying your creditors.

Before you do business with any debt relief service, check it out with your state Attorney General and local consumer protection agency. They can tell you if any consumer complaints are on file about the firm you are considering doing business with. Ask your state Attorney General if the company is required to be licensed to work in your state and, if so, whether it is.

If you are thinking about getting help to stabilize your financial situation, do some homework first. Find out what services a business provides, how much it costs, and how long it may take to get the results they promised. Do not rely on verbal promises. Get everything in writing, and read your contracts carefully.

Credit Counseling

Reputable credit counseling organizations can advise you on managing your money and debts, help you develop a budget, and offer free educational materials and workshops. Their counselors are certified and trained in consumer credit, money and debt management, and budgeting. Counselors discuss your entire financial situation with you, and help you develop a personalized plan to solve your money problems. An initial counseling session typically lasts an hour, with an offer of follow-up sessions.

Most reputable credit counselors are nonprofits and offer services through local offices, online, or on the phone. If possible, find an organization that offers in-person counseling. Many universities, military bases, credit unions, housing authorities, and branches of the U.S. Cooperative Extension Service operate nonprofit credit counseling programs. Your financial institution, local consumer protection agency, and friends and family also may be good sources of information and referrals.

But, be aware that "nonprofit" status does not guarantee that services are free, affordable, or even legitimate. In fact, some credit counseling organizations charge high fees, which they may hide, or urge their clients to make "voluntary" contributions that can cause more debt.

Debt Management Plans

If your financial problems stem from too much debt or your inability to repay your debts, a credit counseling agency may recommend that you enroll in a debt management plan (DMP). A DMP alone is not credit counseling, and DMPs are not for everyone. Do not sign up for one of these plans unless and until a certified credit counselor has spent time thoroughly reviewing your financial situation, and has offered you customized advice on managing your money. Even if a DMP is appropriate for you, a reputable credit counseling organization still can help you create a budget and teach you money management skills.

In a DMP, you deposit money each month with the credit counseling organization. It uses your deposits to pay your unsecured debts, such as your credit card bills, student loans, and medical bills, according to a payment schedule the counselor develops with you and your creditors. Your creditors may agree to lower your interest rates or waive certain fees. But, it is a good idea to check with all your creditors to be sure they offer the concessions that a credit counseling organization describes to you. A successful DMP requires you to make regular, timely payments; it could take 48 months or more to complete your DMP. Ask the credit counselor to estimate how long it will take for you to complete the plan. You may have to agree not to apply for – or use – any additional credit while you are participating in the plan.

Debt Settlement Programs

Debt settlement programs typically are offered by for-profit companies, and involve them negotiating with your creditors to allow you to pay a "settlement" to resolve your debt – a lump sum that is less than the full amount that you owe. To make that lump sum payment, the program asks that you set aside a specific amount of money every month in savings. Debt settlement companies usually ask that you transfer this amount every month into an escrow-like account to accumulate enough savings to pay off any settlement that is eventually reached. Further, these programs often encourage or instruct their clients to stop making any monthly payments to their creditors.

Debt Settlement Has Risks

Although a debt settlement company may be able to settle one or more of your debts, there are risks associated with these programs to consider before enrolling:

- These programs often require that you deposit money in a special savings account for 36 months or more before all your debts will be settled. Many people have trouble making these payments long enough to get all (or even some) of their debts settled, and end up dropping out the programs as a result. Before you sign up for a debt settlement program, review your budget carefully to make sure you are financially capable of setting aside the required monthly amounts for the full length of the program.
- Your creditors have no obligation to agree to negotiate a settlement of the amount you owe. So there is a possibility that your debt settlement company will not be able to settle some of your debts – even if you set aside the monthly amounts required by the program. Also, debt settlement companies often try to negotiate smaller debts first, leaving interest and fees on large debts to continue to mount.
- Because debt settlement programs often ask or encourage you to stop sending payments directly to your creditors, they may have a negative impact on your credit report and other serious consequences. For example,

your debts may continue to accrue late fees and penalties that can put you further in the hole. You also may get calls from your creditors or debt collectors requesting repayment. You could even be sued for repayment. In some instances, when creditors win a lawsuit, they have the right to garnish your wages or put a lien on your home.

Debt Settlement and Debt Elimination Scams

Some companies offering debt settlement programs may not deliver on their promises, like their "guarantees" to settle all your credit card debts for 30 to 60 percent of the amount you owe. Other companies may try to collect their fees from you before they settle any of your debts. The FTC's Telemarketing Sales Rule prohibits companies that sell debt settlement and other debt relief services on the phone from charging a fee before they settle or reduce your debt. Some companies may not explain the risks associated with their programs, including that many (or most) of their clients drop out without settling their debts, that their clients' credit reports may suffer, or that debt collectors may continue to call them.

Before you enroll in a debt settlement program, do your homework. You are making a big decision that involves spending a lot of your money that could go toward paying down your debt. Enter the name of the company with the word "complaints" into a search engine. Read what others have said about the companies you are considering, including whether they are involved in a lawsuit with any state or federal regulators for engaging in deceptive or unfair practices.

Fees

If you do business with a debt settlement company, you may have to put money in a dedicated bank account, which will be administered by an independent third party. The funds are yours and you are entitled to the interest that accrues. The account administrator may charge you a reasonable fee for account maintenance, and is responsible for transferring funds from your account to pay your creditors and the debt settlement company when settlements occur.

Disclosure Requirements

Before you sign up for the service, the debt relief company must give you information about the program:

- **Price and terms.** The company must explain its fees and any conditions on its services.
- **Results.** The company must tell you how long it will take to get results – how many months or years before it will make an offer to each creditor for a settlement.
- **Offers.** The company must tell you how much money or what percentage of each outstanding debt you must save before it will make an offer to each creditor on your behalf.

How to Spot Fake Debt Collectors

Not everyone who calls saying that you owe a debt is a real debt collector. Some are scammers who are just trying to take your money. So how can you tell?

A caller may be a fake debt collector if they:

- Want you to repay a debt you do not recognize
- Refuse to give you their mailing address or phone number
- Pressure you, or try to scare you into paying by threatening to report you to law enforcement or have you arrested

(Source: "Fake and Abusive Debt Collectors," Federal Trade Commission (FTC).)

- **Nonpayment.** If the company asks you to stop making payments to your creditors – or if the program relies on your not making payments – it must tell you about the possible negative consequences of your action.

The debt relief company also must tell you:

- That the funds are yours and you are entitled to the interest earned,
- The account administrator is not affiliated with the debt relief provider and does not get referral fees, and
- That you may withdraw your money at any time without penalty.

Tax Consequences

Depending on your financial condition, any savings you get from debt relief services can be considered income and taxable. Credit card companies and others may report settled debt to the IRS, which the IRS considers income, unless you are "insolvent." Insolvency is when your total debts are more than the fair market value of your total assets. Insolvency can be complex to determine. Talk to a tax professional if you are not sure whether you qualify for this exception.

Use Caution When Shopping for Debt

Avoid any debt relief organization – whether it is credit counseling, debt settlement, or any other service – that:

- Charges any fees before it settles your debts or enters you into a DMP plan
- Pressures you to make "voluntary contributions," which is really another name for fees
- Touts a "new government program" to bail out personal credit card debt
- Guarantees it can make your unsecured debt go away
- Tells you to stop communicating with your creditors, but does not explain the serious consequences
- Tells you it can stop all debt collection calls and lawsuits
- Guarantees that your unsecured debts can be paid off for pennies on the dollar

- Would not send you free information about the services it provides without requiring you to provide personal financial information, such as your credit card account numbers, and balances
- Tries to enroll you in a debt relief program without reviewing your financial situation with you
- Offers to enroll you in a DMP without teaching you budgeting and money management skills
- Demands that you make payments into a DMP before your creditors have accepted you into the program

Debt Consolidation

You may be able to lower your cost of credit by consolidating your debt through a second mortgage or a home equity line of credit. But, these loans require you to put up your home as collateral. If you cannot make the payments – or if your payments are late – you could lose your home.

What is more, consolidation loans have costs. In addition to interest, you may have to pay "points," with one point equal to one percent of the amount you borrow. Still, these loans may provide certain tax advantages that are not available with other kinds of credit.

Bankruptcy

Personal bankruptcy also may be an option, although its consequences are long-lasting and far-reaching. People who follow the bankruptcy rules receive a discharge – a court order that says they do not have to repay certain debts. However, bankruptcy information (both the date of the filing and the later date of discharge) stay on a credit report for 10 years and can make it difficult to get credit, buy a home, get life insurance, or sometimes get a job. Still, bankruptcy is a legal procedure that offers a fresh start for people who have gotten into financial difficulty and cannot satisfy their debts.

There are two main types of personal bankruptcy: Chapter 13 and Chapter 7. Each must be filed in federal bankruptcy court. Filing fees are several hundred dollars.

Chapter 13 allows people with a steady income to keep property, like a mortgaged house or a car, that they might otherwise lose through the bankruptcy process. In Chapter 13, the court approves a repayment plan that allows you to use your future income to pay off your debts during three to five years, rather than surrender any property. After you make all the payments under the plan, you receive a discharge of your debts.

Chapter 7 is known as "straight bankruptcy;" it involves liquidating all assets that are not exempt. Exempt property may include automobiles, work-related tools, and basic household furnishings. Some of your property may be sold by a court-appointed official, called a "trustee," or turned over to your creditors.

Both types of bankruptcy may get rid of unsecured debts and stop foreclosures, repossessions, garnishments and utility shut-offs, as well as debt collection activities. Both also provide exemptions that let you keep certain assets, although exemption amounts vary by state. Personal bankruptcy usually does not erase child support, alimony, fines, taxes, and some student loan obligations. And, unless you have an acceptable plan to catch up on your debt under Chapter 13, bankruptcy usually does not allow you to keep property when your creditor has an unpaid mortgage or security lien on it.

You must get credit counseling from a government-approved organization within six months before you file for any bankruptcy relief. You can find a state-by-state list of government-approved organizations at the U.S. Trustee Program, the organization within the U.S. Department of Justice that supervises bankruptcy cases and trustees. Also, before you file a Chapter 7 bankruptcy case, you must satisfy a "means test." This test requires you to confirm that your income does not exceed a certain amount. The amount varies by state and is publicized by the U.S. Trustee Program.

Debt Scams

Advance Fee Loans. Some companies guarantee you a loan if you pay them a fee in advance. The fee may range from $100 to several hundred dollars. Resist the temptation to follow up on these advance-fee loan guarantees. They may be illegal. It is true that many legitimate creditors offer extensions of credit through telemarketing and require an application or appraisal fee in advance. But, legitimate creditors never guarantee that you will get the loan – or even represent that a loan is likely. Under the FTC's Telemarketing Sales Rule, a seller or telemarketer who guarantees or represents a high likelihood of your getting a loan or some other extension of credit may not ask for – or accept – payment until you get the loan.

Credit Repair. Be suspicious of claims from so-called "credit repair clinics." Many companies appeal to people with poor credit histories, promising to clean up their credit reports for a fee. But, anything these companies can do for you for a fee, you can do yourself – for free. You have the right to correct inaccurate information in your file, but no one – regardless of their claims – can remove accurate negative information from your credit report. Only time and a conscientious effort to repay your debts will improve your credit report. Federal – and some state – laws ban these companies from charging you a fee until the services are fully performed.

CHAPTER 27
PREPAYMENT PENALTY

> About This Chapter: Text under the heading "What Is a Prepayment Penalty?" is excerpted from "What Is a Prepayment Penalty?" Consumer Financial Protection Bureau (CFPB), September 25, 2017; Text under the heading "Can You Be Charged a Penalty for Paying off Your Mortgage Early?" is excerpted from "Can I Be Charged a Penalty for Paying off My Mortgage Early?" Consumer Financial Protection Bureau (CFPB), March 18, 2016; Text under the heading "Can You Prepay Your Loan at Any Time without Penalty?" is excerpted from "Can I Prepay My Loan at Any Time without Penalty?" Consumer Protection Bureau Financial (CFPB), June 8, 2016.

What Is a Prepayment Penalty?

A prepayment penalty is a fee that some lenders charge if you pay off all or part of your mortgage early. If you have a prepayment penalty, you would have agreed to this when you closed on your home. Not all mortgages have a prepayment penalty.

Typically, a prepayment penalty only applies if you pay off the entire mortgage balance – for example because you sold your home or are refinancing your mortgage – within a specific number of years (usually three or five years). In some cases, a prepayment penalty could apply if you pay off a large amount of your mortgage all at once. Prepayment penalties do not normally apply if you pay extra principal on your mortgage in small chunks at a time – but it is always a good idea to double-check with the lender.

Can You Be Charged a Penalty for Paying off Your Mortgage Early?

Whether you can be charged a penalty for paying off your mortgage early depends on what type of mortgage you have and the specific terms of your mortgage loan.

Tip: If a loan you are considering has a prepayment penalty, make sure to read the fine print carefully. Make sure you understand exactly the circumstances under which you will have to pay, and how much. Ask your lender for a quote for a similar loan without a prepayment penalty so you can compare total costs and make an informed decision.

Some loans have prepayment penalties during the first years of the loan. These fees may impose substantial costs on homeowners with adjustable rate mortgage loans who want to refinance before their rates increase, and some fixed mortgages have prepayment penalties as well.

Many states have laws that limit the amount or duration of these penalties. Whether your loan carries a prepayment penalty must have been disclosed in your loan documents. Sometimes it is only disclosed in something called the "Addendum to the Note" – look at the Note and anything with "Addendum" in the title.

Can You Prepay Your Loan at Any Time without Penalty?

Whether you can pay off your auto loan early without a penalty depends on your contract and on your state's law.

If the lender wants to charge you a penalty or fee to pay off the loan early, the contract has to contain a prepayment penalty clause. Review your Truth in Lending disclosures and the contract before you sign the agreement. These documents will tell you whether there is a penalty for paying early. You should also ask your lender, or the dealer if you are getting dealer financing if there is a prepayment penalty. If there is, you can negotiate to have the penalty removed from the contract or ask for a different loan.

Why it matters: If your loan has a high-interest rate, you may later be able to refinance at a lower interest rate and payment. When you refinance, you prepay the original loan in full. Ask your bank, credit union, or other lenders about interest rates.

CHAPTER 28
SEEKING CREDIT COUNSELING

About This Chapter: This chapter includes text excerpted from "What Is Credit Counseling?" Consumer Financial Protection Bureau (CFPB), February 2, 2018.

What Is Credit Counseling?

Credit counseling organizations can advise you on your money and debts, help you with a budget, and offer money management workshops.

Credit counseling organizations are usually nonprofit organizations. Typically, their counselors are certified and trained in the areas of consumer credit, money and debt management, and budgeting. Counselors discuss your financial situation with you and help you develop a personalized plan to solve your money problems. Here are some examples of what credit counselors might do:

- Advise you on managing your money and debts
- Help you develop a budget
- Help you get a copy of your credit report and scores
- May offer free educational materials and workshops
- Organize a "debt management plan" to pay down your debts

> **Tip:** If you are having trouble making payments on your debts, a credit counselor may be able to help you with advice or by organizing a "debt management plan" for all your debts. Typically, under a debt management plan you make a single payment to the credit counseling organization each month or pay period and the credit counseling organization makes monthly payments to each of your creditors. Under debt management plans, credit counselors usually do not negotiate any reduction in the amounts you owe – instead, they can lower your overall monthly payment. They do so by negotiating extensions of the periods over which you can repay a loan and by asking creditors to lower the interest rates and waive certain fees.

How Do You Find a Credit Counselor?

Most credit counselors offer services through in-person meetings at local offices, the Internet, or on the telephone. To get started, you can try the Financial Counseling Association of America, on their website (fcaa.org) or by phone at 800-450-1794, or the National Foundation for Credit Counseling, on their website (www.nfcc.org) or by phone at 800-388-2227.

Once you have developed a list of potential credit counseling organizations, check them out with your state attorney general (www.naag.org/current-attorneys-general.php) and state consumer protection agency (www.usa.gov/state-consumer). Ask the counselors for free information about their services.

How Do You Choose the Right Credit Counselor?

A reputable credit counseling organization should be willing to send you free information about itself and the services it provides without requiring you to provide any details about your situation. If a service does not do that, consider this a red flag and go elsewhere for help.

Here are some questions to ask to help you find the best credit counseling service for you:

What Services Do You Offer?

Look for an organization that offers a range of services, including budget counseling and classes for managing spending and debt. Avoid organizations that push a debt management plan as your only option before they have spent a significant amount of time analyzing your financial situation.

How Is Credit Counseling Offered?

Services may be offered in-person, by phone, or online. An initial counseling session typically lasts an hour, with an offer of follow-up sessions.

Do You Offer Free Educational Materials?

Avoid organizations that charge for information.

What Are Your Fees?

Are there set-up or monthly fees? Get a specific price quote in writing. Although most credit counseling organizations are nonprofits, credit counselors may charge fees for some of their services that they take out of the payments you make to them.

What If You Cannot Afford to Pay Your Fees or Make Contributions?

If an organization would not help you because you cannot afford to pay, look elsewhere.

Will You Have a Formal Written Agreement or Contract with You?

Do not sign anything without reading it first. Make sure all verbal promises are also in writing. As with any contract, do not sign anything that you do not understand.

What Are the Counselor's Qualifications?

Is the organization or counselor accredited or certified? What are the qualifications of its credit counselors? Find out about what training or professional certifications the counselor has received.

How Are Your Employees Paid?

Are the employees paid more if I sign up for certain services, if I pay a fee, or if I make a contribution to your organization? If the answer is yes, consider this a red flag and go elsewhere.

CHAPTER 29
CREDIT/DEBT AND YOUR CONSUMER RIGHTS

About This Chapter: This chapter includes text excerpted from "Credit and Your Consumer Rights," Federal Trade Commission (FTC), June 2017.

A good credit rating is very important. Businesses inspect your credit history when they evaluate your applications for credit, insurance, employment, and even leases. They can use it when they choose to give or deny you credit or insurance, provided you receive fair and equal treatment. Sometimes, things happen that can cause credit problems: a temporary loss of income, an illness, even a computer error. Solving credit problems may take time and patience, but it does not have to be an ordeal.

The Federal Trade Commission (FTC) enforces the credit laws that protect your right to get, use and maintain credit. These laws do not guarantee that everyone will receive credit. Instead, the credit laws protect your rights by requiring businesses to give all consumers a fair and equal opportunity to get credit and to resolve disputes over credit errors. This brochure explains your rights under these laws and offers practical tips to help you solve credit problems.

Your Credit Report
Your credit report contains information about where you live, how you pay your bills, and whether you have been sued, or filed for bankruptcy. Credit reporting companies sell the information in your report to businesses that use it to evaluate your applications for credit, insurance, employment, or renting a home.

The federal Fair Credit Reporting Act (FCRA) promotes the accuracy and privacy of information in the files of the nation's credit reporting companies.

Under the Fair Credit Reporting Act:
- You have the right to receive a copy of your credit report. The copy of your report must contain all the information in your file at the time of your request.

- Each of the nationwide credit reporting companies – Equifax, Experian, and TransUnion – is required to provide you with a free copy of your credit report, at your request, once every 12 months.
- Under federal law, you are also entitled to a free report if a company takes adverse action against you, like denying your application for credit, insurance, or employment, and you ask for your report within 60 days of receiving notice of the action. The notice will give you the name, address, and phone number of the credit reporting company. You are also entitled to one free report a year if you are unemployed and plan to look for a job within 60 days; if you are on welfare; or if your report is inaccurate because of fraud, including identity theft.

Your Credit Application

When creditors evaluate a credit application, they cannot engage in discriminatory practices.

The Equal Credit Opportunity Act (ECOA) prohibits credit discrimination on the basis of sex, race, marital status, religion, national origin, age, or receipt of public assistance. Creditors may ask for this information (except religion) in certain situations, but they may not use it to discriminate against you when deciding whether to grant you credit.

The ECOA protects consumers who deal with companies that regularly extend credit, including banks, small loan and finance companies, retail and department stores, credit card companies, and credit unions. Everyone who participates in the decision to grant credit, including real estate brokers who arrange financing, must follow this law. Businesses applying for credit also are protected by this law.

Under the Equal Credit Opportunity Act:
- You cannot be denied credit based on your race, sex, marital status, religion, age, national origin, or receipt of public assistance.
- You have the right to have reliable public assistance considered in the same manner as other income.
- If you are denied credit, you have a legal right to know why.

Your Credit Billing and Electronic Fund Transfer Statements

It is important to check credit billing and electronic fund transfer account statements regularly because these documents may contain mistakes that could damage your credit status or reflect improper charges or transfers. If you find an error or discrepancy, notify the company and dispute the error immediately. The Fair Credit Billing Act (FCBA) and Electronic Fund Transfer Act (EFTA) establish procedures for resolving mistakes on credit billing and electronic fund transfer account statements, including:
- Charges or electronic fund transfers that you – or anyone you have authorized to use your account – have not made

- Charges or electronic fund transfers that are incorrectly identified or show the wrong date or amount
- Math errors
- Failure to post payments, credits, or electronic fund transfers properly
- Failure to send bills to your current address – provided the creditor receives your change of address, in writing, at least 20 days before the billing period ends
- Charges or electronic fund transfers for which you ask for an explanation or written proof of purchase along with a claimed error or request for clarification

The FCBA generally applies only to "open end" credit accounts – credit cards and revolving charge accounts, like department store accounts. It does not apply to loans or credit sales that are paid according to a fixed schedule until the entire amount is paid back, like an automobile loan. The EFTA applies to electronic fund transfers, like those involving automatic teller machines (ATMs), point-of-sale debit transactions, and other electronic banking transactions.

Your Debts and Debt Collectors

You are responsible for your debts. If you fall behind in paying your creditors, or if an error is made on your account, you may be contacted by a "debt collector." A debt collector is any person, other than the creditor, who regularly collects debts owed to others, including lawyers who collect debts on a regular basis. You have the right to be treated fairly by debt collectors.

The Fair Debt Collection Practices Act (FDCPA) applies to personal, family, and household debts. This includes money you owe for the purchase of a car, for medical care, or for charge accounts. The FDCPA prohibits debt collectors from engaging in unfair, deceptive, or abusive practices while collecting these debts. Under the FDCPA:

- Debt collectors may contact you only between 8 a.m. and 9 p.m.
- Debt collectors may not contact you at work if they know your employer disapproves.

- Debt collectors may not harass, oppress, or abuse you.
- Debt collectors may not lie when collecting debts, such as falsely implying that you have committed a crime.
- Debt collectors must identify themselves to you on the phone.
- Debt collectors must stop contacting you if you ask them to do so in writing.

Solving Your Credit Problems

Your credit report can influence your purchasing power, as well as your opportunity to get a job, rent or buy an apartment or a house, and buy insurance. When negative information in your report is accurate, only the passage of time can assure its removal. A credit reporting company can report most accurate negative information for seven years and bankruptcy information for 10 years. Information about an unpaid judgment against you can be reported for seven years or until the statute of limitations runs out, whichever is longer. There is no time limit on reporting information about criminal convictions; information reported in response to your application for a job that pays more than $75,000 a year; and information reported because you have applied for more than $150,000 worth of credit or life insurance. There is a standard method for calculating the seven-year reporting period. Generally, the period runs from the date that the event took place.

If you are having problems paying your bills, contact your creditors immediately. Try to work out a modified payment plan with them that reduces your payments to a more manageable level. Do not wait until your account has been turned over to a debt collector.

Here are some additional tips for solving credit problems:
- If you want to dispute a credit report, bill or credit denial, write to the appropriate company and send your letter "return receipt requested."
- When you dispute a billing error, include your name, account number, the dollar amount in question, and the reason you believe the bill is wrong.
- If in doubt, request written verification of a debt.
- Keep all your original documents, especially receipts, sales slips, and billing statements. You will need them if you dispute a credit bill or report. Send copies only. It may take more than one letter to correct a problem.
- Be skeptical of businesses that offer instant solutions to credit problems: There are not any.
- Be persistent. Resolving credit problems can take time and patience.
- There is nothing that a credit repair company can charge you for that you cannot do for yourself for little or no cost.

If you are not disciplined enough to create a workable budget and stick to it, work out a repayment plan with your creditors, or keep track of mounting bills, consider contacting a credit counseling organization. Many credit counseling organizations are nonprofit and work with you to solve your financial problems. But, not all are reputable. For example, just because an organization says it is "nonprofit," there is no guarantee that its services are free, affordable, or even legitimate. In fact, some credit counseling organizations charge high fees, or hide their fees by pressuring consumers to make "voluntary" contributions that only cause more debt.

Most credit counselors offer services through local offices, the Internet, or on the telephone. If possible, find an organization that offers in-person counseling. Many universities, military bases, credit unions, housing authorities, and branches of the U.S. Cooperative Extension Service operate nonprofit credit counseling programs. Your financial institution, local consumer protection agency, and friends and family also may be good sources of information and referrals.

Reputable credit counseling organizations can advise you on managing your money and debts, help you develop a budget, and offer free educational materials and workshops. Their counselors are certified and trained in the areas of consumer credit, money and debt management, and budgeting. Counselors discuss your entire financial situation with you, and help you develop a personalized plan to solve your money problems. An initial counseling session typically lasts an hour, with an offer of follow-up sessions.

The FTC works to prevent fraudulent, deceptive and unfair business practices in the marketplace and to provide information to help consumers spot, stop and avoid them. To file a complaint or get free information on consumer issues, visit ftc.gov or call toll-free, 877-FTC-HELP (877-382-4357); toll-free TTY: 866-653-4261.

PART 4 | SMART SPENDING

CHAPTER 30
IMPULSE BUYING

About This Chapter: "Impulse Buying," © 2022 Infobase.

Impulse buying is when you decide to make a purchase on the spur-of-the-moment, without planning ahead or taking into consideration whether you really need or can afford the item. Everyone makes impulsive purchases once in a while. You might grab a pack of gum while waiting in the supermarket checkout line, for instance, or give in to the urge to buy a shirt that is on sale. Although this common behavior is not always dangerous or harmful, it can create problems if it becomes excessive or out of control.

There are many psychological factors that can feed your desire to buy things. Social and cultural factors can also influence your spending decisions. In addition, most retail stores and websites are specifically designed to encourage impulse buying. But, recognizing your personal triggers and warning signs can help you resist the urge and control your spending. Since impulse buying can lead to anxiety, buyer's remorse, unhappiness, and debt, avoiding it can improve your emotional well-being as well as your financial health.

Psychological Factors That Drive Impulse Buying

To make smarter purchasing decisions, it is important to understand the psychological factors that can lead you toward poorly-planned, impulsive spending decisions. Some of the key psychological drivers of impulse buying include the following:

- **Concern about social status.** If you spend a lot of time worrying about your appearance, image, or social status, you may tend to buy things on impulse that you think will impress other people. You may also feel driven to buy things that you see other people wearing or using in an effort to increase your status.

- **Seeking pleasure.** If you enjoy shopping just for fun, you probably imagine yourself owning many of the products you see in stores. Many people make impulsive purchases in order to continue experiencing this pleasurable feeling of owning a new thing. Research has shown that people who love to shop experience an increase in endorphins in their brains when they buy something.

- **Improving mood.** If you immediately head to the mall after a bad day at work or school, you may be using shopping as a way to relieve stress or improve your mood. A Harris Interactive poll showed that 31 percent of women have used shopping as a form of "retail therapy."

- **Relieving boredom.** If you go shopping because you are looking for a way to fill empty spots in your schedule, you may fall into the psychological trap of spending money to relieve boredom.

- **Competing for limited items.** Retailers take advantage of your natural competitive instincts by offering great deals on a limited number of items. People flock to Black Friday sales on the day after Thanksgiving in pursuit of such deals. Although the competition pulls shoppers in, even those who do not get the promotional deal are likely to purchase other items on impulse – even if they cannot afford them.

- **Saving by spending.** Another trick retailers use to get you to spend money is shifting your focus toward savings instead. That is why stores offer coupons, discounts, and sales – to make you feel good about being a smart, economical shopper and saving lots of money. In reality, of course, you can never save money by spending money, and "savings" often provide a justification for impulse buying.

- **Grabbing "last-chance" deals.** Retailers also encourage impulse buying by offering flash sales, last-minute deals, and special opportunities that are only available for short periods of time. They hope that these offers will create a sense of panic that will drive you to purchase things you do not really need. Many online retailers bombard customers with daily e-mails designed to tempt them to visit the website and take advantage of these offers before the flash sale ends.

How Retailers Encourage Impulse Buying

In addition to the methods retailers use to create a psychological desire for customers to buy things, they also strategically organize their floor space to entice you to spend more money. Retail stores try to appeal to all of your senses with their visual displays, pleasant music, interesting textures, and tempting aromas. By understanding some of the tactics retailers use, you can be prepared to resist the urge to make impulsive or needless purchases:

- **The relaxing entryway.** Upon entering the store, you encounter a friendly greeter, inviting displays, and sale racks offering some of the retailer's best deals. This area, sometimes called the "decompression zone," is intended to put you in the frame of mind to shop and lure you further into the store.

- **The front section.** As you move past the entryway, you are likely to encounter promotional and sale items. This section of the store is designed to offer enough deals to tempt you to keep shopping. In a grocery store, it usually includes the produce section, bakery, and deli, with its assortment of tasty, convenient, prepared foods.

- **The middle.** By the time you reach the center of the store, you are likely to encounter full-priced items. The retailer's aim is to make you walk past and take notice of these items in order to reach the clearance section in the back of the store. You might even mistakenly think these items are on sale since they are sandwiched between promotional and sale items. By the time you notice the price tag, you may have already decided to buy. Grocery stores tend to put junk food and convenience items in the middle so you have to pass by them in order to reach the staple items in the back, such as milk and eggs.
- **The checkout lane.** After you complete your shopping, you have to walk through the entire store again in order to reach the checkout stands in front and pay for your purchases. If you manage to avoid impulse buying up until that time, you still face the challenge of resisting the novelty items, candy bars, and other goodies that are strategically placed near the cash register. Retailers hope you will give in to temptation and toss a few inexpensive trinkets into your cart at the last minute.

These layout strategies have been developed by psychologists and retail consultants to maximize the opportunities for customers to make impulse purchases. By recognizing these common tactics, however, you will be less likely to fall for them.

Free Trial Offers
A chance to try something out for free? What have you got to lose?

If you are interested in a particular product or service, trying before you buy might seem like a no-brainer. But, what starts as a free trial – or for a very low cost – might end up costing you real money.

The Federal Trade Commission, the nation's consumer protection agency, wants you to know that some companies use free trials to sign you up for more products – sometimes lots of products – which can cost you lots of money as they bill you every month until you cancel.

(Source: ""Free" Trial Offers?" Federal Trade Commission (FTC).)

How to Avoid Impulse Buying
If you often fall victim to impulse buying, the following suggestions may help you resist the urge to splurge:

- Make a list and stick to it to avoid unplanned purchases.
- Plan your route through the store ahead of time and only visit the aisles where the items on your list are located.
- Pay in cash whenever possible to limit your ability to impulse buy. Studies show that people who pay in cash spend around 15 percent less per shopping trip than those who use credit cards.

- Shop for groceries on a full stomach in order to resist the call of junk food.
- Reward yourself with experiences rather than purchases.
- Replace shopping with other activities that alleviate boredom, relieve stress, and improve mood, such as listening to music, writing in a journal, talking to a friend, getting some exercise, or reading a book.
- Impose a mandatory waiting period before purchasing a frivolous or unnecessary item. Carry it around in your cart for a while, then take a picture of it with your phone and put it back. If you still want it a week later, then you can go back to the store and buy it.
- Avoid shopping in groups because it encourages spending. Studies show that people who browse in stores with friends make 7 percent more impulse purchases than those who shop alone. If you do shop with friends, be sure to designate one person to help keep your spending in check.
- Make a policy of donating, giving away, or throwing out one item you already own before you allow yourself to buy something new. This strategy not only reminds you how much stuff you already have, but also helps you declutter your life.
- Ask yourself tough questions before you buy something, such as: Do I really need this, or do I just want it? Do I already have something like it? Will it improve my life in some way? Can I live without it? If you answer these questions honestly and the purchase still seems practical and necessary, then you can buy it.
- Set long-term goals and save toward accomplishing them. Whether it is paying off debt, saving for college, or planning a vacation, remembering your financial goals can help fortify your willpower to avoid impulse buying.
- Save the receipt if you slip up and make an impulse purchase. Many stores have generous return policies that allow you to bring items back if you get buyer's remorse.

References

1. Brenner, Julia. "Eight Secrets of Shoppers Who Resist Impulse Buying," Apartment Therapy, September 5, 2016.
2. Curtis, Jacqueline. "How Retailers Encourage Impulse Buys," Money Crashers, 2017.
3. Curtis, Jacqueline. "Seven Psychological Triggers That Cause Spending," Money Crashers, 2017.
4. Davis, Rebecca. "How to Say No to Impulse Buying," WebMD, 2017.
5. Yeager, Jeff. "Twelve Ways to Avoid Impulse Buying," AARP, October 2012.
6. Zimmerman, Ian. "What Motivates Impulse Buying," Psychology Today, July 18, 2012.

CHAPTER 31
SOCIAL MEDIA AND OPINION-BASED SHOPPING

The social media usage has exploded in the United States from the early twenty-first century. Research shows that 70 percent of Americans used social media in 2016, up from only 5 percent a decade earlier. In 2021, around 72.3 percent of Americans are known to have a social media account. Facebook is the most popular social media platform, followed by Pinterest, Instagram, LinkedIn, and Twitter. As social media usage has grown, people started looking at these platforms for information and advice on deciding what to buy. Studies show that nearly half of all American consumers under the age of 25 are influenced by social media in their purchasing decisions. Social media has not only affected the way people shop, but also affects how companies promote their products and engage with their customers.

Changing the Way People Shop

A few ways that social media influence people's shopping behavior are as follows:

- **Product awareness and advertisement.** When it comes to increasing brand awareness, social media has a big influence on the customers. The purpose of any business is to influence its consumer's behavior. Awareness of a product, details, availability, quality, and various other details are advertised on various social media networks. Technology has improved drastically such that when a person searches for a product online, she or he starts seeing ads relevant to that product on various other platforms they use. Her or his interest toward the product increases once it starts getting displayed quite often. About 65 percent of respondents used social media to engage with retailers and brands by viewing advertisements.
- **Promotional offers and discount deals.** Many people on social media have joined groups and sites that they are interested in. Sales, discounts, and

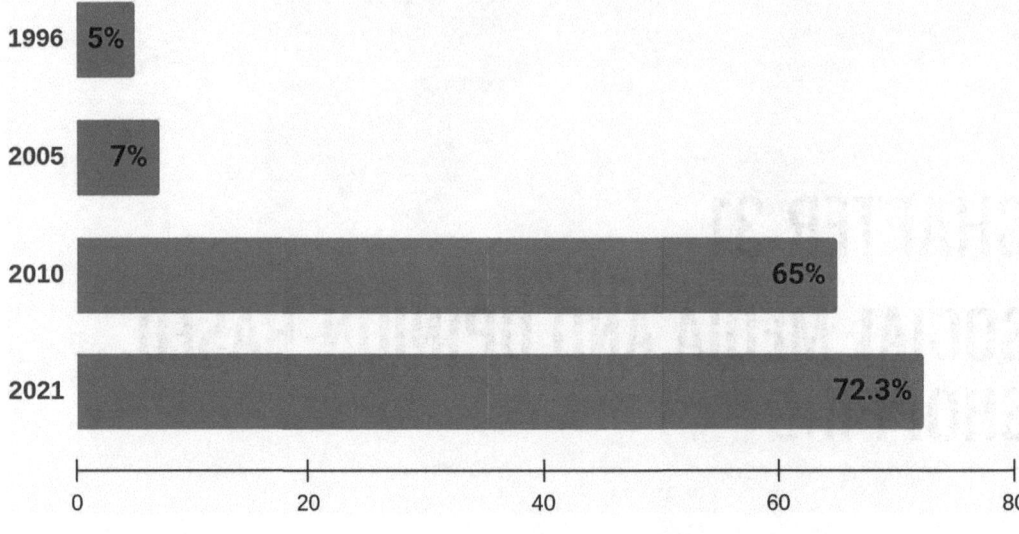

Figure 31.1. Social Media Usage over the Years

offers that consumers see on social media affect their purchase decisions. Liking a company's Facebook group or following a brand's Twitter handle, Instagram page, Pinterest profile, and other similar pages often provides customers with exclusive deals and savings opportunities.

- **Social proof influence.** Social media has resulted in the evolution of social proof (psychological behavior where people copy others actions) as a greater force for buying decisions. Customers who are pleased with their purchases are more likely to publicize/promote them on social media with their reviews and comments. To build brand trust and enhance conversion rates, marketers make the social sphere more visible by posting reviews, comments, likes, tweets, and pins from delighted consumers.

- **Learning about fashion trends.** About 80 percent of respondents use social media to gather information about the latest fashion trends, styles, and products. This information might come from friends, product ads, retailer promotions, designers, or celebrities. Actress and singer Ariana Grande and football player Christiano Ronaldo are the most-followed personalities on Instagram with each having more than 250 million followers. Research shows that endorsement of a product on social media amplifies the post by 69 percent.

According to a Deloitte study, consumers who are influenced by social media are four times more likely to invest more money. Furthermore, the impact can be so effective that 29 percent of users are more likely to purchase a product the same day they see it on social media.

Changing the Way Companies Sell Products

Retailers have watched the growing influence of social media on consumers' shopping and buying habits with great interest. Many have tried to harness the power of social media to help build their brands and connect with customers. Some of the ways companies use social media include the following:

- **Collecting information about customers.** People freely give out lots of personal information about themselves on social media. Some companies are collecting and analyzing this data to gain insight into consumer preferences and buying behavior. They can use this information to identify trends and develop new products that meet customer demands.
- **Building brands and reputations.** Social media places a great deal of power in the hands of consumers. Opinions and feedback about products or shopping experiences – whether positive or negative – can influence thousands of potential customers around the world within minutes. Many retailers recognize this reality and carefully manage their brands and protect their reputations online.
- **Improving customer service.** Many businesses use social media to connect with their customers and improve their shopping experience. For instance, the retailer Nordstrom encourages shoppers in stores to download an app to help them locate items, learn about sales and discounts, and make purchases without waiting in line.
- **Advertising and generating interest.** An increasing number of companies are using social media content to engage with customers and generate interest in their products. The GoPro video camera, for instance, posted videos of people doing daredevil stunts and enjoying outdoor activities on social media to raise product awareness. The launch video for its HERO4 model received 18 million views within three months.
- **Converting awareness into sales.** The biggest challenge facing retailers is convincing social media users to actually purchase their products. Although 75 percent of shoppers became aware of products through social media, only 1.5 percent of online sales could be attributed to social media campaigns in 2016. The potential customers who discover a product on social media also tend to use social media to research other options, read product reviews, and shop around for the best deal. In many cases, these activities lead them to purchase something else instead of the original product they viewed or shared. Many retailers are experimenting with targeted advertising and dynamic content in an effort to engage customers all the way through the shopping process to the final purchase.

References

1. Fernandez, Chantal. "Snapchat, Facebook, or Instagram: Who Is Winning the Social Media Shopping Race?" Business of Fashion, December 20, 2016.

2. Griffiths, Jacqui. "Social Shopping: The Digital Future of Retail," Compass, 2013.

3. Haviland, Mark. "The Second Opinion Phenomenon," *Digital Marketing Magazine*, December 17, 2014.

4. "How Social Media Influences Buying Behavior," eMarketer, March 17, 2016.

5. Kenyon, Jennifer. "Social Commerce: Combining Social Media and Shopping," Catalyst, December 18, 2013.

6. Roesler, Peter. "How Social Media Influences Consumer Buying Decisions," *The Business Journals*, May 29, 2015.

7. "How Does Social Media Influence Consumer Behavior?" Clootrack, February 15, 2020.

CHAPTER 32
SHOPPING FOR HIGH-SPEED INTERNET SERVICE

About This Chapter: This chapter includes text excerpted from "Shopping for High-Speed Internet Service," Federal Trade Commission (FTC), September 2011.

You can get high-speed Internet access through a variety of services, including:
- Cable
- Fiber optic
- Satellite
- Wireless

When you are shopping for Internet service, it helps to understand the differences and know what questions to ask.

Types of High-Speed Internet Service

The type of Internet service available to you depends on what technology your local providers offer:
- Cable modems provide access to the Internet through cable lines without interfering with your cable TV service; cable companies provide this service.
- Fiber optic service provides Internet, phone, and TV services delivered simultaneously through one fiber optic line.
- Satellite Internet service is available in most areas from providers of satellite television services. Extreme weather conditions can disrupt service.

There also are wireless Internet options available in some areas:
- Mobile wireless services, often referred to as 3G or 4G networks, are available from mobile phone companies. You access them through mobile devices or a computer with a built-in or plug-in air card.

- Fixed wireless broadband connects a home or business to the Internet using a radio link between your location and the service provider's tower.
- Wi-Fi hotspots are available in many airports, city parks, bookstores, and other public locations.

How Fast Is Fast?

Speeds depend on a variety of factors, including what type of service you are using, what level or tier of service you purchase, and how congested your network and the Internet are at any time.

- Typically, fiber is faster than cable.
- Speeds are expressed in kilobits (kbps) – thousands of bits per second, or megabits (Mbps) – millions of bits per second.

Most providers have different speeds for uploading and downloading content. Download speeds usually are faster than upload speeds.

Some processes – like watching high-definition movies or playing real-time video games – require a high-speed connection, but even basic web browsing goes faster with one.

If speed matters to you, ask providers what speeds you can expect.

The web is full of free speed testing programs, but they do not all test speed the same way. If you test your connection speed and you are not getting what you expected, ask your provider why and whether you can improve it.

Questions to Ask When Shopping

Ask providers:

Is There a Discount If You Order More than One Service from Their Company?

Buying a bundle of services from one provider can be a good deal. At the same time, it can make it more difficult to change providers for any one service if you are tied into a long-term contract. In addition, promotional prices may have time limits. Ask how long they last, and what the postpromotion cost will be. Get that in writing.

Are You Offering Any Specials?

Special promotion prices may be enticing, but get all the details. The promotion price probably does not include taxes, the cost of extra equipment, or additional fees, like activation or early termination fees. Ask the provider to explain the one-time, recurring, and special charges, including taxes and fees. Get all these quotes in writing.

Some deals are available only online or by phone. Even if you have to order your service online, call the provider first. Review all the information presented on the websites, the minimum system requirements, and the fine-print terms and conditions. Read the entire customer service agreement, and file it for future reference.

Is There Anything You Need to Know about Setting Up Your Connection?

Some promotions require you to install cables, modems, routers, satellite dishes or software yourself. Find out early on what you will need to do and whether support will be available on the phone or online if you have trouble. Message boards on a manufacturer's website can be helpful for troubleshooting.

What Speeds Can You Expect?

Be aware that low promotional pricing may be for the lowest speeds. Make sure the listed download and upload speeds are the ones that you are expecting, and if there is a trial period to test the service to see if it meets your expectations. Actual transmission speeds depend on many factors, including the type of application you are using and the number of people using it at the same time, and may be slower than the maximum potential speed your provider touts.

Can You Change Plans before Your Contract Expires?

Ask about options and costs for changing your plan to reflect your use.

Is There a Cancellation Fee?

Some plans include early-termination fees. Be sure you understand what the fees are and how they are calculated before you sign up.

Whom Do You Call If the Service Goes Out?

Ask if customer service or tech support is available 24 hours a day, seven days a week, and whether it is by telephone or the Internet. Is it free?

What Happens If Your Power Goes Out?

Check with the provider to find out whether phone and Internet service will be available in the event of a power outage. Services provided over a landline typically work during short term power outages, but services provided over cable or fiber may not. Remember that your computer needs a battery or other power supply to work during a power outage.

What Security Measures Does the Provider Include, and What Is the Cost?

Some Internet providers include antivirus and antispyware software with your service, and sometimes it is free. Ask about it, and take these other steps to ensure basic computer security.

> Signing up for broadband can be a significant commitment. Be sure you understand your contract, including whether the price is a promotion that will expire, and any early termination fees for switching service before your contract is up. Understand whether you are paying an additional fee for your modem.
>
> *(Source: "Broadband Service for the Home: A Consumer's Guide," Federal Communications Commission (FCC).)*

Get Help

If you have a problem with your Internet service, first contact your service provider to resolve the issue. If you cannot get satisfaction, consider contacting your public-utility commission or other appropriate state or local regulator.

CHAPTER 33
BUYING A CAR

About This Chapter: Text beginning with the heading "Buying Your New Car" is excerpted from "Buying a New Car," Federal Trade Commission (FTC), November 2012; Text under the heading "Before You Buy a Used Car" is excerpted from "Buying a Used Car From a Dealer," Federal Trade Commission (FTC), May 2021.

Buying Your New Car

Think about what car model and options you want and how much you are willing to spend. Do some research. You will be less likely to feel pressured into making a hasty or expensive decision at the showroom and more likely to get a better deal.

Consider these suggestions:

- Check publications and websites that discuss new car features and prices. These may provide information on the dealer's costs for specific models and options.
- Shop around to get the best possible price by comparing models and prices in ads and at dealer showrooms. You also may want to contact car-buying services and broker-buying services to make comparisons.
- Plan to negotiate on price. Dealers may be willing to bargain on their profit margin, often between 10 and 20 percent. Usually, this is the difference between the manufacturer's suggested retail price (MSRP) and the invoice price.
- Because the price is a factor in the dealer's calculations regardless of whether you pay cash or finance your car – and also affects your monthly payments – negotiating the price can save you money.
- Consider ordering your new car if you do not see what you want on the dealer's lot. This may involve a delay, but cars on the lot may have options you do not want – and that can raise the price. However, dealers often want to sell their current inventory quickly, so you may be able to negotiate a good deal if an in-stock car meets your needs.

Learning the Terms

Negotiations often have a vocabulary of their own. Here are some terms you may hear when you are talking price.

- **Invoice price** is the manufacturer's initial charge to the dealer. This usually is higher than the dealer's final cost because dealers receive rebates, allowances, discounts, and incentive awards. Generally, the invoice price should include freight (also known as "destination and delivery"). If you are buying a car based on the invoice price (e.g., "at invoice," "$100 below invoice," "two percent above invoice") and if freight is already included, make sure freight is not added again to the sales contract.
- **Base price** is the cost of the car without options, but includes standard equipment and factory warranty. This price is printed on the Monroney sticker.
- **Monroney sticker price (MSRP)** shows the base price, the manufacturer's installed options with the manufacturer's suggested retail price, the manufacturer's transportation charge, and the fuel economy (mileage). Affixed to the car window, this label is required by federal law, and may be removed only by the purchaser.
- **Dealer sticker price,** usually on a supplemental sticker, is the Monroney sticker price plus the suggested retail price of dealer-installed options, such as additional dealer markup (ADM) or additional dealer profit (ADP), dealer preparation, and undercoating.

Financing Your New Car

If you decide to finance your car, be aware that the financing obtained by the dealer, even if the dealer contacts lenders on your behalf, may not be the best deal you can get. Contact lenders directly. Compare the financing they offer you with the financing the dealer offers you. Because offers vary, shop around for the best deal, comparing the annual percentage rate (APR) and the length of the loan. When negotiating to finance a car, be wary of focusing only on the monthly payment. The total amount you will pay depends on the price of the car you negotiate, the APR, and the length of the loan.

Sometimes, dealers offer very low financing rates for specific cars or models, but may not be willing to negotiate on the price of these cars. To qualify for the special rates, you may be required to make a large down payment. With these conditions, you may find that it is sometimes more affordable to pay higher financing charges on a car that is lower in price or to buy a car that requires a smaller down payment.

Before you sign a contract to purchase or finance the car, consider the terms of the financing and evaluate whether it is affordable. Before you drive off the lot, be sure to have a copy of the contract that both you and the dealer have signed and be sure that all blanks are filled in.

Some dealers and lenders may ask you to buy credit insurance to pay off your loan if you should die or become disabled. Before you buy credit insurance, consider the cost, and whether it is worthwhile. Check your existing policies to avoid duplicating benefits. Credit insurance is not required by federal law. If your dealer requires you to buy credit insurance for car financing, it must be included in the cost of credit. That is, it must be reflected in the APR. Your state Attorney General also may have requirements about credit insurance. Check with your state Insurance Commissioner or state consumer protection agency.

You can get the invoice price by looking at the dealer's invoice or reviewing car publications.

Leasing a Car

With the cost of cars today, you may consider financing or leasing your next car. If you do, here are some things to keep in mind.

Before you lease a car, determine how much you can afford. According to the Federal Trade Commission, look at your financial situation to make sure you have enough income to cover your monthly living expenses.

Should you take on a new monthly payment? Finance or lease a car only when you can afford to take on a new payment. Saving for a down payment or trading in a car can reduce the amount you need to finance or lease, which then lowers your financing or leasing costs.

The most common type of auto lease is a closed-end lease. With a closed-end lease, you may return the vehicle at the end of the lease term, pay any end-of-lease costs, and walk away.

The best return for your money, is to try to lease a car soon after the model comes out.

(Source: "Leasing a Car: Getting Started," MyCreditUnion.gov.)

Trading in Your Old Car

Discuss the possibility of a trade-in only after you have negotiated the best possible price for your new car and after you have researched the value of your old car. Find out what your current vehicle is worth before you negotiate the purchase of a new car. Check the National Automobile Dealers Association's (NADA) Guides, Edmunds, and Kelley Blue Book. This information may help you get a better price from the dealer. Though it may take longer to sell your car yourself, you generally will get more money than if you trade it in.

Considering a Service Contract

Service contracts that you may buy with a new car provide for the repair of certain parts or problems. These contracts are offered by manufacturers, dealers, or independent companies and may or may not provide coverage beyond the manufacturer's warranty. Remember that a warranty is included in the price of the car while a service contract costs extra.

Before deciding to purchase a service contract, read it carefully and consider these questions:

- What is the difference between the coverage under the warranty and the coverage under the service contract?
- What repairs are covered?
- Is routine maintenance covered?
- Who pays for the labor? The parts?
- Who performs the repairs? Can repairs be made elsewhere?
- How long does the service contract last?
- What are the cancellation and refund policies?

Before You Buy a Used Car

Before you start shopping for a used car from an auto dealer, do some homework. It may save you serious money. Consider the kind of car you need, how you will use it, and your budget. Do not forget other costs like registration, insurance, gas, and maintenance. Research models, options, repair records, safety tests, and mileage.

Once you have a car (or cars) in mind, ask for the out-the-door prices in writing from dealers before you visit. Use those quotes to:

- Confirm that advertised prices, discounts, rebates, etc., are actually being applied
- Confirm that the vehicle is actually on the lot
- Spot add-ons and other charges that the dealer may try to introduce at the last minute

Then, find out about the dealer before you visit. Contact your state and local consumer protection agencies to find out if any unresolved complaints are on file about a particular dealer. You also can check out a dealer's reputation by searching online for the company's name with words like "scam," "review," or "complaint."

CHAPTER 34
TAKING YOUR MONEY ON A TRIP

About This Chapter: This chapter includes text excerpted "Is It Time for Your Financial Checkup?"
Federal Deposit Insurance Corporation (FDIC), 2014.

Your suitcase is packed, you have got your travel itinerary, and you are prepared for the weather where you are going. But, are you all set financially? Unless you have taken the time to consider your money needs, including safety precautions, that pleasure or business trip could turn into a big disappointment and a major expense. Here are few suggestions before you leave.

Decide on the Amount of Cash You May Need

You may want to take some cash to pay for small purchases where credit cards may not be accepted. But, for your own security, it is not a good idea to take a lot of cash anywhere. If your cash is lost or stolen, you cannot replace it.

Take a Couple of Credit Cards

They are generally widely accepted (even in other countries), easy to replace if lost or stolen, and your maximum legal liability for unauthorized use is $50 per card. "Just as when you are not travelling, it is best not to carry any more cards than what you expect to use, in case you lose your wallet," advised Luke W. Reynolds, Chief of the FDIC's Outreach and Program Development Section.

And, Reynolds suggested taking two credit cards, each with a different payment network logo on the front, such as American Express, Discover, MasterCard or Visa. That is to increase the likelihood, particularly when you are travelling internationally, that you can pay with plastic if a merchant does not accept cards licensed or issued by a certain payment network you want to use.

> **Note:** Using your credit card at an ATM or in a bank to get a cash advance can cost you substantial fees.

Consider Other Alternatives to Cash

Debit cards, which can be used at stores and at ATMs, deduct funds automatically from a bank account. Prepaid debit cards, which are generally not linked to your bank account, allow you to load a specific amount of money on the card for purchases and ATM cash withdrawals. With these or other alternatives, research the potential costs, limitations on their use, and your protections if they are lost or stolen.

Do Not Flaunt Your Cash, Bank Cards, Jewelry or Other Valuables

"When you travel, modesty is not only the best policy, it may also deter a robber," said Michael Benardo, manager of the FDIC's Financial Crimes Section. If possible, leave your jewelry and other valuable items in a safe deposit box at your financial institution or leave expensive items at home. Pickpockets thrive in certain communities, so do not ever leave your purse, wallet or keys out in the open. Consider hiding extra money under removable insoles in your shoes and putting your credit card in your inside pocket or a waist pack under your shirt or jacket. "You could take a backup or 'emergency' credit card with you, but make sure to lock it up in the hotel safe," Benardo added.

In general, it makes sense to keep your cash, cards, wallets and passports in separate places. If you have a travel companion and you share the same credit card accounts, it may be a good idea to carry one card each from different accounts so you can avoid losing all your cards at once.

Pay Your Bills before You Go, Especially If You Are Going to Be Away for Two or More Weeks

Doing so will eliminate hassles when trying to pay bills from the road, which could include finding a secure Internet connection to log into your financial accounts. You will also avoid the risk of forgetting to make a payment during your trip and incurring late fees.

Make a List of Key Numbers and Copy Important Documents in Case They Get Lost or Stolen

Your list could include phone numbers for your credit card companies, banks and insurance companies. Consider scanning and e-mailing this list along with a copy of your driver's license and (if you are going abroad) your passport identification page to a secure place, such as your own e-mail address or the e-mail of a trusted friend or family member.

If You Are Traveling Outside of the Country, Make Additional Preparations

Notify your bank and credit card companies where and when you will be traveling so that transactions would not be denied based on incorrect assumptions that your credit or debit card has been stolen. Also remember to verify that any credit card or debit card you plan to use can be used internationally.

Unless you only plan to use plastic, become familiar with the look and the value of the local coins and bills so that you do not get short-changed or cheated. And as noted in the Summer 2014 issue of *FDIC Consumer News*, if you are planning to visit Europe and you do not have one of the new credit or debit cards that contains a computer chip for security purposes, you may want to request one from your financial institution. That is because many European merchants no longer accept magnetic stripe cards.

CHAPTER 35
FACTS FOR CONSUMERS: HOW TO RIGHT A WRONG

About This Chapter: This chapter includes text excerpted from "Solving Customer Problems: Returns, Refunds, and Other Resolutions," Federal Trade Commission (FTC), May 2021.

Disappointed by a product or service? These strategies can help you get your money back or reach another resolution.

Return to the Store or Website

Explain the Problem

Is the product faulty? Damaged? Did you get poor service or repairs that did not fix the problem? Explain the issue. Reputable businesses want to know about problems their customers encounter so they can take action and avoid future complaints.

> **Pro tip:** If you go to the store, try to go when it is not busy. Avoid weekends. Bring your receipt. It also helps if you have the tags and original packaging.

Have Your Documents Ready

These might be receipts, warranties, canceled checks, credit card statements, invoices, contracts, or other documents. If you need to submit any documents, submit copies and keep the originals.

> **Pro tip:** You might be able to find return policies, customer service numbers, and other important information on receipts, product packaging, or warranties, or on a seller's website.

Be Clear about What You Are Asking For

If you want a full refund, ask for that, but be flexible if you can. Other options might include an exchange, a store credit, a markdown on the item you bought, or a percentage discount on a future purchase. If you want a specific remedy, explain why.

> **Pro tip:** Sellers often are more willing to offer a store credit than a refund. It is less expensive for them, and it also means they have a chance to keep you as a customer.

Do Not Wait

Many stores limit the time you have to return or exchange something. Returning an undamaged item sooner also gives the seller a better chance of reselling it and might encourage the store to work with you.

> **Pro tip:** For damaged and defective products, you might have to contact the manufacturer if you are trying to return a product after the seller's return period has expired.

Ask to Speak with a Manager

If a customer representative does not offer the resolution you want, stay calm and polite, but be persistent and ask for a manager or supervisor. A manager will likely have more flexibility and authority to resolve the issue. With each person you speak with, explain the problem – and what you want them to do – calmly and accurately.

> **Pro tip:** Keep notes about your efforts to resolve the problem, including who you spoke with, the date of your conversation, and what action they promised. If you chat online with customer service, see if you can save the chat or take a picture of the screen before you exit the chat.

Write a Letter

If you cannot resolve the problem by going back to the store or website, use this sample letter and these tips to write an effective complaint:

- **Be clear and concise.** Describe the product or service you bought and important details of the transaction. These can include the name of the product, its serial or model number, and the date and place of the purchase.
- **Explain the problem.** For example, you might say the product does not work, you were billed incorrectly, something was not disclosed clearly, or a product's features were misrepresented.
- **Ask for specific action to resolve the problem.** For example, do you want a refund, repair, exchange, or store credit?

1 Gather your paperwork related to the purchase
- Receipts
- Contracts
- Warranties
- Order confirmations

2 Write/call/email:
- Contact the local seller
- Contact corporate offices/consumer affairs departments
- Contact 3rd parties (state licensing boards, consumer protection offices, local regulators)

3 Take legal action
Resolve your complaint in court

Figure 35.1. Steps to File a Consumer Complaint *(Source: "Filing a Consumer Complaint," USA.gov.)*

- Include copies of relevant documents, such as receipts, repair orders, and warranties. Keep the originals.
- **Tell the company how long you are willing to wait for a response.** Give time for the company to take action, but let the company know you will report the matter to your state attorney general or consumer protection office if you do not hear back soon.

Pro Tips
- Do not write an angry, sarcastic, or threatening letter. The person reading your letter probably is not responsible for the problem, but may be very helpful in resolving it.
- Give your name, address, and phone number. If an account is involved, include the account number.
- Send your letter by certified mail, return receipt requested, and keep a copy.
- If you file your complaint online, print the screen or take a screenshot before you hit "submit." That way, you will have a record of your complaint.

Get Outside Help

If you are not satisfied with a business's response to your complaint, consider these steps:

- **Contact your state attorney general or consumer protection office.** These government agencies may mediate complaints, conduct investigations, and prosecute those who break consumer protection laws.
- **Contact a national consumer organization.** Groups such as Call for Action (callforaction.org) and Consumer Action (complaints.consumer-action.org/forms/english-form/complaint_form) try to help people with complaints.
- **Contact your local Better Business Bureau.** The Better Business Bureau (www.bbb.org) is made up of organizations supported by local businesses. Local Better Business Bureaus try to resolve customer complaints.
- **File a report with the Federal Trade Commission (FTC).** The FTC does not resolve individual complaints, but your report helps law enforcement detect patterns of wrongdoing and may lead to an investigation. File your report at ReportFraud.ftc.gov.
- **Visit USA.gov/consumer.** You will find information on filing complaints about specific types of products, steps to filing a complaint with a seller or manufacturer, links to product recall information, and more.

Post an Online Review

If you cannot resolve the problem and feel the company has been unfair, you may want to warn other people by writing an online review. The Consumer Review Fairness Act protects your ability to share your honest opinions about a business's products, services, or conduct, in any forum, including social media.

The law makes it illegal for companies to threaten or penalize you for posting honest reviews. Many companies monitor social media and may reply if they see you are dissatisfied with their response to your complaint.

> **Pro tip:** Your post will be most effective if you use a reasonable tone and explain the problem clearly.

Consider Dispute Resolution Alternatives

- **Research dispute resolution programs online.** Many consumers and businesses use dispute resolution programs – mediation and arbitration – as alternatives to going to court.
  - Mediation involves a neutral third party who helps you and the other party try to resolve the problem. However, it is up to you and the other party to reach an agreement.
  - Arbitration is less formal than court, although you and the other party may appear at hearings, present evidence, or call and question each other's witnesses. Unlike mediation, an arbitrator or panel makes a decision or award once you have presented your case. The decision may be legally binding.

- **Is the program voluntary or mandatory?** Many dispute resolution programs are voluntary. Whether to use them is your decision. In some states, however, a court may order you to try mediation or arbitration. Some companies require you to arbitrate your dispute and give up your right to go to court. Check your contract or product packaging for details. Your state consumer protection office or bar association may be able to suggest alternative dispute resolution programs in your area.
- **Consider small claims court.** Small claims courts can resolve many financial disputes. The dollar limits on claims vary by state, but some states set the limit as high as $25,000. The costs are relatively low, procedures are simple, and lawyers usually are not needed. Check with your local small claims court for information about how to file your lawsuit.
- **If all else fails, you may want to consider a lawsuit.** You can sue for damages or any other type of relief the court awards, including legal fees. A lawyer can advise you how to proceed.

PART 5 | UNDERSTANDING LATEST TRENDS IN FINANCIAL TECHNOLOGY

CHAPTER 36
WHAT IS FINANCIAL TECHNOLOGY?

About This Chapter: "What Is Financial Technology?" © 2022 Infobase.

Financial technology, commonly known as "Fintech," is a broad term used to define any use of technology in businesses that provide financial services. Financial technology can be a software, service, or a company's product that provides digitally relevant financial services that are more efficient than traditional banking processes. Financial technology is a rapidly growing industry that primarily serves young adults and teenagers who are predominantly online. The popularity of financial technology lies in the fact that it brings present-day relevance to financial services along with precision and ease of use for younger consumers.

Financial technology digitizes money and helps monetize real-time consumer data for digital platforms. Several companies use technology such as artificial intelligence (AI) and blockchain in traditional financial services for safety, efficiency, and speed. As it is a booming sector, companies invest in different aspects of financial technology such as investments, saving plans, loan payments, stocks, and credit scores. Some popular financial technology companies include Stripe, Ripple, Chime, Coinbase, and Opendoor. These companies provide services ranging from real estate (Opendoor), mobile-only banking that facilitates no-fee checking accounts (Chime), secure cryptocurrency exchange (Coinbase), and international exchange (Ripple) to simple online payments (Stripe).

How Does Financial Technology Work?

Financial technology has been part of the economic sectors since the introduction of credit cards, ATMs, personal finance applications, and online trading. The latest technologies that work within financial technology include machine learning software and blockchain algorithms to simplify financial processes such as running credit risks and investing in hedge funds. It is unique to each service being provided and varies between different applications and adapts to automated customer services, chatbots, and artificial intelligence interfaces that also help reduce employment costs.

Types of Services

There are three categories to Fintech services that include:

- **Consumer-to-consumer (C2C).** A financial technology service that is involved in digital money transactions. These services allow consumers to interact with each other without mediators such as banks. They are used in money exchange applications such as Venmo. This kind of application is instantaneous, free of charge, and convenient.
- **Business-to-business (B2B).** These tools help integrated businesses function efficiently. Services such as cash management between businesses are the most prioritized in these tools. These services are beneficial for businesses as they provide liquidity, protection, and higher rates of return for businesses and their cash reserves.
- **Business-to-consumer (B2C).** Businesses that interact with customers, such as in the traditional banking sector or retail sector, make the most use of these services. PayPal is a clear example of B2C financial technology service. Such benefits of financial technology enable businesses to keep their customers satisfied by providing transparency in transactions.

Benefits of Financial Technology

- Greater security is guaranteed since Fintech employs data encryption and biometrics to secure consumer data. Many businesses are choosing to enlist financial technology for the monetary services they provide to assure consumers of security.
- Enhanced customer service and returns are the primary goals of financial institutions that use financial technology. These technologies provide better and digitally relevant services that help retain customers and thereby increase revenue.
- **Wider reach for businesses.** By integrating financial technology and mobile technology, companies can tap into a larger demographic since a significant section of the population belongs to the teenage and young adult age group that is continuously adapting to mobile and digital-based living.
- Convenience is a significant benefit of financial technology. It completely removes the need for mediators and lets the customer handle their finances directly along with improved connectivity. The ease with which finance services are obtained with financial technology instead of traditional methods is a bonus, especially for teenagers who wish to personally handle their finances.
- **Relevant payment approaches.** Recent advances in financial technology can ensure that businesses can provide invoices and collect money payments online with higher accuracy.

- **Better access to financial advice.** Individuals such as teenagers interested in managing their finances can avail the services of robo-advising for generalized topics. Many institutions utilize automated technology as the first point of contact for novice customers. With this approach, there is a lower risk of fraud or mismanagement as the algorithm employed is curated to provide accurate and real-time advice without the input of a human thereby also reducing errors.
- **Financial inclusivity.** Financial technology has led to ease of access to financial services previously reserved for a particular section of society, such as lending platforms, investment banking, and loan approvals. People across age groups and economic strata now have the opportunity to be financially literate.
- **Changing the insurance landscape.** Financial technology is bringing a change in traditional insurance provision by taking a majority of the procedures online such as online policy and data handling, and providing customized insurance policies.
- **Helping businesses manage cash more efficiently.** Financial technology services ranging from managing deposits for businesses to handling escrow (a legal concept where a neutral third party holds money for two parties during a business transaction) help simplify transactions, keep related documents secure and avoid outsourcing.

Technologies Involved in Financial Technology

Various technologies contribute to the efficiency of financial technology, such as:
- Blockchain is a system of recording valuable data which cannot be hacked or changed. It is highly preferred as it allows for secure storage of data and transaction records. All transactions with blockchain are encrypted, which reduces the risk of cyber-attacks. Blockchain is primarily used in managing cryptocurrencies.
- **Big data, data analytics.** Market and consumer data, though extensive, is valuable for financial technology companies. Collecting such data can help improve predictive analytics algorithms that can predict customer behavior about investments and other preferences.
- **Artificial intelligence (AI), machine learning (ML).** These technologies use algorithms to detect patterns in online processes and money transactions. These can also be used to detect fraudulent transactions, improve wealth management and credit scoring.
- Robotic process automation (RPA) involves robotics that can be used instead of human labor for repetitive actions in financial services. Robotics can be used for data collection, statistical analysis, communication through chatbots and automated e-mail systems, and managing transactions.

Applications and Uses of Fintech

Financial technology comes with various benefits and is slowly finding its way into all digital platforms that offer financial services. Financial technology is primarily used in fields such as:

- Banking
- Lending
- Mobile payments
- Trading
- Investments and savings
- Cryptocurrency
- Insurance
- Robo-advising
- Microfinance
- Crowdfunding platforms
- Online payments

Safety and Regulations in Financial Technology

Financial technology, though advantageous, has its share of risks. This drives the legal regulations that control the processes and how various corporations and governments use or misuse financial technology. It now comes with a set of regulatory technologies called "regtech" that helps companies address compliance and regulation policies.

Since financial technology finds applications in different industries, a comprehensive regulatory approach is necessary; combining existing and customized regulations that can help prevent threats of misuse and unnecessary exposure to hackers and misuse of data.

References

1. "Fintech," Built In, May 25, 2019.
2. "What Is Financial Technology or Fintech and Its Benefits?" Automeme, November 20, 2019.
3. Pack, Tyler. "Few Advantages of Financial Technology in the Retail Banking Industry," Fintech Weekly, February 28, 2020.
4. Walden, Stephanie. "What Is Fintech and How Does It Affect How I Bank?" Forbes Advisor, August 3, 2020.
5. Kagan, Julia. "Financial Technology – Fintech," Investopedia, August 28, 2020.
6. "Fintech (Financial Technology)," Corporate Finance Institute, January 31, 2020.
7. "Fintech Definition," Fintech Weekly, n.d.
8. "What Is Fintech – Financial Technology?" The American Deposit Management Company (ADM), September 29, 2020.
9. Kauflin, Jeff. "The 10 Biggest Fintech Companies in America 2020," *Forbes*, February 12, 2020.

CHAPTER 37
ELECTRONIC BANKING

About This Chapter: Text under the heading "Online Banking" is excerpted from "Online and Mobile Banking Tips for Beginners," Consumer Financial Protection Bureau (CFPB), May 5, 2020; Text under the heading "Online Payment Services" is © 2022 Infobase; Text under the heading "Mobile Payments and Mobile Wallets" is excerpted from "Mobile Payments and Mobile Wallets," MyCreditUnion.gov, November 28, 2018.

Online Banking

As long as you have a computer or smartphone with access to the Internet and an account with a bank or credit union account eligible for internet banking, it's easy to get started.

1. Gather your account numbers
   Your account numbers should be on your paper statement. Your account number will also be on the bottom of your checks or deposit slips. They are needed to enroll your account.
2. Find your bank or credit union's website
   Look on one of your paper statements or on the back of your debit or credit card to find the website, rather than googling or clicking on links in an e-mail or text. If you visit your bank's website from your smartphone, you may be prompted to download the bank or credit union's mobile app that you can use from your phone.
3. Register for access to your bank or credit union's online banking platform
   The first time you visit, you will follow the prompts to create an online account. You will answer questions to prove it is really you, choose a username and password, and set up security features and preferences. Be sure to create strong passwords and do not use the same password for all accounts. Do not use information such as addresses and birthdays in your passwords.
4. Log in and take a tutorial
   If it is offered by your bank or credit union to learn your way around the platform.

What Can You Do with Online and Mobile App Banking?

- Most transactions can be done online or through your financial institution's mobile app on your smartphone.
- Check your account balances online at any time. You now can catch errors such as unauthorized activity earlier – without having to wait for your paper statement. You usually can notify your bank or credit union account of errors through the online or mobile banking app or chat functions.
- Often, you can see deposits and charges that are pending, meaning they have not posted to your account yet. Note that for pending debit card transactions, the amounts you see may not be the same as the final amount that posts to your account. Be sure to check your bank's or credit union's funds availability policy before assuming that pending deposits are available for making payments or withdrawals.
- Consider whether you would like to continue to receive paper versions of your periodic statements and other documents. Your bank or credit union may prompt you to go paperless while you set up online banking.
- Most banks and credit unions allow you to set up automatic notifications to help you manage your account and alert you when any of the following happen: A direct deposit is received, a large payment is charged, your balance falls below a certain amount, your account is in overdraft, and more. Often, bank and credit union online portals offer you the ability to sign up to get these alerts via text, e-mail, or both. These alerts can help ensure you stay informed without having to log in to your account several times a day.
- Most banks and credit unions will allow you to deposit checks using your smartphone and a mobile app. You might not be able to deposit all types of checks this way, so check with your bank or credit union if you have any questions. The mobile app makes it easy to deposit a check in a few steps:
  - Download your bank or credit union's app on your smartphone if you have not already.
  - Understand any rules your bank or credit union has about mobile check deposit.
  - Follow the directions in the mobile app to deposit the check
  - Hold onto the check for several days after deposit until you are sure it has posted to your account meaning that it is no longer pending and any holds your institution has placed have expired.
  - Destroy the check once it's cleared by shredding it or tearing or cutting it up.
- If you need to transfer money between accounts, or even between financial institutions, your online banking or mobile app likely offers you options to do that. Make sure you understand the terms and conditions of your transfer and double check that you are using the correct account and routing numbers when making any transfers.

- There is a good chance your financial institution offers a way to send money person to person, too. Before you use any mobile payment services, check out our best practices guide to make sure your transactions are done safely. You can test it out by transferring a small amount, like a dollar, back and forth. That way you'll be sure your money goes where you want and you receive money you're owed.
- Instead of writing checks and mailing them, you can pay most bills online or through the mobile app for your financial institution.
- Banking online or through your mobile device is secure, as long as you follow best practices for keeping the information on your mobile device safe. Your financial institution may offer additional services to help you keep your account safe, including turning off your debit card if you suspect fraud. Check with your bank or credit union to learn more about additional protections they may offer.

How Do You Get Help with Online Banking?

If you run into any issues, ask for help! If you need specific guidance, contact your bank or credit union directly. Customer service associates are available by phone, online chat, or video in some cases. The financial institution staff will help you set up your account and answer questions. They will also help you figure out what you can and cannot do online or through their app. Please note that during this pandemic crisis, many bank and credit union call centers are experiencing high call volumes and may be delayed in responding to inquiries.

Online Payment Services

An increasing numbers are using online payment services, such as PayPal, Venmo, Zelle®, etc., to process their transactions and the advantages are clear. From the seller perspective, merchants do not need to set up complicated technology and financial infrastructure to take funds via the web. Instead they pay a fee to the service, which handles the transaction. And buyers enjoy advantages such as convenience, payment flexibility and a higher level of information security.

Using Online Payment Services

Online payments can be made in a variety of ways, including with credit cards, debit cards, gift cards, eChecks, and mobile phone apps. But more and more, online payment services are becoming a method of choice, both for individual sellers and for the websites of large companies. Although services vary somewhat, here is how the process generally works:

- Go to the payment service's website and sign up for a free account.
- Link the account to your credit card, debit card, or bank account.
- Send money to anyone with an e-mail address.
- Receive money from anyone who has an account with that service.

When you send money, it is charged to your credit card or deducted from your bank account. When you receive money, it can be deposited directly into your account or you can request a check in the mail. Some services also have their own debit cards that allow you to get cash from an ATM or make purchases.

Advantages and Disadvantages of Online Payment Services

Online payment services have become so popular because they offer a number of advantages over other forms of making purchases on the Web. Some of these include:

- **Convenience.** Online retailers and auction sites that take payments from services generally link to those services making it easy for you to transfer funds.
- **Security.** Rather than having your credit card number or other financial information held by every online store and individual you do business with, that data can be maintained by just one service.
- **Flexibility.** Most online payment services allow you to shop with online merchants, buy from individual sellers, have money sent to you at college, and send funds to someone who needs it.
- **Easy access to funds.** When you sell something or get money from an individual, you can generally use your payment service account to buy goods and services online, have money sent to you as a check or bank transfer, or, in some cases, get a debit card that can be used anywhere.

Of course, there are some disadvantages, as well, such as:

- **There can be fees.** Most online payment services allow buyers to create an account and conduct certain transactions at no cost, but some have limits on the amount of business that can be transacted for free, after which fees are added. And all of them charge sellers a fee that is usually based on the amount sold.
- **Lack of regulation.** Online payment services function in many ways such as a bank, taking in money, holding it, and paying it out when requested. Yet they are not subject to the same regulations as banks. For example, money held by a payment service is not insured by the Federal Deposit Insurance Corporation (FDIC) as it would be when deposited in a bank.
- **Fraud.** Since many transactions handled by payment services are between individual buyers and sellers, rather than through company websites, there is always the possibility that you could find yourself doing business with an unscrupulous person. If you buy something and do not get it if it is not what you thought you were buying, or if you sell something and do not get your payment, there will be a process for resolving the issue, but it could take some time.

- **Hacking.** While it is true that online payment services offer the security of having your card or bank account information stored in just one place, there is always the chance that the service's system could be invaded by a hacker stealing customer data. In such a case, it is likely that account holders will eventually be compensated, but the process could be complex and take a long time.
- **Slow customer service.** With many payment services, if something goes wrong with a transaction, it can be difficult to speak to a customer service representative. Most of the services are set up to take complaints online, with automated responses. There is almost always a way to resolve problems, but it can be time-consuming and frustrating.

Some Common Online Payment Services

There are quite a few online payment services available to buyers and sellers. Some are aimed at facilitating individual transactions, like auctions, while others are designed for use by merchants with their own dedicated websites. A few of these services include:

- Amazon Payments
- Dwolla
- PayPal
- Skrill
- 2Checkout
- Venmo
- Zelle®

Online Payment Security

Payment security issues are not the exclusive domain of online transactions, of course – they can also be a problem at physical stores – but online payments cause extra concern on the part of consumers, so it pays to be familiar with some of the steps you can take to protect yourself:

- Do some research before committing to an online payment service. Go to their websites and see what kind of security measures they use. Also, do a web search for reviews of the service to see what other consumers have to say about them.
- Use strong passwords. Even if online payment websites do not require complex passwords, you can create your own by using a combination of numbers, symbols, and a mix of capital and lowercase letters.
- Use different passwords for each online account or payment service. Once a hacker figures out one of your passwords, you do not want the criminal to have access to all your online accounts. At least use different passwords for online purchases and other financial transactions than you do for e-mail and social media.

EFT Stop Payment Privileges

When you use an electronic fund transfer, the EFT Act does not give you the right to stop payment. If your purchase is defective or your order is not delivered, it is as if you paid cash: it is up to you to resolve the problem with the seller and get your money back. There is one exception. If you arranged for recurring payments out of your account to third parties, such as insurance companies or utilities, you can stop payment if you notify your institution at least three business days before the scheduled transfer. You can notify the bank orally or in writing.

(Source: "Electronic Fund Transfers," MyCreditUnion.gov.)

- Install antivirus and antimalware software and a firewall on your computer. This is all-around good practice, but it is especially important if you do any financial transactions online, including sending funds through a payment service.

References

1. Hord, Jennifer. "How Electronic Payment Works," HowStuffWorks.com, October 19, 2005.
2. McIver, Rich. "Online Payment Processing 101," CleverBridge.com, November 4, 2015.
3. O'Brien, Russell. "Online Payment Basics," HubPages.com, December 15, 2016.
4. Smith, Aaron; Monica Anderson. "Online Shopping and E-commerce," Pew Research Center, December 19, 2016.
5. Whitehouse, Jordan. "Types of eCommerce Payment Systems," Techwalla.com, March 31, 2015.

Mobile Payments and Mobile Wallets
What Is a Mobile Payment?

A mobile payment uses your mobile phone or other mobile device, online or in person, to provide information electronically to make a payment. There are many different technologies and processes used to make mobile payments and new ones are always around the corner.

Common Types of Mobile Payments

- **Near Field Communication (NFC) mobile wallet payment.** NFC enables you to tap or wave your mobile device close to a "reader" next to a cash register or on a vending machine, turnstile, parking meter, etc. Your mobile device sends the account information that you are going to use for the payment through a radio signal with a short range of about four inches. The mobile wallet app stores your account number in a secure chip in the phone or in a secure file server linked to the mobile wallet app. Examples include Apple Pay and Google Android Pay.

- **Mobile web payments (WAP).** Use the web browser on your mobile device or a mobile app to make a purchase on the Internet and charge it to your credit, debit, prepaid or bank account.
- **QR code (quick response) scans.** Your mobile device produces a QR code on the screen to be scanned at the register. The QR code provides the link to the payment information. Usually you download a mobile app for the merchant (such as Starbucks) or a mobile wallet (such as LevelUp) that allows you to create the QR code on your mobile device.
- **Mobile text payments (SMS).** Send a code by text message to the seller using your mobile device to approve the payment. The purchase is charged to your wireless service bill or a prepaid account held by the mobile operator. Personal information, such as payment account number, should not be sent via SMS.
- **Direct mobile billing.** Provide your mobile phone number as your account number to the merchant. The purchase is charged to your wireless service bill. These are normally low-dollar digital payments for items such as ring tones, screen savers, or apps, with most mobile operators establishing a transaction and consolidated dollar limit.

Protecting Your Privacy and Security When You Make Mobile Payments

Did you know that now you can use a smartphone, tablet or other mobile devices to pay for some purchases? Mobile payments can be convenient – no need to write a check or to pull out your wallet for cash or plastic. No need to type in your payment information to buy something online. But, are mobile payments safe? What about your privacy? Those are good questions to ask when you consider using any new technology. Because you usually carry your phone or other mobile device with you, it is 'on' most of the time, and it may contain very sensitive personal information, it is especially important to keep it, and its contents, safe and secure, especially if you want to use it to make mobile payments or conduct other financial business.

What Is a Mobile Wallet?

A mobile wallet stores payment card information on your mobile device or smartwatch and allows you to make electronic purchases.

Mobile wallet security. Purchases made using a mobile wallet may be more secure than physical cards. This is because mobile wallets use methods such as data encryption and tokenization to monitor and secure your personal and payment card account information.

Mobile Wallet Services Protection*

Many consumers use their smartphones, tablets and other mobile devices as mobile wallets to pay for goods and services, using apps to make both online and in-person purchases. As our use of mobile payment services increases, so does the need to protect mobile devices, apps and associated data from theft and cyberattacks.

How to Safeguard Your Mobile Wallet

- Never leave your smartphone unattended in a public place or visible in an unattended car.
- Consider your surroundings and use your smartphone or mobile device discreetly.
- Never use mobile payment services over an unsecured Wi-Fi network.
- Choose unique passwords for all your mobile apps.
- Install and maintain security software on your smartphone. Apps are available to:
- Locate your smartphone from any computer.
- Lock your smartphone to restrict access.
- Wipe sensitive personal information and mobile wallet credentials from your smartphone.
- Make your smartphone emit a loud sound ("scream") to help you or the police locate it.
- Be careful about using social networking apps, which may pose a security risk and may possibly allow unwanted access to personal information, including your mobile financial data.
- Monitor financial accounts linked to in-mobile apps for any fraudulent charges. Review the service agreements for these accounts to find out what steps to take if your smartphone is lost, stolen or hacked, and what charges you may be responsible for paying.
- The police may need your smartphone's unique identifying information if it is stolen or lost. Write down the make, model number, serial number and unique device identification number – either the International Mobile Equipment Identifier (IMEI) or the Mobile Equipment Identifier (MEID) number. Some phones display the IMEI/MEID number when you dial *#06#. The IMEI/MEID also can be found on a label located beneath the phone's battery or on the box that came with the phone.

Text excerpted from "Mobile Wallet Services Protection," Federal Communications Commission (FCC), February 25, 2020.

CHAPTER 38

ONLINE SHOPPING: A GUIDE FOR E-CONSUMERS

You can buy virtually anything online today, from clothing and electronics to hand-made craft items and groceries. No matter what you are looking for, you are likely to find a website that sells it. The infinite variety of goods available on the Internet, along with the ease and convenience of online shopping, has led to tremendous growth in electronic commerce (e-commerce).

Benefits of Online Shopping

Online shopping has grown tremendously as consumers have recognized the many benefits it offers, which include the following:

- **Convenience.** You can shop from home on your computer or from anywhere on your smartphone, at any time of the day or night.
- **Time savings.** You do not have to drive to the store or wait in a checkout line, and the product will be delivered right to your doorstep.
- **Comparison shopping.** You can easily compare the prices and selection available on different websites.
- **Cost savings.** You can find clearance sales or research online coupons to save money.
- **Product reviews.** You can ask questions or read reviews posted by other people who have purchased a product.
- **Wide selection.** You can buy specialty items that are difficult to find or out of season.
- **Customer support.** Many websites offer online customer service via e-mail or chat functions.

- **Easy returns and exchanges.** Most reputable online sellers have generous return policies that allow you to simply put the item back in the box and drop it off at a nearby shipping location.

Types of Online Shopping Sites

Once you have made the decision to shop online, the next step is to figure out what type of online store to visit. The different types of shopping websites available include the following:

- **Online marketplaces.** Amazon is the world's largest online retailer, offering more than 480 million products for sale on its website and serving more than 300 million customers worldwide. Many other online shopping sites provide one-stop shopping for a variety of general merchandise, including Target, WalMart, Overstock.com, and Wayfair.
- **Manufacturer websites.** Many companies that produce consumer goods, such as clothing or electronics, offer their products for sale on their own websites. Buying direct from the manufacturer often provides better product information, customer service, and warranties, but you may be able to find better prices elsewhere.
- **Price comparison websites.** A number of search engine sites are available to help consumers compare the deals available through various online retailers. Sites such as PriceGrabber, Bizrate, and Shopzilla gather information from multiple online stores in one location, although advertising sometimes influences what sites are listed.
- **Online auction sites.** A wide variety of goods are available at bargain prices on auction sites such as eBay, Listia, uBid, and ShopGoodwill. Name-brand merchandise is sometimes listed at deep discounts, and vendors often have collector's items and hard-to-find pieces for sale as well. To participate in an auction, you simply register as a user and place your bids. The security risk is somewhat higher than manufacturer sites, but most auction sites provide ratings to help you evaluate sellers' past history.
- **Online classifieds.** Sites such as Craigslist and Recycler are similar to the classified advertisements that appear in newspapers. People place ads for items that they wish to buy or sell and connect with others online to complete the transaction. Although these sites may provide good deals on used merchandise, you should proceed with caution because it can be difficult to evaluate the honesty of the seller.

Making an Online Purchase

Once you have found an item that you are interested in buying online, there are a number of important steps to follow before you complete your purchase, such as:

- **Read the fine print.** Be sure to read and understand all the terms and conditions of the sale. Double check the product description, price, taxes, delivery date, and shipping costs. See if the product comes with a warranty, if the seller accepts returns, and how the retailer handles complaints or disputes.

- **Look for secure checkout.** Before entering a credit card number or other personal information, make sure the online shopping site offers secure checkout. You might see a padlock next to the URL in your browser's status bar, or the website might begin with https (with the "s" meaning secure). Most online shopping sites use Secure Sockets Layer (SSL) technology to encrypt your payment details as the information travels through the Internet.

- **Check the privacy policy.** Reputable websites provide customers with access to a privacy policy that outlines exactly what personal information is collected, how it is used, and whether it is stored or shared with third parties. Many websites use "cookies," or small files that are placed on your computer, to store information about you and your browsing habits. Some retailers sell customer information and buying preferences to market research firms or telemarketers.

- **Choose a payment method.** Many experts recommend using credit cards for online purchases since they offer cardholder protections against unauthorized or fraudulent transactions. If you do not feel safe giving your credit card number to online retailers, third-party payment services such as PayPal can be a good option. These services allow you to send money directly to anyone through the Internet and to link your payment account to a bank account or credit card. PayPal also provides automatic currency conversions for international transactions.

Staying Safe While Shopping Online

Despite the many benefits of online shopping, many people continue to voice concerns about the security of their personal information. They worry that shopping online might expose them to data breaches, identity theft, credit card fraud, hacking, or scams. To protect your privacy and shop online safely, experts recommend taking the following precautions:

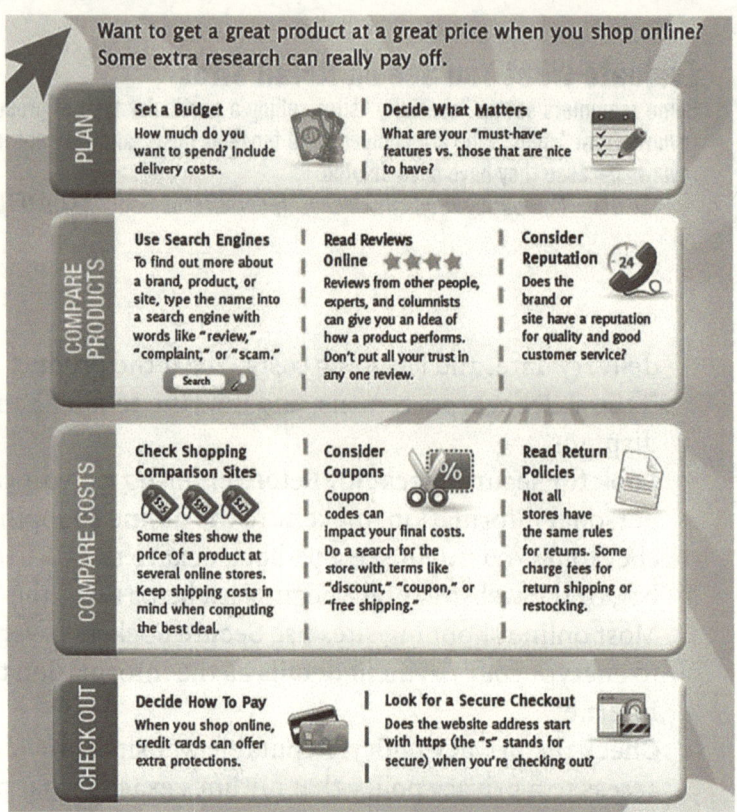

Figure 38.1. Shopping Online *(Source: "Shopping Online Infographic," Federal Trade Commission (FTC).)*

- Stick with familiar, reputable, trusted websites whenever possible. When visiting an online retailer for the first time, check their customer satisfaction ratings and read the user comments. The Better Business Bureau (BBB) is a good resource to find out whether sellers have complaints lodged against them for product, delivery, or return issues.
- Go directly to the online shopping website through your Internet browser, rather than clicking on coupon links or product advertisements that may have originated from a different source. Be sure to type in the website name correctly, because misspellings sometimes lead to fake "copycat" sites that try to trick you into giving away your personal information.
- Never make online purchases from public computers, like the ones at the library or the computer lab at school. If you must use a shared machine, make sure no one is looking over your shoulder when you input payment information, and be sure to log out of the store website and clear the browser history, cookies, and page cache when you are done. Otherwise, the next person who uses the computer could gain access to all of your private information.

- Only provide the minimum information required to complete the transaction. Never give online retailers your Social Security number (SSN), birthday, mother's maiden name, or other data that could be used to steal your identity.
- Keep your computer, tablet, and smartphone updated and protected against viruses and malware. Be sure to use strong passwords when creating accounts on e-commerce sites, and never share your passwords with anyone.
- Use private browsing while online shopping to avoid cookies and pop-up ads related to your product searches.
- Keep track of your online purchases and save a copy of your receipts and any correspondence with retailers. Check the online statements for your credit card, debit card, and bank accounts regularly for any suspicious or fraudulent charges. Notify your bank or credit card company immediately if you notice any problems.
- Order a free copy of your credit report annually and check carefully for mistakes or fraudulent accounts.
- Use common sense to avoid falling victim to scams. If an online shopping site offers a deal that seems too good to be true, it probably is.

References

1. Alford, Catherine. "The Ultimate Guide to Online Shopping," Simple Dollar, May 15, 2015.
2. Farber, Madeline. "Consumers Are Now Doing Most of Their Shopping Online," *Fortune*, June 8, 2016.
3. Griffith, Eric. "Eleven Tips for Safe Shopping Online," *PC Magazine*, November 21, 2011.
4. Kollmorgen, Andy. "Stretch Your Shopping Dollar Further Online," Choice, September 3, 2014.
5. O'Donnell, Andy. "Ten Tips for Shopping Safely Online," Lifewire, December 30, 2016.

CHAPTER 39
CRYPTOCURRENCY

About This Chapter: This chapter includes text excerpted from "What to Know about Cryptocurrency and Scams," Federal Trade Commission (FTC), April 2021.

Confused about cryptocurrencies, such as bitcoin and Ethereum? You are not alone. Before you use or invest in cryptocurrency, know what makes it different from cash and other payment methods, and how to spot cryptocurrency scams or detect cryptocurrency accounts that may be compromised.

What to Know about Cryptocurrency
What Is Cryptocurrency?
Cryptocurrency is a type of digital currency that generally only exists electronically. There is no physical coin or bill unless you use a service that allows you to cash in cryptocurrency for a physical token. You usually exchange cryptocurrency with someone online, with your phone or computer, without using an intermediary like a bank. Bitcoin and Ether are well-known cryptocurrencies, but there are many different cryptocurrency brands, and new ones are continuously being created.

How Do People Use Cryptocurrency?
People use cryptocurrency for quick payments, to avoid transaction fees that regular banks charge, or because it offers some anonymity. Others hold cryptocurrency as an investment, hoping the value goes up.

How Do You Get Cryptocurrency?
You can buy cryptocurrency through an online exchange platform. Some people earn cryptocurrency through a complex process called "mining," which requires advanced computer equipment to solve highly complicated math puzzles.

Where and How Do You Store Cryptocurrency?

Cryptocurrency is stored in a digital wallet, which can be online, on your computer, or on an external hard drive. But, if something unexpected happens – your online exchange platform goes out of business, you send cryptocurrency to the wrong person, you lose the password to your digital wallet, or your digital wallet is stolen or compromised – you are likely to find that no one can step in to help you recover your funds. And, because you typically transfer cryptocurrency directly without an intermediary like a bank, there is often no one to turn to if you encounter a problem.

How Is Cryptocurrency Different from U.S. Dollars?

There are important differences between cryptocurrency and traditional currency.

- **Cryptocurrency accounts are not backed by a government.** Cryptocurrency accounts are not insured by a government like U.S. dollars deposited into a bank account. If you store cryptocurrency with a third-party company, and the company goes out of business or is hacked, the government has no obligation to step in and help get your money back.

- **Cryptocurrency values change constantly.** The value of a cryptocurrency can vary rapidly, even changing by the hour. It depends on many factors, including supply and demand. An investment that is worth thousands of dollars today might be worth only hundreds tomorrow. And, if the value goes down, there is no guarantee it will go up again.

Paying with Cryptocurrency

If you are thinking about paying with cryptocurrency, know that it is different from paying with a credit card or other traditional payment methods.

- **Cryptocurrency payments do not come with legal protections.** Credit cards and debit cards have legal protections if something goes wrong. For example, if you need to dispute a purchase, your credit card company has a process to help you get your money back. Cryptocurrencies typically do not.

- **Cryptocurrency payments typically are not reversible.** Once you pay with cryptocurrency, you can usually only get your money back if the person you paid sends it back. Before you buy something with cryptocurrency, know the seller's reputation, where the seller is located, and how to contact someone if there is a problem. Confirm these details by doing some research before you pay.

- **Some information about your transactions will likely be public.** People talk about cryptocurrency transactions as anonymous. But, the truth is not that simple. Some cryptocurrencies record some transaction details on a public ledger, called a "blockchain." That is a public list of every cryptocurrency transaction – both the payment and receipt sides.

Depending on the cryptocurrency, the information added to the blockchain can include details like the transaction amount and the sender's and recipient's wallet addresses. A wallet address is a long string of numbers and letters linked to your digital wallet. Even though you can use a fake name to register your digital wallet, it is possible to use transaction and wallet information to identify the people involved in a specific transaction. And when you buy something from a seller who collects other information about you, like a shipping address, that information can be used to identify you later on.

How to Avoid Cryptocurrency Scams

Scammers are always finding new ways to steal your money using cryptocurrency. One sure sign of a scam is anyone who says you have to pay by cryptocurrency. In fact, anyone who tells you to pay by wire transfer, gift card, or cryptocurrency is a scammer. Of course, if you pay, there is almost no way to get that money back. Which is what the scammers are counting on. Here are some cryptocurrency scams to watch out for.

Investment and Business Opportunity Scams

- Some companies promise that you can earn lots of money in a short time and achieve financial freedom.
- Some scammers tell you to pay in cryptocurrency for the right to recruit others into a program. If you do, they say, you will get recruitment rewards paid in cryptocurrency. The more cryptocurrency you pay, the more money they promise you will make. But these are all fake promises, and false guarantees.
- Some scammers start with unsolicited offers from supposed "investment managers." These scammers say they can help you grow your money if you give them the cryptocurrency you have bought. But, once you log in to the "investment account" they opened, you will find that you cannot withdraw your money unless you pay fees.
- Some scammers send unsolicited job offers to help recruit cryptocurrency investors, sell cryptocurrency, mine cryptocurrency, or help with converting cash to bitcoin.
- Some scammers list scam jobs on job websites. They will promise you a job (for a fee), but end up taking your money or personal information.

Look for claims like these to help you spot the companies and people to avoid:
- **Scammers guarantee that you will make money.** If they promise you will make a profit, that is a scam. Even if there is a celebrity endorsement or testimonials. (Those are easily faked.)
- **Scammers promise big payouts with guaranteed returns.** Nobody can guarantee a set return, say, double your money. Much less in a short time.

Figure 39.1. Social Media Scams

What Risks Come with Virtual Currencies?
While virtual currencies have potential benefits, the market overall is largely unregulated, so beware.
Virtual currencies:
- Are commonly targeted by hackers and fraudsters
- Have no assurance of recourse if stolen
- Involve e-wallets or storage that present cybersecurity risks
- Carry speculative risk plus fraud and manipulation risks

(Source: "Bitcoin Basics," U.S. Commodity Futures Trading Commission (CFTC).)

- **Scammers promise free money.** They will promise it in cash or cryptocurrency, but free money promises are always fake.
- **Scammers make big claims without details or explanations.** Smart business people want to understand how their investment works, and where their money is going. And good investment advisors want to share that information.

Before you invest, check it out. Research online for the name of the company and the cryptocurrency name, plus words such as "review," "scam," or "complaint." See what others are saying. And read more about other common investment scams.

Blackmail E-mails
Scammers will often send e-mails that say they have embarrassing or compromising photos, videos, or personal information about you. Then, they threaten to make it public unless you pay them in cryptocurrency. Do not do it. This is blackmail and a criminal extortion attempt. Report it to the FBI immediately.

How to Report Cryptocurrency Scams

Report fraud and other suspicious activity involving cryptocurrency to:

- The FTC at ReportFraud.ftc.gov
- The Commodity Futures Trading Commission (CFTC) at CFTC.gov/complaint
- The U.S. Securities and Exchange Commission (SEC) at sec.gov/tcr
- The cryptocurrency exchange company you used to send the money

PART 6 | AVOIDING FINANCIAL PITFALLS

CHAPTER 40

AVOIDING COMMON MISTAKES WITH MONEY

About This Chapter: This chapter includes text excerpted from "FDIC Consumer News Spring 2005 – A Special Guide for Young Adults," Federal Deposit Insurance Corporation (FDIC), July 3, 2014.

Everybody makes mistakes with their money. The important thing is to keep them to a minimum. And one of the best ways to accomplish that is to learn from the mistakes of others. Here is our list of the top mistakes young people (and even many not-so-young people) make with their money, and what you can do to avoid these mistakes in the first place.

Buying Items You Do Not Need and Paying Extra for Them in Interest

Every time you have an urge to do a little "impulse buying" and you use your credit card but you do not pay in full by the due date, you could be paying interest on that purchase for months or years to come. Spending money for something you really do not need can be a big waste of your money. But, you can make the matter worse, a lot worse, by putting the purchase on a credit card and paying monthly interest charges.

Research major purchases and compare prices before you buy. Ask yourself if you really need the item. Even better, wait a day or two, or just a few hours, to think things over rather than making a quick and costly decision you may come to regret.

There are good reasons to pay for major purchases with a credit card, such as extra protections if you have problems with the items. But, if you charge a purchase with a credit card instead of paying by cash, check or debit card (which automatically deducts the money from your bank account), be smart about how you repay. For example, take advantage of offers of "zero-percent interest" on credit card purchases for a certain number of months (but understand when and how interest charges could begin).

229

> If you pay only the minimum payment due on a $1,000 computer, let us say it is about $20 a month, your total cost at an annual percentage rate (APR) of more than 18 percent can be close to $3,000, and it will take you nearly 19 years to pay it off.

And, pay the entire balance on your credit card or as much as you can to avoid or minimize interest charges, which can add up significantly.

Getting Too Deeply in Debt

Being able to borrow allows us to buy clothes or computers, take a vacation or purchase a home or a car. But, taking on too much debt can be a problem, and each year millions of adults of all ages find themselves struggling to pay their loans, credit cards and other bills.

Learn to be a good money manager by following the basic strategies outlined in this special report. Also recognize the warning signs of a serious debt problem. These may include borrowing money to make payments on loans you already have, deliberately paying bills late, and putting off doctor visits or other important activities because you think you do not have enough money.

If you believe you are experiencing debt overload, take corrective measures. For example, try to pay off your highest interest-rate loans (usually your credit cards) as soon as possible, even if you have higher balances on other loans. For new purchases, instead of using your credit card, try paying with cash, a check or a debit card.

Paying Bills Late or Otherwise Tarnishing Your Reputation

Companies called "credit bureaus" prepare credit reports for use by lenders, employers, insurance companies, landlords and others who need to know someone's financial reliability, based largely on each person's track record paying bills and debts. Credit bureaus, lenders and other companies also produce "credit scores" that attempt to summarize and evaluate a person's credit record using a point system.

While one or two late payments on your loans or other regular commitments (such as rent or phone bills) over a long period may not seriously damage your credit record, making a habit of it will count against you. Over time you could be charged a higher interest rate on your credit card or a loan that you really want and need. You could be turned down for a job or an apartment. It could cost you extra when you apply for auto insurance. Your credit record will also be damaged by a bankruptcy filing or a court order to pay money as a result of a lawsuit.

So, pay your monthly bills on time. Also, periodically review your credit reports from the nation's three major credit bureaus – Equifax, Experian and TransUnion – to make sure their information accurately reflects the accounts you have and your payment history, especially if you intend to apply for credit for something important in the near future.

Having Too Many Credit Cards

Two to four cards (including any from department stores, oil companies and other retailers) is the right number for most adults. Why not more cards?

The more credit cards you carry, the more inclined you may be to use them for costly impulse buying. In addition, each card you own – even the ones you do not use – represents money that you could borrow up to the card's spending limit. If you apply for new credit you will be seen as someone who, in theory, could get much deeper in debt and you may only qualify for a smaller or costlier loan.

Also be aware that card companies aggressively market their products on college campuses, at concerts, ball games, or other events often attended by young adults. Their offers may seem tempting and even harmless – perhaps a free T-shirt or Frisbee, or 10 percent off your first purchase if you just fill out an application for a new card – but you have got to consider the possible consequences.

Not Watching Your Expenses

It is very easy to overspend in some areas and take away from other priorities, including your long-term savings. Our suggestion is to try any system – ranging from a computer-based budget program to hand-written notes – that will help you keep track of your spending each month and enable you to set and stick to limits you consider appropriate.

Not Saving for Your Future

It is tough to scrape together enough money to pay for a place to live, a car and other expenses each month. But, experts say it is also important for young people to save money for their long-term goals, too, including perhaps buying a home, owning a business or saving for your retirement (even though it may be 40 or 50 years away).

Start by "paying yourself first." That means even before you pay your bills each month you should put money into savings for your future. Often the simplest way is to arrange with your bank or employer to automatically transfer a certain amount each month to a savings account or to purchase a U.S. Savings Bond or an investment, such as a mutual fund that buys stocks and bonds.

Even if you start with just $25 or $50 a month you will be significantly closer to your goal. Banking institutions pay interest on savings accounts that they offer.

However, bank deposits are not the only way to make your money grow. "Investments, which include stocks, bonds and mutual funds, can be attractive alternatives to bank deposits because they often provide a higher rate of return over long periods, but remember that there is the potential for a temporary or permanent loss in value," said James Williams, an FDIC Consumer Affairs Specialist. "Young people especially should do their research and consider getting professional advice before putting money into investments."

Paying Too Much in Fees

Whenever possible, use your own financial institution's automated teller machines or the ATMs owned by financial institutions that do not charge fees to noncustomers. You can pay $1 to $4 in fees if you get cash from an ATM that is not owned by your financial institution or is not part of an ATM "network" that your bank belongs to.

Try not to "bounce" checks – that is, writing checks for more money than you have in your account, which can trigger fees from your financial institution (about $15 to $30 for each check) and from merchants. The best precaution is to keep your checkbook up to date and closely monitor your balance, which is easier to do with online and telephone banking. Remember to record your debit card transactions from ATMs and merchants so that you will be sure to have enough money in your account when those withdrawals are processed by your bank.

Financial institutions also offer "overdraft protection" services that can help you avoid the embarrassment and inconvenience of having a check returned to a merchant. But, be careful before signing up because these programs come with their own costs.

Pay off your credit card balance each month, if possible, so you can avoid or minimize interest charges. Also send in your payment on time to avoid additional fees. If you do not expect to pay your credit card bill in full most months, consider using a card with a low interest rate and a generous "grace period" (the number of days before the card company starts charging you interest on new purchases).

Not Taking Responsibility for Your Finances

Do a little comparison shopping to find accounts that match your needs at the right cost. Be sure to review your bills and bank statements as soon as possible after they arrive or monitor your accounts periodically online or by telephone. You want to make sure there are no errors, unauthorized charges or indications that a thief is using your identity to commit fraud.

Keep copies of any contracts or other documents that describe your bank accounts, so you can refer to them in a dispute. Also remember that the quickest way to fix a problem usually is to work directly with your bank or other service provider.

Final Thoughts

Even if you are fortunate enough to have parents or other loved ones you can turn to for help or advice as you start handling money on your own, it is really up to you to take charge of your finances. Doing so can be intimidating for anyone. It is easy to become overwhelmed or frustrated. And everyone makes mistakes. The important thing is to take action.

Start small if you need to. Stretch to pay an extra $50 a month on your credit card bill or other debts. Find two or three ways to cut your spending. Put an extra $50 a month into a savings account. Even little changes can add up to big savings over time.

CHAPTER 41

WATCH OUT FOR PREDATORY LENDING PRACTICES

About This Chapter: Text beginning with the heading "What Is Predatory Lending?" is excerpted from "Predatory Lending," U.S. Department of Justice (DOJ), April 16, 2015; Text under heading "Payday Loans and Cash Advances" is excerpted from "Payday Loans and Cash Advances," Federal Trade Commission (FTC), September 28, 2012.

What Is Predatory Lending?

Predatory lending practices, broadly defined, are the fraudulent, deceptive, and unfair tactics some people use to dupe us into mortgage loans that we cannot afford. Burdened with high mortgage debts, the victims of predatory lending cannot spare the money to keep their houses in good repair. They strain just to keep up their mortgage payments. Often, the strain is too much. They succumb to foreclosure. Their houses have been taken or stolen from them.

Run down and vacant houses, the inevitable result of inevitable predatory lending wreak havoc on neighborhoods. Property values fall. People move away. Once sturdy neighborhoods start to crack, then crumble. Something that has been so important for so many people lays in ruins. Everyone who lived in a neighborhood destroyed by predatory lending becomes a victim.

The United States Attorney's Office (USAO) has made combating predatory lending a priority. The Office is taking a comprehensive approach to addressing the problem of predatory lending through education, prosecution, and remediation.

Education

An educated consumer is the predatory lending syndicate's worst customer. Educated consumers know what loans are right for them and where to find them. The United States Attorney's Office has prepared a brochure with some helpful information about preventing mortgage fraud. You can print it out, double-sided, and fold it in thirds to hand it out.

Prosecution

The Office has prosecuted and will continue to prosecute the worst predatory lenders. The Office can use your help. Pay attention to what is going on in your community. If something looks suspicious, check it out. Report it.

Tips to Protect Your Home

- **Get help!** There are scores of housing and credit counselors who can help you decide whether a loan is right for you. Look on the back of this brochure for contact numbers.

- **Know your credit rating.** Get your credit report. We list credit agencies in this brochure. If you have credit trouble, fix it.

- **Trust your instincts**. If it sounds too good, it probably is not true. Many predatory lenders are slick salesmen. They know how to talk. They do not always tell you the whole truth. If a deal does not sound right to you, then do not do it.

- **Ask questions; demand answers.** Predatory lenders will try to fool you by making your loan confusing. If you do not understand anything, ask. Demand an answer.

- **Read everything.** Get all the loan documents before closing. Do not sign anything until you have read it. If there is something incorrect, fix it. If you are confused about something, ask.

- **Do not fall for a "bait and switch."** If what you read in your loan papers is not what you wanted, expected, or agreed to, do not sign. Be prepared to walk out.

- **Learn about your loan.** There are many organizations that produce publications that can be helpful. We have listed some of them in this brochure.

- **Shop around.** There are lots of people who may be willing to give you a loan. Most of them are honest, responsible people. Find them. Call as many banks as you can. Look in your newspaper's real estate section for advertisements. Go to the library and search the Internet; try "mortgage," "mortgage rate," and "mortgage companies."

- **Take your time**. A predatory lender will try to rush you so you cannot ask questions. Take all the time you need to understand what your deal is.

- **Say "No."** Do not let someone talk you into something you really do not want or need. Also, it is okay to change your mind.

- **Never let a contractor get a loan for you.** If you are doing home improvements, a contractor may tell you that he can get a loan for you. Do not let him. Find the loan yourself; it will be cheaper.

- **Do not make final payment to a contractor until all the work is done.** Some contractors may ask you to sign over checks to them or to sign so-called "completion certificates" before they finish the work on your house. Do not.

Make sure you are happy with the work on your house before you give any money to a contractor.

- **Avoid prepayment penalties.** If possible, do not take a loan that penalizes you for refinancing. You may get stuck in a loan that you cannot get out of.
- **Do not lie.** No matter what anyone else may tell you, it is not okay to lie on a form, even a little. If you get a loan based on false documents, you may be getting in over your head. You would not be able to afford the loan.
- **Report wrongdoing.** If you learn that someone did something illegal, report it. There are contact numbers on this brochure.

Red Flags

- **Aggressive solicitations.** Whose idea was it to get this loan? Did someone sell it to you? Be wary of anyone who came to you trying to sell you a loan. If you need a loan, shop around for it yourself.
- **Loan flipping.** Loan flipping is pressuring you to refinance your loan over and over. Before you refinance, make sure a new loan makes you better off. For instance, do not refinance a low interest loan into one with a higher interest rate. See a housing counselor.
- **High fees.** Look at your Good Faith Estimate of Costs and your settlement sheet. Do you know what each fee is for? If not, ask. If your total fees are more than 5 percent of your loan, that is probably too much.
- **Property taxes.** If you do not save enough money to pay your tax bill, a predatory lender will try to lend you money for your taxes. You may want to have your taxes "escrowed." That means that you will put aside some money each month for your taxes.
- **Balloon Payments.** A balloon payment is one very large payment you make at the end of the loan. Predatory lenders like balloon payments because they can tell you that your monthly payment is low. The problem is that you may not be able to make the payment and will need to refinance. You will need a new loan with new fees and costs.
- **Consolidating debt.** It is not always a good idea to pay off your credit cards with a mortgage loan. If you cannot pay your credit cards, it is almost impossible for someone to take your house. If you consolidate, however, your house is collateral. Consolidating means you risk losing your house to pay your credit cards.

Payday Loans and Cash Advances
What Is a Payday Loan or Cash Advance Loan?

A payday loan or a cash advance loan is a loan for a short time. You pay a fee to borrow the money, even if it is for a week or two.

A payday loan or cash advance loan can be very expensive. Before you get one of these loans, consider other ways to borrow.

What Are Some Other Ways to Borrow Money?

You might be able to borrow money from:
- Family or friends
- A bank or credit union
- Your credit card

You might ask for more time to pay your bills. You can talk to a credit counselor to get help.

How Does a Payday Loan or Cash Advance Loan Work?

- You give the lender a check for the amount of money you want to borrow – plus a fee.
- The lender keeps your check and gives you cash – less the fee they charge.
- On your next payday, you have to pay the lender in cash. You owe the amount you borrowed plus the fee.

How Much Do These Loans Cost?

A payday loan or cash advance loan can cost a lot. Even if you only borrow money for a week or two until you get your paycheck.

For example:
- You borrow $500. The fee is $75.
- You give the lender a check for $575.
- The lender keeps your check and gives you $500 in cash.
- After two weeks, you give the lender $575 in cash and you get your check back.
- The bottom line: You paid $75 to borrow $500 for two weeks.

How Do You Compare Costs?

Most loans have an annual percentage rate (APR). The APR is how much it costs you to borrow money for one year. The APR on payday loans and cash advances is very high.

When you get a payday loan or cash advance loan, the lender must tell you the APR and the cost of the loan in dollars.

What Does Happen If You Cannot Pay the Lender the Money You Owe?

If you cannot pay the lender the money you owe, you borrow the money for two more weeks. This is called a "rollover," or "rolling over" the loan. To roll over the loan, you pay another fee. If you roll over the loan a few times, you will pay a lot to borrow the money. It becomes harder to get back to where you started.

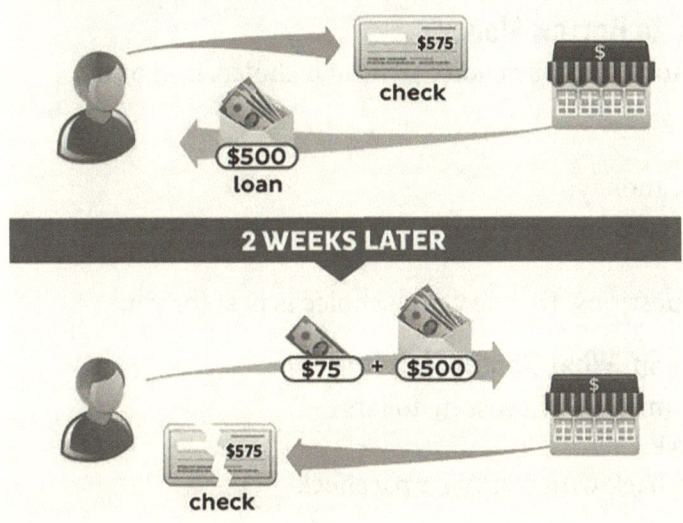

You borrow $500
The fee is $75

$575
check

$500
loan

2 WEEKS LATER

$75 + $500

$575
check

Figure 41.1. How a Payday Loan Works

What Is an Annual Percentage Rate?

The annual percentage rate (APR), is based on:
- The amount of money you borrow
- The monthly finance charge or interest rate
- How much you pay in fees
- How long you borrow the money

For example:
- You borrow $500. You pay a $75 fee to get the money. But, in two weeks you cannot repay the loan.
- You pay another $75 to roll over the loan. But, in two more weeks, you still cannot repay the loan.
- Every two weeks, you pay another $75 fee. You might pay the lender more in fees than you first borrowed. But, you would still owe the original $500.

What Should You Do before You Get a Payday Loan or a Cash Advance Loan?

Before you get one of these loans, ask yourself the following questions:
- Can I get a loan from a bank or credit union?
- Can I get more time to pay my bills by talking with creditors or a credit counselor?
- Do I have any money saved that I can use?

- Can I borrow money from family or friends?
- Can I use a credit card instead?

How Do You Choose Which Way to Borrow Money?

Compare the costs, if you have more than one choice. For each choice, find out:

- What is the APR?
- What are the fees?
- How soon must I repay the money?
- What happens if I cannot repay?

Write the answers to these questions. Decide which choice is best for you.

You Decided to Get a Payday Loan. What Should You Do?

- Ask the lender to tell you how much it will cost in dollars
- Ask the lender to tell you the APR
- Borrow only what you can pay back with your next paycheck

CHAPTER 42

IF YOUR CREDIT, ATM, OR DEBIT CARDS ARE LOST OR STOLEN

About This Chapter: Text beginning with the heading "Report Loss or Theft Immediately" is excerpted from "Lost or Stolen Credit, ATM, and Debit Cards," Federal Trade Commission (FTC), August 2012; Text under the heading "Four Steps You Can Take If You Think Your Credit or Debit Card Data Was Hacked" is excerpted from "Four Steps You Can Take If You Think Your Credit or Debit Card Data Was Hacked," Consumer Financial Protection Bureau (CFPB), January 27, 2014.

Report Loss or Theft Immediately

Acting fast limits your liability for charges you did not authorize. Report the loss or theft of your card to the card issuer as quickly as possible. Many companies have toll-free numbers and 24-hour service for such emergencies. Once you report the loss of your ATM or debit card, federal law says you cannot be held liable for unauthorized transfers that occur after that time.

- **Follow up with a letter or e-mail.** Include your account number, the date and time when you noticed your card was missing, and when you first reported the loss.
- **Check your card statement carefully** for transactions you did not make. Report these transactions to the card issuer as quickly as possible. Be sure to send the letter to the address provided for billing errors.
- **Check if your homeowner's or renter's insurance policy covers your liability** for card thefts. If not, some insurance companies will allow you to change your policy to include this protection.

How to Report Fraudulent Transactions

- Contact your ATM or debit card issuer.
  - Report the fraudulent transaction.
  - Act as soon as you discover a withdrawal or purchase you did not make.

- Write a follow up letter to confirm that you reported the problem.
  - Keep a copy of your letter.
  - Send it by certified mail and ask for a return receipt.
- Update your files.
  - Record the dates you made calls or sent letters.
  - Keep copies of letters in your files.

How to Limit Your Losses

The Fair Credit Billing Act (FCBA) and the Electronic Fund Transfer Act (EFTA) offer protection if your credit, ATM, or debit cards are lost or stolen.

Credit Card Loss or Fraudulent Charges

Under the FCBA, your liability for unauthorized use of your credit card tops out at $50. However, if you report the loss before your credit card is used, the FCBA says you are not responsible for any charges you did not authorize. If your credit card number is stolen, but not the card, you are not liable for unauthorized use.

ATM or Debit Card Loss or Fraudulent Transfers

If you report an ATM or debit card missing before someone uses it, the EFTA says you are not responsible for any unauthorized transactions. If someone uses your ATM or debit card before you report it lost or stolen, your liability depends on how quickly you report it:

If someone makes unauthorized transactions with your debit card number, but your card is not lost, you are not liable for those transactions if you report them within 60 days of your statement being sent to you.

Table 42.1. Reporting of ATM or Debit Card Loss or Fraudulent Transfers

If You Report	Your Maximum Loss
Before any unauthorized charges are made.	$0
Within 2 business days after you learn about the loss or theft.	$50
More than 2 business days after you learn about the loss or theft, but less than 60 calendar days after your statement is sent to you.	$500
More than 60 calendar days after your statement is sent to you.	All the money taken from your ATM/debit card account, and possibly more; for example, money in accounts linked to your debit account.

How to Protect Your Cards and Account Information
For Credit and ATM or Debit Cards
- Do not disclose your account number over the phone unless you initiate the call.
- **Guard your account information.** Never leave it out in the open or write it on an envelope.
- Keep a record of your account numbers, expiration dates, and the telephone numbers of each card issuer so you can report a loss quickly.
- Draw a line through blank spaces on charge or debit slips above the total so the amount cannot be changed.
- Do not sign a blank charge or debit slip.
- Tear up copies and save your receipts to check against your monthly statements.
- Cut up old cards – cutting through the account number – before you throw them away.
- Open your monthly statements promptly and compare them to your receipts. Report mistakes or discrepancies as soon as possible.
- Carry only the cards you will need.

For ATM or Debit Cards
- Do not carry your PIN in your wallet, purse, or pocket – or write it on your ATM or debit card. Commit it to memory.
- Never write your PIN on the outside of a deposit slip, an envelope, or other papers that could be lost or looked at.
- Carefully check your ATM or debit card transactions; the funds for this item will be quickly transferred out of your checking or other deposit account.
- Periodically check your account activity, especially if you bank online. Compare the current balance and transactions on your statement to those you have recorded. Report any discrepancies to your card issuer immediately.

Four Steps You Can Take If You Think Your Credit or Debit Card Data Was Hacked

Keep a close eye on your account activity and report suspicious transactions immediately to your bank or credit card provider. The sooner you tell your provider about any unauthorized debits or charges, the better off you will be.

1. Check Your Accounts for Unauthorized Charges or Debits and Continue Monitoring Your Accounts

If you have online or mobile access to your accounts, check your transactions as frequently as possible. If you receive paper statements, be sure to open them and review them closely. If your provider offers it, consider signing up for e-mail or text alerts.

Report even small problems right away. Sometimes thieves will process a small debit or charge against your account and return to take more from your bank account or add more charges to your credit card if the first smaller debit or charge goes through. And keep paying attention – fraudulent charges to your card or fraudulent debits to your bank account might occur many months after the theft of your information during a data breach.

2. Report a Suspicious Charge or Debit Immediately

Contact your bank or card provider immediately if you suspect an unauthorized debit or charge. If a thief charges items to your account, you should cancel the card and have it replaced before more transactions come through. Even if you are not sure that PIN information was taken, consider changing your PIN just to be on the safe side.

If your physical credit card has not been lost or stolen, you are not responsible for unauthorized charges. You can protect yourself from being liable for unauthorized debit card charges by reporting those charges immediately after you find out about them or they show up on your bank statement.

If you spot a fraudulent transaction, call the card provider's toll-free customer service number immediately. Follow up with a written letter. Your monthly statement or error resolution notice will tell you how and where to report fraudulent charges or billing disputes.

When you communicate in writing, be sure to keep a copy for your records. Write down the dates you make follow-up calls and keep this information together in a file.

If your card or PIN was lost or stolen, different rules may apply. Your timeline for reporting after your card, PIN, or other access device is lost or stolen is tied to when you discover the loss or theft or when unauthorized transactions show up on your bank statement. Therefore, you should make the report as soon as you know that there is a problem.

3. Submit a Complaint If You Have an Issue with Your Bank or Card Provider's Response

Debit card issuers should investigate the charges (generally within 10 business days) and take action quickly (generally within 3 business days). For your credit card, it can take longer, but you do not have to pay the charge while it is under investigation. You also have a right to see the results of their investigations.

If you have an issue with their response, you can submit a complaint online or by calling 855-411-2372. For TTY/TDD, call 855-729-2372.

If you have other questions about billing disputes and your debit and credit card protections, you can Ask CFPB.

4. Know When to Ignore Anyone Contacting You to "Verify" Your Account Information by Phone or E-mail

This could be a common scam, often referred to as "phishing," to steal your account information. Banks and credit unions never ask for account information through phone or e-mail that they initiate. If you receive this type of contact, you should immediately call your card provider (using a customer service number that you get from a different source than the initial call or e-mail) and report it.

CHAPTER 43
IDENTITY THEFT AND IDENTITY FRAUD

About This Chapter: Text beginning with the heading "What Is Identity Theft?" is excerpted from "What to Know about Identity Theft," Federal Trade Commission (FTC), March 2021; Text under the heading "New Protections Available for Minors under 16" is excerpted from "New Protections Available for Minors under 16," Federal Trade Commission (FTC), March 11, 2019.

What Is Identity Theft?

Identity theft is when someone uses your personal or financial information without your permission.

They might steal your name and address, credit card, or bank account numbers, Social Security number, or medical insurance account numbers. And they could use them to.

- Buy things with your credit cards.
- Get new credit cards in your name.
- Open a phone, electricity, or gas account in your name.
- Steal your tax refund.
- Use your health insurance to get medical care.
- Pretend to be you if they are arrested.

How to Protect Yourself against Identity Theft

Taking steps to protect your personal information can help you avoid identity theft. Here is what you can do to stay ahead of identity thieves.

What Do Thieves Do with Your Information?

Once identity thieves have your personal information, they can drain your bank account, run up charges on your credit cards, open new utility accounts, or get medical treatment on your health insurance. An identity thief can file a tax refund in your name and get your refund. In some extreme cases, a thief might even give your name to the police during an arrest.

(Source: "Warning Signs of Identity Theft," IdentityTheft.gov, Federal Trade Commission (FTC).)

Protect Documents That Have Personal Information

Keep your financial records, Social Security and Medicare cards, and any other documents that have personal information in a safe place. When you decide to get rid of those documents, shred them before you throw them away. If you do not have a shredder, look for a local shred day, or use a marker to block out account numbers.

If you get statements with personal information in the mail, take your mail out of the mailbox as soon as you can.

Ask Questions before Giving Out Your Social Security Number

Some organizations need your Social Security number to identify you. Those organizations include the IRS, your bank, and your employer. Organizations like these that do need your Social Security number will not call, e-mail, or text you to ask for it.

Other organizations that might ask you for your Social Security number might not really need it. Those organizations include a medical provider, a company, or your child's school. Ask these questions before you give them your Social Security number:

- Why do you need it?
- How will you protect it?
- Can you use a different identifier?
- Can you use just the last four digits of my Social Security number?

Protect Your Information from Scammers Online and on Your Phone

If you are logging in to an online account, use a strong password.

Add multifactor authentication for accounts that offer it. Multifactor authentication offers extra security by requiring two or more credentials to log in to your account. The additional credentials you need to log in to your account fall into two categories: something you have – like a passcode you get via text message or an authentication app, or something you are – like a scan of your fingerprint, your retina, or your face. Multifactor authentication makes it harder for scammers to log in to your accounts if they do get your username and password.

Do not give your personal information to someone who calls, e-mails, or texts you. It could be a scammer trying to steal your information.

How to Know If Someone Stole Your Identity

In addition to taking steps to protect your information, it pays to know how to tell if someone stole your identity. There are things you can do yourself to detect identity theft. There also are companies that sell credit and identity monitoring services.

If you discover that someone is misusing your personal information, visit IdentityTheft.gov to report and recover from identity theft.

What You Can Do to Detect Identity Theft

Here is what you can do to spot identity theft:

- **Track what bills you owe and when they are due.** If you stop getting a bill, that could be a sign that someone changed your billing address.
- **Review your bills.** Charges for things you did not buy could be a sign of identity theft. So could a new bill you did not expect.
- **Check your bank account statement.** Withdrawals you did not make could be a sign of identity theft.
- **Get and review your credit reports.** Accounts in your name that you do not recognize could be a sign of identity theft. Here is how you can get your free credit reports.

Monitoring Services, Recovery Services, and Identity Theft Insurance

Many companies sell identity theft protection services that may include credit monitoring, identity monitoring, identity recovery services, and identity theft insurance. These services also might be offered by your:

- Bank or credit union
- Credit card provider
- Employer's benefits program
- Insurance company

Credit Monitoring Services

Credit monitoring services scan activity that shows up on your credit reports. They might monitor activity at one, two, or all three of the major credit bureaus – Equifax, Experian, and TransUnion.

Credit monitoring services will usually alert you when:

- A company checks your credit history
- A new loan or credit card account appears on your credit reports
- A creditor or debt collector says your payment is late
- Public records show that you filed for bankruptcy
- Someone files a lawsuit against you
- Your credit limit changes
- Your personal information, such as your name, address, or phone number, changes

Credit monitoring services will not alert you when:

- Someone withdraws money from your bank account
- Someone uses your Social Security number to file a tax return and collect your refund

If you are considering using a credit monitoring service, here are some questions you can ask them:

- How often do you check credit reports for changes?
- Which of the three credit bureaus do you monitor?
- Is there a limit to how often I can review my credit reports?
- Will I be charged each time I review my credit reports?
- Are other services included, like access to my credit score?

Identity Monitoring Services

Companies that offer identity monitoring services check databases that collect different types of information to see if they contain new or inaccurate information about you. Those could be a sign that someone is using your personal information. These services can detect uses of your personal information that will not show up on your credit report.

Identity monitoring services may tell you when your information shows up in:

- A change of address request
- Court or arrest records
- Orders for new utility, cable, or wireless services
- An application for a payday loan
- A request to cash a check
- On social media
- On websites that identity thieves use to trade stolen information

Most identity monitoring services will not alert if someone uses your information to:

- File a tax return and collect your refund
- Get Medicare benefits
- Get Medicaid benefits
- Get welfare benefits
- Claim Social Security benefits
- Claim unemployment benefits

Identity Recovery Services

Companies that sell credit and identity monitoring services also may offer identity recovery services to help you fix any damage caused by identity theft. These services may be included or cost extra. Some of the services they offer may be things you can do on your own for little or no cost.

Identity recovery services typically give you access to counselors or case managers who will help you recover your identity. They may

- Help you write letters to creditors and debt collectors
- Place a freeze on your credit report to prevent an identity thief from opening new accounts in your name
- Guide you through documents you have to review

Some services will represent you in dealing with creditors or other institutions if you formally grant them authority to act on your behalf.

Identity Theft Insurance

Companies that sell monitoring services also may offer identity theft insurance. These services may be included or cost extra.

Identity theft insurance may cover

- Out-of-pocket expenses directly associated with reclaiming your identity, such as
  - The cost of copying documents
  - Postage costs for sending documents
  - Costs for getting documents notarized
- Wages you lost
- Legal fees you paid

Identity theft insurance generally will not reimburse you for money stolen or financial loss resulting from the theft. Most policies will not pay if your loss is covered by your homeowner's or renter's insurance. If you are considering getting identity theft insurance, ask about the deductible and find out what is covered and what is not.

New Protections Available for Minors under 16

Young people now have more protection from identity theft and fraud, thanks to a new federal law that went into effect September 21, 2018. The new law lets parents and child welfare representatives of people under 16, as well as legal guardians, request a security freeze, also called a "credit freeze," on their behalf. Taking this step can help protect a young person from identity theft and fraud – and it is free.

Identity theft happens when someone misuses your personal information, such as a Social Security number, to open accounts, file taxes, or make purchases. Hackers, thieves, and even people you know might steal your identity. Minors typically do not have credit reports, which means that a young person may not find out about issues with their credit reports until they first try to get credit – perhaps even years later.

While a security freeze will not affect anything already on your credit report, it restricts access to your report. That makes it harder for identity thieves to open new accounts using your personal information. With the new law, it is free to freeze and unfreeze your credit file at the three nationwide consumer reporting agencies – Equifax,

Experian, and TransUnion. To find contact information for placing a free credit freeze, visit IdentityTheft.gov/credit bureau contacts.

The new law also lets people like parents, guardians, and representatives acting on behalf of a young person in foster care proactively protect a young person's credit file by freezing it.

If the nationwide credit reporting agencies do not have a file on the child, they will create one so they can freeze it. This record cannot be used for credit purposes. It is there just to make sure the child's record is frozen and protected against identity theft and fraud.

Depending on the adult's relationship to the child, there are different procedures to put a freeze in place. Parents need to show proof of their authority, like a birth certificate, to freeze or unfreeze the credit file for their child under 16. The new law says that child welfare or probation agency representatives acting on behalf of a young person in foster care can request a security freeze for that child. They have to show documentation certifying that the child is in the agency's care, such as a written communication or an official letter from the child welfare or probation agency or its designee. Child welfare agencies who already work with consumer reporting agencies to pull and review credit reports for youth in their care can use the same company contacts and liaisons to facilitate the security freeze process.

CHAPTER 44

CON ARTISTS WANT YOUR MONEY: AVOID THESE SCAMS AND SCHEMES

About This Chapter: This chapter includes text excerpted from "Common Scams and Frauds," USA.gov, June 2, 2021.

COVID-19 Scams, Rumors, and Price Gouging

During the COVID-19 pandemic, scammers may try to take advantage of you. They might get in touch by phone, e-mail, postal mail, text, or social media. Protect your money and your identity. Do not share personal information such as your bank account number, Social Security number, or date of birth. Learn how to recognize and report a COVID vaccine scam and other types of coronavirus scams.

Common Coronavirus Scams

Scammers change their methods frequently. Current coronavirus scams include:

- **Identity theft when people post a photo of their vaccination card on social media.** Do not post a photo of your vaccination card online. Scammers can see and steal your name, birthdate, and other personal information.
- **COVID-19 testing, vaccine, and treatment scams.** Do not trust offers to get early access to the approved vaccine. And be aware that scammers are also targeting Medicare recipients. They are offering COVID-19 testing in an attempt to steal personal information.
- **Charity scams.** Fake charities pop up during disasters. And scammers can also claim to be from real charities. Learn how to research charity claims and protect your money.
- **Checks from the government.** Scammers say they are from the IRS or another government agency. They ask for your personal information or try to charge you fake fees for getting your stimulus check or offer you a way to get the money early.

- **FDIC and banking.** People pretend to call from the Federal Deposit Insurance Corporation (FDIC) or your bank. They say your bank account or your ability to get cash are in danger and ask for your personal information.
- **Grandparent and military service member scams.** A scammer pretends to be a grandchild or a military service member. They say they are sick or in trouble because of the coronavirus. They contact you asking to wire them money to pay for fake medical or travel expenses.
- **COVID-19 funeral assistance scam.** Scammers pretend to be from FEMA's COVID-19 Funeral Assistance Program and call to offer program registration to family members of people who have died from COVID-19. In this way, the scammers can steal the family members' Social Security numbers and other forms of identification.

Report COVID-19 Scams

- Contact the National Center for Disaster Fraud hotline at 866-720-5721 or e-mail disaster@leo.gov.
- Report a scam to the FBI at tips.fbi.gov.
- If it is an online scam, submit your complaint through the Internet Crime Complaint Center (IC3).

Coronavirus Rumors

Rumors, myths, and conspiracy theories about the coronavirus can be frightening and misleading. Go to FEMA's Rumor Control page (www.fema.gov/disasters/coronavirus/rumor-control) to check out the real answers about the rumors you are hearing.

Report Price Gouging

During times of high demand, sellers may raise prices to a very high and unfair level on needed items such as:

- Face masks
- Hand sanitizer
- Household or personal-care items

This is called "price gouging" and it is illegal. If you suspect price gouging, report it to your state attorney general (www.usa.gov/state-attorney-general).

Telephone Scams

Telephone scammers try to steal your money or personal information. Scams may come through phone calls from real people, robocalls, or text messages. Callers often make false promises, such as opportunities to buy products, invest your money, or receive free product trials. They may also offer you money through free grants and lotteries. Some scammers may call with threats of jail or lawsuits if you do not pay them.

Report Telephone Scams

It is important to report phone scams to federal agencies. They cannot investigate individual cases. But, your report can help them collect evidence for lawsuits against scammers.

- Report telephone scams online to the Federal Trade Commission. You can also call 877-382-4357. The FTC is the primary government agency that collects scam complaints.
- Report all robocalls and unwanted telemarketing calls to the Do Not Call Registry.
- Report caller ID spoofing to the Federal Communications Commission. You can report either online or by phone at 888-225-5322.

Protect Yourself from Telephone Scams

Remember these tips to avoid being a victim of a telephone scam:

Dos

- Register your phone number with the National Do Not Call Registry. You may register online or by calling 888-382-1222. If you still receive telemarketing calls after registering, there is a good chance that the calls are scams.
- Be wary of callers claiming that you have won a prize or vacation package.
- Hang up on suspicious phone calls.
- Be cautious of caller ID. Scammers can change the phone number that shows up on your caller ID screen. This is called "spoofing."
- Independently research business opportunities, charities, or travel packages that the caller offers.

Don'ts

- Do not give in to pressure to take immediate action.
- Do not say anything if a caller starts the call asking, "Can you hear me?" This is a common tactic for scammers to record you saying "yes." Scammers record your "yes" response and use it as proof that you agreed to a purchase or credit card charge.
- Do not provide your credit card number, bank account information, or other personal information to a caller.
- Do not send money if a caller tells you to wire money or pay with a prepaid debit card.

Banking Scams

Banking scams involve attempts to access your bank account. Use this information to recognize, report, and protect yourself from them.

Popular Banking Scams

The most common banking scams include:

- **Overpayment scams.** A scam artist sends you a counterfeit check. They tell you to deposit it in your bank account and wire part of the money back to them. Since the check was fake, you will have to pay your bank the amount of the check, plus you will lose any money you wired.
- **Unsolicited check fraud.** A scammer sends you a check for no reason. If you cash it, you may be authorizing the purchase of items or signing up for a loan you did not ask for.
- **Automatic withdrawals.** A scam company sets up automatic debits from your bank account to qualify for a free trial or to collect a prize.
- **Phishing.** You receive an e-mail message that asks you to verify your bank account or debit card number.

Report Banking Scams

The proper organization to report a banking scam depends on which type of scam you experienced.

- Report fake checks you receive by mail to the US Postal Inspection Service.
- Report counterfeit checks to the Federal Trade Commission, either online or by phone at 877-382-4357.
- Contact your bank to report and stop unauthorized automatic withdrawals from your account.
- Forward phishing e-mails to the Federal Trade Commission at spam@uce.gov.

How to Protect Yourself

Remember these tips to avoid a banking scam:

Dos

- Be suspicious if you are told to wire a portion of funds from a check you received back to a company.
- Be wary of lotteries or free trials that ask for your bank account number.
- Verify the authenticity of a cashier's check with the bank that it is drawn on before depositing it.
- When verifying a check or the issuer, use contact information on a bank's website.

Don'ts

- Do not trust the appearance of checks or money orders. Scammers can make them look legitimate and official.
- Do not deposit checks or money orders from strangers or companies you do not have a relationship with.

- Do not wire money to people or companies you do not know.
- Do not give your bank account number to someone who calls you, even for verification purposes.
- Do not click on links in an e-mail to verify your bank account.
- Do not accept a check that includes an overpayment.

Census-Related Fraud

Census scams happen when someone pretends to work for the Census Bureau to steal your personal information. Use this information to learn how these scams work, and protect yourself against them.

How Census Related Fraud Works

Some scam artists may pretend to be working for the Census Bureau. They will try to collect your personal information to use for fraud or to steal your identity. These scam artists may send you letters that seem to come from the U.S. Census Bureau. Others may come to your home to collect information about you.

Report Census-Related Fraud

If you suspect fraud, report it to the Census Bureau's regional office for your state. Forward scam e-mails to the Census Bureau at ois.fraud.reporting@census.gov.

How to Protect Yourself

Follow these tips to ensure that your personal information stays safe:

Dos
- Verify that the study is legitimate. Check the survey name on the Census Bureau's list of surveys.
- If someone comes to your home and claims to be a census worker, verify that they work for the Census Bureau.
- Look up the employee's name in the Census Bureau staff directory.
- Ask to see their badge. A Census Bureau badge has a picture of the field agent, a Department of Commerce watermark, and an expiration date.
- Follow these tips to help you spot census scams, so you do not become a victim.

Don'ts
- Do not share your full Social Security number, bank or credit card account numbers, or your mother's maiden name. The Census Bureau would not ask for this type of information.
- Do not trust e-mails claiming to be from the Census Bureau. This agency sends letters to invite individuals to take part in its surveys. If you get an e-mail from the Census Bureau, it is probably a scam.
- Do not trust caller ID. Call the Census Bureau's National Processing Center to verify a telephone survey.

Government Grant Scams

Government grant scammers try to get your money by guaranteeing you a grant for costs like college or home repairs. They ask for your checking account information. With it, they say they will "deposit the grant money into your account" or withdraw a "one-time processing fee."

In reality, government grants are rarely awarded to individuals. They usually go to state and local governments, universities, and other organizations. The money is awarded to help pay for research and projects that benefit the public.

Report Grant Scams

If you think you have been a victim of a government grant scam, report it to the Federal Trade Commission. You can file a complaint with the FTC:

- Online
- By calling toll-free 877-FTC-HELP (877-382-4357); toll-free TTY: 866-653-4261

The FTC enters fraud-related complaints into a database available to law enforcement agencies in the U.S. and abroad.

If you have paid a fee to learn about or apply for a government grant, you can report it to your state consumer protection office. The government does not charge for information or applications for federal grants.

Protect Yourself from Grant Scams

Remember these tips to avoid being a victim of a grant scam:

Dos

- Be wary of advertisements and calls about free government grants. These are usually scams.
- Register your phone number with the National Do Not Call Registry. This may reduce the number of telemarketing calls you receive. You can register:
  - Online at donotcall.gov
  - By calling 888-382-1222 (TTY: 866-290-4236) from the phone number you wish to register

Don'ts

- Do not give your bank account information to anyone you do not know.
- Do not pay any money for a government grant. You can get information about government grants for free at public libraries and online at Grants. gov. Government agencies do not charge processing fees for grants they have awarded.
- Do not believe callers who claim they are from an official-sounding government agency with news about a grant. Check out the name of the agency online or in the phone book – it may be fake.

- Do not assume a phone call is originating from the area code displayed on your caller ID. Some scam artists use technology to disguise their location and make it appear as if they are calling from Washington, DC.

Investment Scams

Investment scams promise high returns, without financial risk. Use this information to report and protect your investments.

Report Investment Scams

Report investment scams, if you have been a victim.
- File a complaint about an investment or an investment account with the Securities and Exchange Commission (SEC).
- Report pyramid or Ponzi schemes to the Federal Trade Commission (FTC).
- Report investment scams by state-licensed companies to your state's securities administrator.

The SEC may forward your complaint to the investment company. It will request that the company reply to your complaint. The FTC will not research your individual case of investment fraud.

How to Protect Yourself

Remember these tips to avoid being a victim of an investment scam:

Dos
- Research investment opportunities and investment professionals. Your state securities regulator and the Financial Industry Regulatory Authority offer information.
- Learn where the investment and the investment professional have registered. It may be in your state or with other regulators.
- Get all the details of an investment in writing, but still do your own research.
- Ask questions about costs, timing, risks, and other issues.

Don'ts
- Do not give in to pressure to invest immediately.
- Do not be influenced by promises that seem too good to be true. These promises may include "guaranteed earnings" or "risk-free" investments.
- Do not invest just because the investment professional seems nice, trustworthy, or has professional titles.
- Do not invest based on claims that other people, "just like you," have invested.
- Do not feel obligated to invest, even if the professional gave you a gift, lunch, or reduced their fees.

Lottery and Sweepstakes Scams

Prize scammers try to get your money or personal information through fake lotteries, sweepstakes, or other contests. Many claim that you have won a prize but must pay a fee to collect it. Others require you to provide personal information to enter a "contest." These scams may reach you by postal mail, e-mail, phone call, robocall, or text message.

Report Lottery and Sweepstakes Scams

To report a prize scam:
- Contact the Federal Trade Commission online or by phone at 877-382-4357.
- Contact a postal inspector if the scam uses the U.S. mail.
- Report robocalls and unwanted telemarketing calls to the Do Not Call Registry.

Federal agencies investigate scams and pursue criminal charges against the scammers. They do not, however, investigate individual cases. State consumer protection offices (www.usa.gov/state-consumer) might pursue individual cases as well as investigate scams.

Protect Yourself from Lottery and Sweepstakes Scams

Remember these tips to avoid being a victim of a lottery or sweepstakes scam:

Dos
- Check the postage on a mailed prize notice. If it was sent bulk rate, it is probably a scam.
- Ask yourself if you entered a particular contest. If you do not remember entering it, the prize notice is likely a fake.
- Some scammers use the names of organizations that run real sweepstakes. Research the company's contact information. Contact them to verify if the prize is legitimate.
- Register your phone number with the National Do Not Call Registry. You may register online or by calling 888-382-1222. If you still receive telemarketing calls after registering, there is a good chance that the calls are scams.
- Report spam text messages to your mobile carrier, then delete them.
- Hang up on suspicious calls.

Don'ts
- Do not pay a fee, taxes, or shipping charges to receive a prize.
- Do not wire money to, or deposit a check from, any organization claiming to run a sweepstakes or lottery.
- Do not provide your credit card number or bank account information to receive a prize.

- Do not believe someone just because they say they are from the government or an official-sounding organization.
- Do not reply to, or click on any links in, a spam text message.
- Do not attend a sales meeting to be eligible to win a prize.
- Do not give in to pressure to take immediate action.
- Do not believe anyone claiming to be from a foreign lottery or sweepstakes. It is illegal to enter foreign contests like these.

Charity Scams

Some scammers set up fake organizations to take advantage of the public's generosity. They especially take advantage of tragedies and disasters.

How to Report Charity Scams
- Your state consumer protection office can accept and investigate consumer complaints.
- File a complaint with the Federal Trade Commission (FTC). The FTC does not resolve individual matters. But, it does track charity fraud claims and sues companies on the behalf of consumers.
- Contact the National Center for Disaster Fraud, if the fraud is because of a natural disaster.

The Do Not Call Registry does not apply to charities. But, you can ask an organization not to contact you again.

How to Protect Yourself from Charity Scams
Follow these tips to detect common charity scam tactics:

Dos
- Check out the charity with your state consumer protection office or the Better Business Bureau.
- Verify the name. Fake charities often choose names that are close to well established charities.

Don'ts
- Do not give in to high pressure tactics such as urging you to donate immediately.
- Do not assume that you can get a tax deduction for donating to an organization. Use the IRS's database of 501(c)3 organizations to find out if it has this status.
- Do not send cash. Pay with a check or credit card.

Pyramid Schemes

Pyramid schemes are scams that need a constant flow of new participants to keep them going. They are marketed as multi-level marketing programs or other types of legitimate businesses. They use new recruits' "investments" to pay "profits" to those participating longer.

Pyramid schemes collapse when they cannot recruit enough new participants to pay earlier investors. These scams always fail – it is mathematically guaranteed.

Report Pyramid Schemes

Report pyramid schemes to:
- Your state consumer protection office
- The Federal Trade Commission (reportfraud.ftc.gov/#/?pid=A)

How to Protect Yourself

Keep these tips in mind to avoid falling for a pyramid scheme:

Dos
- Be wary if you have to recruit more participants to increase your profit, or get your investment back.
- Ask if the company sells nontangible products and services rather than physical products.
- Check out the business with the Better Business Bureau (www.bbb.org), your state attorney general, or state licensing agencies.
- Ask to see financial statements audited by a certified public accountant (CPA). Find out if the company earns income from selling its products or services to customers, not to its sales team.
- Be skeptical of success stories and testimonials of fantastic earnings.

Don'ts
- Do not invest until you have verified that the business is legitimate.
- Do not get involved in businesses that make you recruit new participants.
- Do not buy into franchises that promise big or quick profits.
- Do not invest in any "opportunity" bearing warning signs of a pyramid scheme.

Ponzi Schemes

A Ponzi scheme is a type of investment fraud. Use this information to identify, report, and protect yourself against these scams.

How Ponzi Schemes Work

Ponzi schemes rely on money from new investors to pay "returns" to current investors. To keep the scheme running, organizers need to keep recruiting new investors and try to keep current investors from cashing out. When they cannot, the scheme collapses.

Report Ponzi Schemes

Report Ponzi schemes to:

- The Securities and Exchange Commission (SEC) (www.sec.gov/complaint/select.shtml)
- The Financial Industry Regulatory Authority (www.finra.org/investors/have-problem/file-complaint/complaint-center)
- Your state's securities administrator (www.usa.gov/state-consumer)

How to Protect Yourself from Ponzi Schemes

Keep these tips in mind to protect yourself from Ponzi schemes:

Dos

- Be wary of any investment that regularly pays positive returns regardless of what the overall market is doing.
- Avoid investments if you do not understand them or cannot get complete information about them.
- Be alert to account statement errors, which may be a sign of investment fraud.
- Be suspicious if you do not receive a payment or have difficulty cashing out.

Don'ts

- Do not put your money in investments that promise big returns with little to no risk.
- Do not contribute to any investment that is not registered with the SEC or with state regulators.
- Do not get financially involved with any unlicensed investment professional or unregistered firm.

Ticket Scams

Ticket selling scams happen when a scammer uses tickets as bait to steal your money. The scammer usually sells fake tickets, or you pay for a ticket, but never receive it. They are common when tickets for popular concerts, plays, and sporting events sell out.

Ways That Ticket Scammers Go after Your Money

Scammers, including individuals and fake resale companies, take advantage of ticket shortages by:

- Charging prices much higher than the face value of a ticket
- Creating counterfeit tickets with forged barcodes and logos of real ticket companies
- Selling duplicates of a legitimate ticket and e-mailing it to several buyers
- Pretending to sell tickets online to steal your credit card information

Report Ticket Scams

There are several options to report a ticket scam.

- Contact your state consumer protection office.
- Contact the Federal Trade Commission (FTC) using the Online Complaint Assistant.
- File a local police report, especially if you met the scammer in person or have a picture of them to give the police.
- Report it using the Better Business Bureau's Scam Tracker.
- If you paid by credit card, report the problem to the card company. You may be able to dispute the charge.

How to Protect Yourself

Learn what you can do to avoid becoming a victim:

Dos

- Buy tickets at the venue box office.
- Buy tickets from authorized brokers and third party sellers, with verified contact information.
- Look for red flags in the ticket offer. If the offer has imperfect English or unusual phrases, the offer could be a scam.
- Verify that the seller has a real physical addresses and phone numbers. Scammers often post fake addresses, P.O. Box, or no address on their websites.
- Check the actual web address of the resale ticket seller. Some scammers create phony websites that look like real ticket sellers' websites.
- Search online for negative reviews about the seller. Use the seller's name, e-mail address, and phone number, along with the words "fraud," "scams," and "fake tickets."
- Verify the details on the ticket. Check the date and the time printed on the tickets. Make sure the section and seat numbers actually exist at the venue.
- Have the seller meet you in person in a public place for the ticket exchange.
- Ask the seller for proof that they bought the tickets, if you are buying from an individual.
- Use a credit card to pay third party sellers. Your credit card offers protections, if you need to dispute a charge.
- Check for complaints against a ticket seller with your state's consumer protection agency.

Don'ts

- Do not wire transfer money to pay for tickets.
- Do not trust sellers who want you to pay with a prepaid money card.

- Do not meet an individual ticket seller alone or in a low-traffic area.
- Do not automatically trust online search results for ticket sellers. Search results can include paid ads, sellers that charge high fees, and scams.

CHAPTER 45
TELEMARKETING SCAMS

About This Chapter: This chapter includes text excerpted from "Phone Scams," Federal Trade Commission (FTC), October 2020.

People lose a lot of money to phone scams – sometimes their life savings. Scammers have figured out countless ways to cheat you out of your money over the phone. In some scams, they act friendly and helpful. In others, they might threaten or try to scare you.

One thing you can count on is that a phone scammer will try to get your money or your personal information to commit identity theft. Do not give it to them. Here is what you need to know.

Phone Scams
How to Recognize a Phone Scam

Phone scams come in many forms, but they tend to make similar promises and threats, or ask you to pay certain ways. Here is how to recognize a phone scam.

There Is No Prize

The caller might say you were "selected" for an offer or that you have won a lottery. But if you have to pay to get the prize, it is not a prize.

You Will Not Be Arrested

Scammers might pretend to be law enforcement or a federal agency. They might say you will be arrested, fined, or deported if you do not pay taxes or some other debt right away. The goal is to scare you into paying. But, real law enforcement and federal agencies will not call and threaten you.

You Do Not Need to Decide Now

Most legitimate businesses will give you time to think their offer over and get written information about it before asking you to commit. Take your time. Do not get pressured into making a decision on the spot.

265

There Is Never a Good Reason to Send Cash or Pay with a Gift Card

Scammers will often ask you to pay in a way that makes it hard for you to get your money back – by wiring money, putting money on a gift card, prepaid card or cash reload card, or using a money transfer app. Anyone who asks you to pay that way is a scammer.

Government Agencies Are Not Calling to Confirm Your Sensitive Information

It is never a good idea to give out sensitive information such as your Social Security number to someone who calls you unexpectedly, even if they say they are with the Social Security Administration or IRS.

You Should Not Be Getting All Those Calls

If a company is selling something, it needs your written permission to call you with a robocall. And if you are on the National Do Not Call Registry, you should not get live sales calls from companies you have not done business with before. Those calls are illegal. If someone is already breaking the law calling you, there is a good chance it is a scam. At the very least, it is a company you do not want to do business with.

Examples of Common Phone Scams

Any scam can happen over the phone. But, here are some common angles phone scammers like to use:

Imposter Scams

A scammer pretends to be someone you trust – a government agency such as the Social Security Administration or the IRS, a family member, a love interest, or someone claiming there is a problem with your computer. The scammer can even have a fake name or number show up on your caller ID to convince you.

Debt Relief and Credit Repair Scams

Scammers will offer to lower your credit card interest rates, fix your credit, or get your student loans forgiven if you pay their company a fee first. But, you could end up losing your money and ruining your credit.

Business and Investment Scams

Callers might promise to help you start your own business and give you business coaching, or guarantee big profits from an investment. Do not take their word for it. Learn about the FTC's Business Opportunity Rule, and check out investment opportunities with your state securities regulator.

Charity Scams

Scammers like to pose as charities. Scams requesting donations for disaster relief efforts are especially common on the phone. Always check out a charity before you give, and do not feel pressured to give immediately over the phone before you do.

Extended Car Warranties

Scammers find out what kind of car you drive and when you bought it so they can urge you to buy overpriced – or worthless – service contracts.

"Free" Trials

A caller might promise a free trial but then sign you up for products – sometimes lots of products – that you are billed for every month until you cancel.

Loan Scams

Loan scams include advance fee loan scams, where scammers target people with a poor credit history and guarantee loans or credit cards for an up-front fee. Legitimate lenders do not make guarantees like that, especially if you have bad credit, no credit, or a bankruptcy.

Prize and Lottery Scams

In a typical prize scam, the caller will say you have won a prize, but then say you need to pay a registration or shipping fee to get it. But after you pay, you find out there is no prize.

Travel Scams and Timeshare Scams

Scammers promise free or low cost vacations that can end up costing you a lot in hidden costs. And sometimes, after you pay, you find out there is no vacation. In timeshare resale scams, scammers lie and tell you they will sell your timeshare – and may even have a buyer lined up – if you pay them first.

How to Stop Calls from Scammers
Hang Up

Even if it is not a scammer calling, if a company is calling you illegally, it is not a company you want to do business with. When you get a robocall, do not press any numbers. Instead of letting you speak to a live operator or remove you from their call list, it might lead to more robocalls.

Consider Call Blocking or Call Labeling

Scammers can use the Internet to make calls from all over the world. They do not care if you are on the National Do Not Call Registry. That is why your best defense against unwanted calls is call blocking. Which type of call-blocking (or call-labeling) technology you use will depend on the phone – whether it is a mobile phone, a traditional landline, or a home phone that makes VoIP (voice over Internet Protocol) calls. See what services your phone carrier offers, and look online for expert reviews. For mobile phones, you also can check out the reviews for different call-blocking apps in your online app store.

Do Not Trust Your Caller ID

Scammers can make any name or number show up on your caller ID. That is called "spoofing." So even if it looks like it is a government agency like the Social Security Administration calling, or like the call is from a local number, it could be a scammer calling from anywhere in the world.

What to Do If You Already Paid a Scammer

Scammers often ask you to pay in ways that make it tough to get your money back. If you have paid a scammer, the sooner you act, the better.

If you paid a scammer with a credit or debit card, you may be able to stop the transaction. Contact your credit card company or bank right away. Tell them what happened, and ask for a "chargeback" to reverse the charges.

If you paid a scammer with a gift card, prepaid card, or cash reload card, contact the company that issued the card right away. Tell them you paid a scammer with the card, and ask if they can refund your money. The sooner you contact them, the better the chance they will be able to get your money back.

If you paid a scammer with a wire transfer, call the money transfer company immediately to report the fraud and file a complaint. Call the complaint department:

- MoneyGram at 800-MONEYGRAM (800-666-3947)
- Western Union at 800-325-6000.

Ask for the money transfer to be reversed. It is unlikely to happen, but it is important to ask.

If you paid a scammer using a money transfer app, contact the company behind the app. If the app is linked to a credit card or debit card, contact your credit card company or bank first.

If you gave a scammer remote access to your computer, update your computer's security software. Then run a scan and delete anything it identifies as a problem.

If you gave your username and password to a scammer, change your password right away. If you use the same password for other accounts or sites, change it there, too. Create a new password that is strong.

If you gave a scammer your Social Security number (SSN), visit identitytheft.gov to learn how to monitor your credit report to see if your SSN is being misused.

If someone calls and offers to "help" you recover money you have already lost, do not give them money or personal information. You are probably dealing with a fake refund scam.

Report Phone Scams

If you have lost money to a phone scam or have information about the company or scammer who called you, report it at ftc.gov/complaint.

National Do Not Call Registry

The National Do Not Call Registry gives you a choice about whether to receive telemarketing calls.

- You can register your home or mobile phone for free.
- After you register, other types of organizations may still call you, such as charities, political groups, debt collectors and surveys. To learn more, read our FAQs.
- If you received an unwanted call after your number was on the National Registry for 31 days, report it to the FTC.

(Source: "National Do Not Call Registry," National Do Not Call Registry, Federal Trade Commission (FTC).)

If you did not lose money and just want to report a call, you can use our streamlined reporting form at donotcall.gov.

Report the number that appears on your caller ID – even if you think it might be fake – and any number you are told to call back. The FTC analyzes complaint data and trends to identify illegal callers based on calling patterns. It also uses additional information you report, such as any names or numbers you are told to call back, to track down scammers.

We take the phone numbers you report and release them to the public each business day. This helps phone carriers and other partners that are working on call-blocking and call-labeling solutions. Your reports also help law enforcement identify the people behind illegal calls.

CHAPTER 46
AVOIDING AND REPORTING SCAMS

About This Chapter: Text beginning with the heading "Signs for Scams" is excerpted from "How to Avoid a Scam," Federal Trade Commission (FTC), November 2020; Text beginning with the heading "What to Do If You Were Scammed" is excerpted from "What to Do If You Were Scammed," Federal Trade Commission (FTC), October 2020.

Signs for Scams

- **Scammers pretend to be from an organization you know.** Scammers often pretend to be contacting you on behalf of the government. They might use a real name, such as the Social Security Administration (SSA), the internal revenue service (IRS), or Medicare, or make up a name that sounds official. Some pretend to be from a business you know, such as a utility company, a tech company, or even a charity asking for donations. They use technology to change the phone number that appears on your caller ID. So the name and number you see might not be real.

- **Scammers say there is a problem or a prize.** They might say you are in trouble with the government. Or you owe money. Or someone in your family had an emergency. Or that there is a virus on your computer. Some scammers say there is a problem with one of your accounts and that you need to verify some information. Others will lie and say you won money in a lottery or sweepstakes but have to pay a fee to get it.

- **Scammers pressure you to act immediately.** Scammers want you to act before you have time to think. If you are on the phone, they might tell you not to hang up so you cannot check out their story. They might threaten to arrest you, sue you, take away your driver's or business license, or deport you. They might say your computer is about to be corrupted.

- **Scammers tell you to pay in a specific way.** They often insist that you pay by sending money through a money transfer company or by putting money on a gift card and then giving them the number on the back. Some will send you a check (that will later turn out to be fake), tell you to deposit it, and then send them money.

What You Can Do to Avoid a Scam

- **Block unwanted calls and text messages.** Take steps to block unwanted calls and to filter unwanted text messages.
- **Do not give your personal or financial information in response to a request that you did not expect.** Legitimate organizations would not call, e-mail, or text to ask for your personal information, such as your Social Security, bank account, or credit card numbers. If you get an e-mail or text message from a company you do business with and you think it is real, it is still best not to click on any links. Instead, contact them using a website you know is trustworthy. Or look up their phone number. Do not call a number they gave you or the number from your caller ID.
- **Resist the pressure to act immediately.** Legitimate businesses will give you time to make a decision. Anyone who pressures you to pay or give them your personal information is a scammer.
- **Know how scammers tell you to pay.** Never pay someone who insists you pay with a gift card or by using a money transfer service. And never deposit a check and send money back to someone.
- **Stop and talk to someone you trust.** Before you do anything else, tell someone – a friend, a family member, a neighbor – what happened. Talking about it could help you realize it is a scam.

What to Do If You Were Scammed

If You Paid a Scammer

Did You Pay with a Credit Card or Debit Card?

Contact the company or bank that issued the credit card or debit card. Tell them it was a fraudulent charge. Ask them to reverse the transaction and give you your money back.

Did a Scammer Make an Unauthorized Transfer from Your Bank Account?

Contact your bank and tell them it was an unauthorized debit or withdrawal. Ask them to reverse the transaction and give you your money back.

Did You Pay with a Gift Card?

Contact the company that issued the gift card. Tell them it was used in a scam and ask if they can refund your money. Keep the gift card itself, and the gift card receipt.

Did You Send a Wire Transfer through a Company Such as Western Union or MoneyGram?

Contact the wire transfer company. Tell them it was a fraudulent transfer. Ask them to reverse the wire transfer and give you your money back.

- MoneyGram at 800-MONEYGRAM (800-666-3947)
- Western Union at 800-325-6000

Did You Send a Wire Transfer through Your Bank?

Contact your bank and report the fraudulent transfer. Ask if they can reverse the wire transfer and give you your money back.

Did You Send Money through a Money Transfer App?

Report the fraudulent transaction to the company behind the money transfer app and ask if they can reverse the payment. If you linked the app to a credit card or debit card, report the fraud to your credit card company or bank. Ask if they can reverse the charge.

Did You Pay with Cryptocurrency?

Contact the company you used to send the money and tell them it was a fraudulent transaction. Ask to have the transaction reversed, if possible.

Did You Send Cash?

If you sent it by U.S. mail, contact the U.S. Postal Inspection Service at 877-876-2455 and ask them to intercept the package.

If you used another delivery service, contact them as soon as possible.

If You Gave a Scammer Your Personal Information

Did You Give a Scammer Your Social Security Number?

Go to IdentityTheft.gov to see what steps you should take, including how to monitor your credit.

Did You Give a Scammer Your Username and Password?

Create a new, strong password. If you use the same password anywhere else, change it there, too.

If a Scammer Has Access to Your Computer or Phone

Does a Scammer Have Remote Access to Your Computer?

Update your computer's security software, run a scan, and delete anything it identifies as a problem. Then take other steps to protect your personal information.

Did a Scammer Take Control of Your Cell Phone Number and Account?

Contact your service provider to take back control of your phone number. Once you do, change your account password.

Also check your credit card, bank, and other financial accounts for unauthorized charges or changes. If you see any, report them to the company or institution. Then go to IdentityTheft.gov to see what steps you should take.

Report Scams to the Federal Trade Commission

When you report a scam, the FTC can use the information to build cases against scammers, spot trends, educate the public, and share data about what is happening in your community. If you were scammed, report it to the FTC at ReportFraud.ftc.gov.

PART 7 | IF YOU NEED MORE HELP OR INFORMATION

CHAPTER 47
RESOURCES FOR FINANCIAL INFORMATION

About This Chapter: Resources in this chapter were compiled from several sources deemed reliable; all contact information was verified and updated in June 2021.

Budgeting and Financial Information

American Bankers Association (ABA)

1120 Connecticut Ave., N.W.
Washington, DC 20036
Toll-Free: 800-BANKERS (800-226-5377)
Website: www.aba.com
E-mail: support@aba.com

American Financial Services Association (AFSA) Education Foundation

919 18th St., N.W., Ste. 300
Washington, DC 20006-5517
Toll-Free: 888-400-7577
Website: www.afsaef.org
E-mail: info@afsaef.org

American Institute of Certified Public Accountants (AICPA)

220 Leigh Farm Rd.
Durham, NC 27707-8110
Toll-Free: 888-777-7077
Phone: 919-402-4500
Fax: 919-402-4505
Website: www.aicpa.org
E-mail: service@aicpa.org

Asset Builders of America

1213 N. Sherman Ave., Ste. 195
Madison, WI 53704
Phone: 608-663-6332
Website: www.assetbuilders.org
E-mail: info@assetbuilders.org

Bloomberg Finance L.P.

731 Lexington Ave.
New York, NY 10022
Phone: 212-318-2000
Website: www.bloomberg.com

Certified Financial Planner Board of Standards, Inc.

1425 K St., N.W., Ste. 800
Washington, DC 20005
Toll-Free: 800-487-1497
Phone: 202-379-2200
Fax: 202-379-2299
Website: www.cfp.net
E-mail: mail@cfpboard.org

Council for Economic Education (CEE)

122 E. 42nd St., Ste. 1012
New York, NY 10168
Phone: 212-827-3600
Fax: 212-827-3610
Website: councilforeconed.org
E-mail: info@councilforeconed.org

Employee Benefit Research Institute (EBRI)

901 D St., S.W., Ste. 802
Washington, DC 20024
Phone: 202-659-0670
Fax: 202-775-6360
Website: www.ebri.org
E-mail: info@ebri.org

Federal Deposit Insurance Corporation (FDIC)

1310 Courthouse Rd.
Arlington, VA 22201
Toll-Free: 877-ASK-FDIC (877-275-3342)
Toll-Free TDD: 800-925-4618
Website: www.fdic.gov

Federal Trade Commission (FTC)

600 Pennsylvania Ave., N.W.
Washington, DC 20580
Phone: 202-326-2222
Website: www.ftc.gov

Financial Planning Association (FPA)

1290 Bdwy., Ste. 1625
Denver, CO 80203
Toll-Free: 800-322-4237
Phone: 303-759-4900
Fax: 303-759-0749
Website: www.onefpa.org
E-mail: info@onefpa.org

Get Out of Debt Guy

Toll-Free: 877-220-0305
Website: getoutofdebt.org
E-mail: info@consumerservicesco.com

InCharge Education Foundation

5750 Major Blvd., Ste. 300
Orlando, FL 32819
Toll-Free: 866-721-3925
Website: www.inchargefoundation.org

Institute for Financial Literacy (IFL)

P.O. Box 1842
Portland, ME 04104
Phone: 207-873-0068
Fax: 207-873-0118
Website: www.financiallit.org

Internal Revenue Service (IRS)

1111 Constitution Ave., N.W.
Washington, DC 20224
Website: www.irs.gov

Iowa State University Extension and Outreach

2150 Beardshear Hall
Ames, IA 50011-2031
Toll-Free: 800-262-3804
Website: www.extension.iastate.edu

JA Worldwide

One Lincoln St.
24th Fl.
Boston, MA 02111
Phone: 617-315-8563
Website: www.jaworldwide.org

Jump$tart Coalition for Personal Financial Literacy

1001 Connecticut Ave., N.W., Ste. 640
Washington, DC 20036
Phone: 202-846-6780
Website: www.jumpstart.org
E-mail: info@jumpstart.org

Junior Achievement USA®

1 Education Way
Colorado Springs, CO 80906
Phone: 719-540-8000
Website: www.juniorachievement.org

The Kiplinger Washington Editors, Inc.

1100 13th St., N.W., Ste. 1000
Washington, DC 20005
Toll-Free: 800-544-0155
Phone: 202-887-6400
Website: www.kiplinger.com
E-mail: sub.services@kiplinger.com

Morningstar, Inc.

22 W. Washington St.
Chicago, IL 60602
Phone: 312-384-4000
Website: www.morningstar.com
E-mail: productinfo@morningstar.com

The Motley Fool

2000 Duke St.
2nd Fl.
Alexandria, VA 22314
Phone: 703-838-3665
Fax: 703-254-1999
Website: www.fool.com

MyMoney.gov

1500 Pennsylvania Ave., N.W.
Washington, DC 20220
Toll-Free: 800-FED-INFO (800-333-4636)
Website: www.mymoney.gov

National Association of Personal Financial Advisors (NAPFA)

8700 W. Bryn Mawr Ave., Ste. 700N
Chicago, IL 60631
Toll-Free: 888-FEE-ONLY (888-333-6659)
Phone: 847-483-5400
Website: www.napfa.org
E-mail: info@napfa.org

National Endowment for Financial Education (NEFE)

1550 Market St., Ste. 475
Denver, CO 80202
Phone: 303-741-6333
Website: www.nefe.org

National Institute of Food and Agriculture (NIFA)

12th St., S.W., Jefferson Dr.
305-A Whitten Bldg.
Washington, DC 20250
Phone: 202-720-2791 (hotline)
Website: nifa.usda.gov
E-mail: nifa@usda.gov

Native Financial Education Coalition (NFEC)

1516 P St., N.W.
Washington, DC 20005
Phone: 202-466-7767
Website: www.nfec.us
E-mail: nfec@ncai.org

Operation HOPE, Inc.

226 Peachtree St., S.W.
Atlanta, GA 30303
Website: www.operationhope.org

Plan Sponsor Council of America (PSCA)

4401 N. Fairfax Dr., Ste. 600
Arlington, VA 22203
Phone: 703-516-9300
Fax: 703-516-9303
Website: www.psca.org
E-mail: customercare@psca.org

Practical Money Skills

900 Metro Center Blvd.
Foster City, CA 94404-2172
Website: www.practicalmoneyskills.com
E-mail: info@practicalmoneyskills.com

Securities Industry and Financial Markets Association (SIFMA)

120 Bdwy., 35th Fl.
New York, NY 10271
Phone: 212-313-1200
Website: www.sifma.org

Society of Financial Service Professionals (FSP)

10 E. Athens Ave., Ste. 224
Ardmore, PA 19003
Phone: 610-526-2500
Website: national.societyoffsp.org

TreasuryDirect KIDS

Website: www.treasurydirect.gov/kids/kids.htm

U.S. Securities and Exchange Commission (SEC)

100 F St., N.E.
Washington, DC 20549
Website: www.sec.gov

USAA Educational Foundation (USAAEF)

9800 Fredericksburg Rd.
San Antonio, TX 78288-0026
Website: www.usaaef.org
E-mail: edfoundation_info@usaa.com

Consumer Information and Insurance

American Consumer Credit Counseling (ACCC)

130 Rumford Ave., Ste. 202
Auburndale, MA 02466-1371
Toll-Free: 800-769-3571
Phone: 617-559-5700
Fax: 617-244-1116
Website: www.consumercredit.com
E-mail: info@consumercredit.com

American Council of Life Insurers (ACLI)

101 Constitution Ave., N.W., Ste. 700
Washington, DC 20001-2133
Toll-Free: 877-674-4659
Phone: 202-624-2000
Website: www.acli.com

Consumer Action

57 Post St., Ste. 611
San Francisco, CA 94104
Phone: 415-777-9635
Fax: 415-777-5267
Website: www.consumer-action.org
E-mail: info@consumer-action.org

Consumer Checkbook

1625 K St., N.W.
8th Fl.
Washington, DC 20006
Toll-Free: 800-213-7283
Website: www.checkbook.org
E-mail: support@checkbook.org

Consumer Federation of America (CFA)

1620 I St., N.W., Ste. 200
Washington, DC 20006
Phone: 202-387-6121
Website: www.consumerfed.org
E-mail: cfa@consumerfed.org

Consumer Financial Protection Bureau (CFPB)

P.O. Box 2900
Clinton, IA 52733-2900
Toll-Free: 855-411-2372
Toll-Free TTY: 855-729-2372
Website: www.consumerfinance.gov

Consumer Reports Online

101 Truman Ave.
Yonkers, NY 10703
Website: www.consumerreports.org

Consumer World

Shore Dr.
Somerville, MA 02145
Website: www.consumerworld.org

Insurance Information Institute (III)

110 William St.
New York, NY 10038
Phone: 212-346-5500
Website: www.iii.org
E-mail: info@iii.org

Kids' Finance

P.O. Box 241775
Los Angeles, CA 90024
Website: www.kidsfinance.com
E-mail: contact@kidsfinance.com

National Consumer Law Center, Inc. (NCLC)

7 Winthrop Sq.
Boston, MA 02110-1245
Phone: 617-542-8010
Fax: 617-542-8028
Website: www.nclc.org
E-mail: consumerlaw@nclc.org

National Consumers League (NCL)

1701 K St., N.W., Ste. 1200
Washington, DC 20006
Phone: 202-835-3323
Fax: 202-835-0747
Website: www.nclnet.org
E-mail: info@nclnet.org

Credit Reporting and Credit Scoring Agencies and Information

Credit Union National Association (CUNA)

99 M St., S.E., Ste. 300
Washington, DC 20003
Toll-Free: 800-356-9655
Website: www.cuna.org

Credit.org

4351 Latham St.
Riverside, CA 92501
Website: www.credit.org

Equifax, Inc.

P.O. Box 740241
Atlanta, GA 30374
Toll-Free: 888-202-4025
Website: www.equifax.com

Experian Information Solutions, Inc.

P.O. Box 1017
Allen, TX 75013-0949
Toll-Free: 888-397-3742
Website: www.experian.com

National Credit Union Administration (NCUA)

1775 Duke St.
Alexandria, VA 22314
Phone: 703-518-6300
Website: www.ncua.gov

PIA (National Association of Professional Insurance Agents)

400 N. Washington St.
Alexandria, VA 22314
Phone: 703-836-9340
Fax: 703-836-1279
Website: www.pianet.org
E-mail: web@pianet.org

TransUnion LLC

2 Baldwin Pl.
P.O. Box 1000
Chester, PA 19016
Toll-Free: 800-888-4213
Website: www.transunion.com

Information about Debt Management, Collection Practices, and Bankruptcy

ACA International

3200 Courthouse Ln.
Eagan, MN 55121-1585
Toll-Free: 800-269-1607
Website: www.acainternational.org

Consolidated Credit, Inc.

5701 W. Sunrise Blvd.
Fort Lauderdale, FL 33313
Toll-Free: 800-320-9929
Website: www.consolidatedcredit.org
E-mail: Counselor@ConsolidatedCredit.org

CuraDebt Systems, LLC.

4000 Hollywood Blvd., Ste. 555-S
Hollywood, FL 33021
Toll-Free: 877-850-3328
Phone: 754-333-5506
Fax: 754-333-5510
Website: www.curadebt.com
E-mail: counselors@curadebt.com

National Foundation for Credit Counseling (NFCC)

2000 M St., N.W., Ste. 505
Washington, DC 20036
Toll-Free: 800-388-2227
Phone: 202-677-4300
Website: espanol.nfcc.org

Navient Solutions, Inc.

P.O. Box 9500
Wilkes-Barre, PA 18773-9500
Toll-Free: 800-428-1039
Website: www.navient.com
E-mail: nvoptout@navient.com

INDEX

INDEX

Page numbers that appear in *Italics* refer to tables or illustrations. Page numbers that have a small 'n' after the page number refer to citation information shown as Notes. Page numbers that appear in **Bold** refer to information contained in boxes within the chapters.